Eg〉.

Egypt

Contested Revolution

Philip Marfleet

PlutoPress
www.plutobooks.com

First published 2016 by Pluto Press
345 Archway Road, London N6 5AA

www.plutobooks.com

Copyright © Philip Marfleet 2016

The right of Philip Marfleet to be identified as the author of this work
has been asserted by him in accordance with the Copyright, Designs
and Patents Act 1988.

British Library Cataloguing in Publication Data
A catalogue record for this book is available from the British Library

ISBN   978 0 7453 3552 0   Hardback
ISBN   978 0 7453 3551 3   Paperback
ISBN   978 1 7837 1794 1   PDF eBook
ISBN   978 1 7837 1796 5   Kindle eBook
ISBN   978 1 7837 1795 8   EPUB eBook

This book is printed on paper suitable for recycling and made from fully
managed and sustained forest sources. Logging, pulping and manufacturing
processes are expected to conform to the environmental standards of the
country of origin.

Typeset by Stanford DTP Services, Northampton, England

Simultaneously printed in the European Union and United States of America

Contents

Acknowledgements

My thanks to many friends and colleagues in Egypt for years of shared experiences, debates and discussions. As I write in early 2016, it would be unwise to identify those who face continuing threats from the military regime.

Thanks especially to Anne Alexander, John Rose and Adrian Budd for their careful reading of drafts of the book; thanks also to Egyptian readers who remain anonymous. The views expressed are very much my own. Given the complexity of events, the obsessive secrecy of successive Egyptian regimes and the difficulty of establishing the pattern of events during crucial phases of the revolution some assessments I have offered may be contentious – and our discussions will continue.

Thanks to David Shulman of Pluto Books for his patience and forbearance, especially when unexpected developments delayed progress. Many thanks to expert editor Thérèse Wassily Saba for her meticulous work on the manuscript and careful monitoring of my transliteration from Arabic. My special thanks to Lynne Hubbard, Ellie Marfleet and Harry Hubbard for putting up with my absences and silences – hugs to you all. Thanks also to friends and colleagues who prompted my interest in Egypt, its people and cultures, especially Talal Asad, Tanya Baker, Enid Hill and the late Tony Cliff.

When I was four or five years old, my father Gerry Marfleet showed me his album of photographs from Egypt. In 1940 he had been conscripted and sent to the Middle East as part of a British army of occupation. Stationed in Iran, Iraq, Syria and Palestine, he was eventually sent to Egypt and encamped at Helwan. Fascinated by the Orient, and especially its literary associations, he had found himself in the 'antique land' of *Ozymandias* – the pharaoh Ramses II who, wrote Shelley, had ordered an inscription on his monumental image constructed at the edge of the desert: 'My name is Ozymandias, king of kings: Look on my works, ye Mighty, and despair!' Almost 60 years later Gerry might have considered another of Shelley's works in the context of Egypt. 'The Mask of Anarchy' had been written to commemorate a massacre of democracy activists in England. It concluded with lines that could have been composed in Arabic by witnesses to events in 2011 that launched sustained struggles against the pharaohs of the twenty-first century:

> Rise, like lions after slumber
> In unvanquishable number!
> Shake your chains to earth like dew
> Which in sleep had fallen on you:
> Ye are many – they are few!

> ....

> The brave men are brave
> The cowards are cowardly
> Come with the brave
> Together to the Square.

Ahmed Fouad Negm

Glossary

Arabic words and phrases

abaya – cloak (for women)

'adl – justice

'amil (pl. *'ummal*) worker

ansar – helpers/supporters (had special status in Islamic history as associates of the Prophet and members of the first *umma*)

awqaf (sing. *waqf*) – religious endowments

'ashwa'iyyat – informal areas, 'slums'

'aysh – bread

'aysh baladi (made with wholewheat flour)

'aysh shami (made with white flour)

baladi – country(side)/of the people/folk

baltagiyya (sing. *baltagi*) – gangs/thugs

batil – illegitimate/false

'eid – feast

feddan – measurement of land area; 4,200 square metres (0.42 hectare); 1.038 acres

fellah – (pl. *fellaheen*) tiller, farmer, peasant

higab/hijab – headscarf for women

feloul – remnants/leftovers

fuul – fava beans

hizb – party

harakat – movement

hadith (pl. *ahadith*) – reports/accounts (of the Prophet's words and deeds)

haram – sanctuary; or impermissable

hukm al-askar – military rule

hurriyya – freedom

ihtijajat fi'awiyya – special (sectional) interests

ikhwan – brotherhood

infitah – opening; *al-infitah al-iqtisadi* – economic opening

insaf – fairness

intifada – uprising

jahiliyya – ignorance (of divine guidance)

jihad – striving, exertion, fight, war

karama – dignity

khedive – governor of a province or region of the Ottoman Empire

kifaya – enough

mazar – place of reverence

manabir – (sing. *minbar*) pulpits

mathaf – museum

midan – (pl. *mayadin*) square

millioneyya – million-strong march

mukhabarat – intelligence (secret police)

mulid – (pl. *mawalid*) festival

murshid – guide (usually of Muslim Brotherhood)

naqabat – unions/syndicates

nizam – order (regime)

riba – usury

salaf – predecessors/forefathers

sha'ab – people

shahid (pl. *shuhada*) – 'witness', martyr

shari'a – laws of Islam

shura – consultation (name of the Upper House of Egyptian parliament)

tahrir – liberation

tali'a – vanguard

tathir – cleansing/purification

thawra – revolution

ultras – hard-core football fans

umma – collective of Muslims, sometimes 'nation'

wasta – connections/influence

State agencies and institutions; political parties and movements

Amn al-Markazi – Central Security [Force] – CSF (riot police)

Destour (Constitution) Party

Gama'at Islamiyya – Islamic groups/associations (Islamist organisations, variously called *Gama'a Islamiya, al-Jamaat al-Islamiya, al-Gama'a al-Islamiyya*)

Haditu (*Al-Harakat al-Dimocratiyya al-Tahrir al-Watani*, or DMNL)
Harakat al-Tagheer – (sing. *Haraket El-Tagheer*) Movements for Change
Hay'aat al-Tahrir – Liberation Agency
Hamla Sha'biyya min Agl al-Tagheer – Popular Campaign for Change
Hizb al-Watani al-Dimuqrati – National Democratic Party (NDP)
Ikhwan al-Muslimin – Muslim Brotherhood
Ittihad al-Qawmi – National Union
Ittihad al-Ishtiraqi – Socialist Union
Ittihadiyya – Federation Palace (presidential palace outside Cairo)
Jihad – Jihad [Islamist organisation]
Jihaz al-Amn al-Dawla (State Security Service)
Jihaz al-Amn al-Qawmi (National Security Service)
Karama (Dignity) Party
Kifaya! – Enough! Slogan of the Egyptian Movement for Change (and
    name by which it is usually known)
Mubahath Amn al-Dawla (General Directorate of State Security Inves-
    tigations, SSI)
Majlis al-Shaab – People's Assembly (Lower House of Parliament)
Majlis al-Shura – Shura Council (Upper House of Parliament)
Mukhabarat al-Aama (General Intelligence and Security Service)
Mukhabarat al-Harbeya (Military Intelligence Service)
Nadi al-Quda – Judges' Club/Association
Tagammu' (Rally/Coalition) – National Progressive Unionist Party
    (NDUP)
Tahaluf (Alliance) – Socialist Popular Alliance Party
Tamarud (Rebellion) – political campaign
Wafd (Delegation) Party, nationalist organisation founded in 1919; New
    Wafd Party founded in 1983
Al-Waqa'e al-Misreya, Egypt's official gazette, giving information on
    laws, regulations and procedures
Wasat (Centre) Party

Abbreviations, acronyms in English

ADNP – Arab Democratic Nasserist Party
AKP – Justice and Development Party (Turkey)
ASU – Arab Socialist Union
CENTO – Central Treaty Organisation (the 'Baghdad Pact')

CSF – Central Security Force (Amn al-Markazi)

CTUWS – Center for Trade Union and Workers Services

EAAT – Egyptian Association Against Torture

ECESR – Egyptian Centre for Economic and Social Rights

Ebda – Egyptian Businesses Development Association

ECP – Egyptian Communist Party

EOHR – Egyptian Organization for Human Rights

EPCSI – Egyptian Popular Committee in Solidarity with the Intifada

ESDP – Egyptian Social Democratic Party

EFITU – Egyptian Federation of Independent Trade Unions

ETUF – Egyptian Trade Union Federation

ERSAP – Economic Reform and Structural Adjustment Programme

FJP – Freedom and Justice Party

NEPAD – New Partnership for Africa's Development

IFI – International Financial Institution

IMF – International Monetary Fund

LCHR – Land Center for Human Rights

MUSIAD – Independent Industrialists' and Businessmen's Association (Turkey)

NAM – Non-Aligned Movement

NDP – National Democratic Party

NSF – National Salvation Front

NSPO – National Service Products Organisation

OpantiSH – Operation Anti-Harrassment

PCSU – Privatization Co-ordination Support Unit

PTA – Property Tax Authority

Retau – Real Estate Property Tax Union

RCC – Revolution Command Council

SSI – State Security Intelligence (*Mubahath Amn al-Dawla*)

SCAF – Supreme Council of the Armed Forces

UNHCR – Office of the United Nations Higher Commissioner for Refugees

USAID – United States Agency for International Development

Preface

I began writing this book almost four years after the first of the events known as the 'Arab Spring'. These had been extraordinary developments, initiated in January 2011 by mass movements in Tunisia and Egypt that emerged apparently without warning. The movements were explosive, creative and – in their initial phases – largely successful. For many participants they involved life-changing experiences – in the case of Egypt, tens of millions of people engaged for the first time in public politics and in a host of novel social and cultural initiatives that marked the events as a 'carnival of the oppressed'. Among the repeated slogans of countless demonstrations and rallies was an insistent, 'We're never going back' – an assertion that return to the autocracy, fear and immiseration of the Mubarak era was unthinkable. But less than three years later Egypt had, apparently, 'gone back'. Military intervention had brought to an end the multiple expressions of democracy from below: individual self-expression evident in public protests, marches and *millioneyya* ('million-man') rallies; new political parties and novel media initiatives; community actions; street theatre and performance art; and collective organisation among workers that placed labour at the centre of the movement. Police and troops had returned to city squares, independent media had been closed, and political parties and networks prominent in the earlier events had been banned and thousands of their members imprisoned. A police state had been reinstalled, as security forces and intelligence agencies operated with the impunity of the Mubarak era. In a demonstrative statement by the new army regime, revolutionary graffiti had been whitewashed. A counter-revolution had taken effect with almost the same speed that characterised the uprising of 2011.

Academic and media analysts had already struggled to understand the movement of 2011. Then, 'expert' opinion was unprepared. Academics who for years focused on the Middle East were among the most perplexed: in a surprisingly frank assessment published as events unfolded, one leading American scholar asked why he and his colleagues had 'missed the Arab Spring' (Gause 2011). These regional specialists were more comfortable identifying the movement's decline – and some did so with indecent haste, for as early as 2012 obituaries were being written for a movement that was still broadening and deepening its influence. For reasons I shall address in this book, it has been extraordinarily difficult for such observers of the events to understand the origins, energies and creative capacities of the Egyptian movement. It has been much easier to interpret the counter-revolution as an assertion of authoritarian rule that confirms an alleged incapacity of the mass of people to sustain collective forms of political engagement and to achieve social change. On this view, the re-establishment of military rule in 2013 was an assertion of the norm. Here, the order of things in the Middle East places politics under the control of regimes that have ruled as part of arrangements in place since the colonial era. Centred on the Arab Gulf and its energy resources, this imperial architecture has rested for some 80 years upon exclusion of the region's people from the political arena. As we shall see, the 'Arab Spring' challenged not only presidents such as Mubarak but also political arrangements across the region. It was with relief that strategic analysts and foreign policy advisers in states of the Global North, and academics sharing their assumptions, greeted counter-revolution in Egypt as the return of business as usual. These experts had 'missed the Arab Spring': could they understand the purposes and dynamics of the mass movement, its successes and failures, and the continuing process of change in Egypt?

What's at stake?

The Egyptian uprising has been the most important mass movement of the twenty-first century. In terms of scale and duration, it may indeed have been one of the most significant expressions of popular participation in modern history. Major public mobilisations such as those in January and February 2011; those marking the first anniversary of the events in January 2012; the Ittihadiyya demonstrations in Cairo of November 2012; and the anti-Mursi marches of 30 June 2013 (with estimates of some 15 million participants) put the uprising in a category of its own. Countless smaller protests, rallies, mass meetings, labour actions and all manner of community mobilisations took place almost continuously between January 2011 and July 2013. The range of these initiatives was extraordinary, including very widespread actions over issues including provision of fresh water, adequate sewage systems, public transport, power supplies, housing and resourcing of local schools. A common cause throughout the events was the issue of *taṭhir* ('cleansing') – the removal of officials associated with the Mubarak regime who were viewed as autocratic, corrupt or compromised. So too in places of work, where managers said to be *feloul* ('remnants') of the former regime were also widely targeted for removal. Tens of thousands of people active in the networks of privilege that sustained Mubarak were affected. Attacks on police stations, security headquarters and symbols of the Mubarak autocracy, including offices of the former president's National Democratic Party (NDP), were also widespread, although these actions were seldom associated with looting and, significantly, private property (and notably the properties of the rich) were rarely affected. In earlier, short-lived uprisings – notably the Auxiliary Forces mutiny of 1986 – protestors had attacked symbols of wealth including hotels, luxury shops and nightclubs. During the events of 2011–2013, among thousands of protest actions few were directed against such targets or against the private gated communities, shopping malls and exclusive clubs for the rich that had appeared during the Mubarak era. The uprising was focused on the old regime, on self-expression and democratisation, and on economic and social reform. These were strengths of a mass movement that drew confidence from its success in removing a dictator. But the movement faltered. As participants turned to political parties old and new to express their aspirations they encountered a general crisis of formal politics, in which an interest in survival of the repressive state brought confusion, paralysis and eventually counter-revolution.

The key issues raised in this book address the political impasse of 2012–2013, in which a movement of unprecedented energy was confronted not only by Egypt's military command but also, paradoxically, by political currents that had been beneficiaries of the uprising. It examines the dynamics of the mass movement: its achievements, potentials and contradictions. It assesses relationships between key actors old and new, including those in authority in the armed forces. It examines the composition and influence of the constituent elements of the movement and their specific interests. It considers the role of Islamism, and especially that of the Muslim Brotherhood. It asks about

Egypt's secular liberals, nationalists and communists, and their relationships with the armed forces. It considers the planning and execution of the coup of 2013 and the implications for upheavals to come. It suggests that the process of change is not over and considers how new movements might be shaped by the experiences of 2011–2013.

The book does not undertake a comprehensive analysis of the political economy of Egypt. Recent work, notably that undertaken by Gilbert Achcar (2013), Adam Hanieh (2013), and Anne Alexander and Mostafa Bassiouny (2014) examines in detail the neo-liberal agenda in Egypt and the wider Middle East, the impact on the Egyptian state and the consequences for the mass of Egyptians. My main aim is to assess the revolutionary process as a lived experience in which millions of people undertook concerted efforts to change their circumstances, engaging in complex interaction with institutions of the state and with political parties that claimed to represent their interests. The book also addresses wider questions about mass movements and radical change. How should we view the Egyptian events? Did the uprising of 2011 launch a movement of protest, or was this a revolution? What forms of organisation were evident? Was this a spontaneous movement, as many analysts have suggested? Was it essentially 'leaderless' – a movement based upon principles of decentralisation and 'horizontalism'? What theories of social action help us to understand the changing dynamics of the movement, including its apparently abrupt rise and fall?

Testimony

This book addresses the upheaval as an engagement by the mass of Egyptians with socio-political structures that have constrained their lives. It argues that, above all, the events of 2011–13 should be seen as expressions of political subjectivity by people long excluded from the political process and from many areas of public activity both formal and informal. It addresses the successes and failures of these efforts as assessed by participants who have expressed their views individually and collectively in various ways: in written form; in radio and television broadcasts; online; at demonstrations, rallies and meetings; in performance; and in interviews with the author. In a mass movement diverse in composition and characterised by uneven levels of participation in a wide range of organisational forms it is not possible, or even meaningful, to offer representative samples of opinion. The observations and analyses presented here are offered as records of experience and as insights from Egyptians with varying levels of engagement in the movement for change. They include personal testimonies of youth activists, workers, students, academics, doctors and lawyers; of members of political currents including social democrats, liberals, nationalists, Marxists and Islamists; and of participants in street actions, labour disputes, campus mobilisations and cultural initiatives. The choice of testimonies reflects a definite standpoint – that of identification with the mass movement and its primary aims, and with the aspirations of the radical left to facilitate a profound change in the current order.

Interviews were undertaken mainly between 2011 and 2013; some date from much earlier (thanks to a former colleague, Nadia Hijab, for her advice: 'Keep your interview notebooks – you'll never know when you'll need them.') When I first envisaged the book, I hoped that it would be possible to identify testimony by name. Interviews conducted between 1976 and 1988 were undertaken with the agreement that they might appear in publications on the Middle East or in reports of human rights organisations. Interviews conducted between 1988 and 2013 were undertaken with the agreement that they might be published, with attribution, as part of academic research. Recent events, and the threat of unwanted attention from the security services, have dictated that they should now be used more sparingly, with care and with the use of pseudonyms. Interviews conducted after July 2013 were undertaken with an assurance that pseudonyms would be used in all cases.

The book combines the experiences and insights of participants with an account of events as they unfolded from January 2011 to the fifth anniversary of the uprising in 2016. It includes historical materials relating to the colonial period and the post-colonial era, focusing on relations between the state and the people, and the development of competing political currents – most importantly those of the Islamist movement and of the left. It addresses debates about the aims and strategies of these currents and their outcomes, especially the implications for the revolutionary movement of 2011. The book draws on academic research from across the Social Sciences, mobilising research in Sociology, Anthropology, Political Science, Labour History, Development Studies,

Urban Studies and Middle East Studies. It also draws on the work of Egyptian journalists who over the past 15 years have established a series of publications, mostly online, which have reported systematically on events and produced analyses of enormous value in establishing a historical record and assisting attempts to understand the course of events. Most references in the book are to English-language materials: wherever possible Internet sources are indicated.

The book falls into three sections. Part I addresses the events of 2011–12, examining the character and dynamics of the revolutionary movement and its confrontations with the state: it includes some contextual historical material. Part II mobilises historical materials more fully, addressing the development of Islamism and of the communist movement, their legacies and the implications for contemporary politics. Part III considers events from 2013–16, including the military coup of July 2013 and its aftermath. It focuses upon key debates about the revolutionary experience now under way in Egypt and more widely among radical activists and academics.

Dedication

I have been a sympathetic observer of struggles for change in Egypt since the 1970s. My first visits to Cairo coincided with a growing anger among Egyptians over the effects of President Anwar Sadat's *infitah* reforms, manifested in campus protests, mass strikes and eventually by the 'bread intifada' of January 1977, when a national uprising against austerity was suppressed by means of military intervention.

On 6 October 1976, I was walking on Meret Pasha Street, close to Tahrir Square in Cairo, when police halted traffic and cleared the road. Among the crowds there was curiosity and some anxiety – there was a long history of violent intervention by security forces in the centre of the city. After some minutes military vehicles approached, followed by scores of outriders and a cavalcade of open cars: in one stood President Anwar Sadat, an unmistakable figure in the uniform of a high-ranking officer with a mass of medal ribbons and glittering epaulettes. He greeted the crowds: it was Armed Forces Day, the anniversary of Sadat's 'War of the Crossing', the 1973 conflict with Israel.[1] His smiles and salutes met with blank stares – all along the street people turned their backs in a spontaneous silent statement that could not be misinterpreted. Sadat faced all manner of protests, surviving in power for a further five years. Almost 35 years later his successor Husni Mubarak was the target for protestors in the very same street. On 2 February 2011 thousands of demonstrators fought for their lives against his riot police and *baltagiyya* ('thugs'/'bullies') in prolonged confrontations that became known as the Battle of the Camel. In an unequal battle the protestors won through, continuing their remarkable occupation of Tahrir Square and of city centres across Egypt. Days later the president was gone, launching more than two years of further mass struggles and political crises.

The uprising of 1977 against Sadat, and the response of the state, might be seen as anticipating the events of 2011 and their outcomes. In more than three decades separating the two episodes there were important changes in Egyptian society, not least further economic reforms that made Egypt a pioneer in the Global South of aggressive neo-liberalism. These were accompanied by consolidation of the authoritarian state and repression of those expressing opposition to immiseration and inequality, and to the stranglehold of the autocracy. What did not change over this long period was the determination of those at the heart of the state to maintain their privileges and power. Their repression produced countless victims: journalists, writers, human rights campaigners, students, workers and peasant activists who were jailed, 'disappeared', or worse. As a Cairo resident in the 1980s and later a frequent visitor to the city, I was able to observe the continuous efforts of Egyptians to maintain resistance, even during the most intensive periods of repression. It was from among activist networks in the 1990s that a new left began to emerge, intent on reasserting the potential of the mass of people to bring change. It was to play a key role when, during the Palestinian intifada of 2000, a movement of solidarity reinstated the practice of public protest and began to enlarge the space for political action. The years before the fall of Mubarak saw a host of new movements for change, together with creative efforts by radical activists to maximise their impact. It also saw intensive debates on the new left about theory, history and the practice of politics. Could the regime be reformed? Was revolution required – if so, who would play the key role? What had been the fate of the old left? Why had it surrendered to the autocracy? How to address the Islamist movement in a period of growing resistance?

Many activists paid for their determination at the hands of the police and the security agencies. This book is dedicated to them: in particular to activists of the new left who worked patiently for years to renew revolutionary traditions that became so relevant in 2011 and remain the key to a transformation of social relations.

Philip Marfleet
25 January 2016

PART I
MAKING REVOLUTION

1

Introduction

Who made Egypt's revolution?

The events of January and February 2011 brought together powerful institutional actors, most importantly those in authority in the Egyptian state, and a vast number of protestors for whom engagement in public politics was a novel experience. Who participated and what was the nature of their involvement? How did they view their experiences and what were their preferred outcomes? Was this a movement of protest, a project of reform or the start of a 'revolution'?

The scale of popular[1] participation in the uprising that began on 25 January 2011 may be unprecedented in modern history. The numbers involved, and the breadth and depth of the movement, suggest extraordinarily high levels of engagement. State officials, police and army chiefs were stunned by the size and energy of demonstrations: Mona El-Ghobasy describes the impact on security forces as one of 'shock and awe' (2011). In a typical exchange on 28 January between officers of the Amn al-Markazi (Central Security Force [CSF], the riot police), a junior officer in the streets of Alexandria told his commander: 'The situation here is beyond belief. I'm telling you, sir, beyond belief.' The CSF was soon ordered to retreat to protect the city's police stations.[2] There were similar incidents in most Egyptian cities, the speed and scale of events surprising both police and protestors. Ibrahim, an organiser of the initial 25 January protest in Cairo relates his experience:

We agreed to meet at the Journalists' Syndicate downtown. On the morning of 25 January we said if there were 500 of us we'd stay for an hour; if a thousand we'd try to march down the street; if more we'd head for Tahrir [Square]. When we found the street was full we marched anyway, then we found there were people in Ramses Street and Gala'

Street and we heard of thousands coming from Shubra and Bulaq –
and we kept moving. We broke into Tahrir from 'Abd al-Mun'im Riyad
Square. The police ran: what a moment of liberation![3]

On the night of 25 January, 10,000 riot police cleared Tahrir Square and
occupied access streets to ensure that protestors did not return. All over
Egypt city centres that had also been occupied by large crowds were
assaulted by CSF detachments using tear gas and live ammunition – by
morning, a Cairo newspaper reported, 'some squares looked like a sea of
black-clad security officers'.[4] The regime had laid down its challenge: if
demonstrators wanted the streets as a stage for their protests, they must
redouble their numbers and be prepared to fight. Activists responded by
declaring 28 January a 'Day of Rage' and government officials ordered
a curfew, denying Internet access and closing mobile phone networks.
At this point the regime's strategists seemed to believe assessments of
the protests as a 'Facebook Revolution'. On this view, repeated widely in
the European and North American press, the events were organised and
led by middle-class youth who were 'tech-savvy', their use of electronic
networks allowing demonstrators to evade the state's usual means of
surveillance and control, so that without the Internet and telephone
networks they could be isolated and protests would peter out.[5] The
notion that protests were the work of highly educated young agitators
complemented a long-standing theme in regime propaganda – the idea
that the government represented the common interests of the people
and that opposition came from a small minority that, in the words of
President Mubarak, 'sought to spread chaos and violence' (2011). As we
shall see, networks of activists long engaged in attempts to contest the
autocracy played a key role in the protests. Most were not 'digital revolutionaries' nor did they possess the influence to initiate events on the scale
of protests now under way.

Sameh Naguib, a radical activist and participant in the initial
mobilisation on 25 January, comments that suspending the Internet and
phone networks had no visible effect, as the vast majority of leaders and
organisers did not have access to Facebook and could easily use more
traditional forms of communication: rather, he suggests, 'it emboldened
the demonstrators even more by proving the regime was desperate
and weak' (Naguib 2011a: 17). On 28 January, the protest movement

answered the regime's challenge by bringing millions of people to city squares. They came from every sector of urban society: in Cairo demonstrations began at many assembly points, drawing participants from prosperous middle-class suburbs, from traditional working-class neighbourhoods and from 'popular quarters' in both inner areas, and from the swathes of informal housing of the *'ashwa'iyyat* that surround the city.[6]

Hussein, a campaigner with long experience in the democracy movement, describes the impact in his suburban area south of Cairo:

> We started off in Ma'adi with a few hundred people. We were all tense and fearful – we knew that anything could happen. As we marched towards the city centre the demonstration grew and grew – but when we got to Dar al-Salam [an 'informal' area] it increased hugely. It seemed as if the whole area was joining in. People left their jobs, students left schools, at each road junction the march swelled and swelled. I'd estimate that at least 40,000 people joined in as we passed through Dar al-Salam – and then more and more as we moved on towards Tahrir through the other poor areas south of the centre.[7]

This picture is confirmed by Marwa, in her account of a march from the middle-class suburb of Medinet Nasr, east of the city centre:

> When we began in Medinet Nasr it was all a gamble. The government had ordered all mobile networks and the Internet to be shut down, so we were calling people to join us by every means. As we headed into the city people came from everywhere – but when we got near the popular quarters an army of people joined us. That was crucial because at Ramses Square the Amn al-Markazi [CSF] put up a serious fight. We beat them, taking many casualties. An unarmed crowd broke through against trained, armed police! In the end we simply exhausted them – they fell back and we poured through. It was all about numbers – a people's insurrection.[8]

By evening, and despite many casualties, Tahrir Square had been secured by demonstrators who were not to leave for many weeks. The pattern was repeated nationwide, especially in cities with large working-class populations. In Port Said, with a population of 600,000, some 80,000 people were said to be on the streets, with demonstrations of comparable proportions in Alexandria, Suez, Damietta and Mansoura (Beaumont and Sherwood 2011). In Suez, *Al Jazeera* reported, 'The police have been quite comprehensively defeated by the power of the people' (Beaumont and Sherwood 2011).

Demonstrators overwhelmed the CSF: they were in effect the shock troops of the movement for change, representing above all Egypt's urban working class and poor. Only in the countryside was participation significantly more modest – and even here many small towns saw protests. Police disappeared from the streets in most cities to be replaced by troops who remained passive, fraternising with the crowds.

What distinguished the movement of January 2011 from earlier protests against the regimes of Mubarak and his predecessor Anwar Sadat was the sheer scale of popular engagement. In this first phase of the uprising the CSF proved inadequate to resist a movement that had mobilised nationwide, paralysing the security agencies. Apparently shaken by the protests, the regime hesitated to order a military offensive, sending troops to the streets ostensibly as guardians of the people – a development that was to have profound long-term implications (see Chapter 4). On 31 January, some 2 million people rallied in Tahrir Square, a million in Martyrs' Square in Alexandria, 750,000 in Mansoura and some 250,000 in Suez – numbers that dwarfed all previous political mobilisations in Egypt (Naguib 2011a: 19). Increasingly desperate, the regime released from its jails thousands of convicted prisoners whom officers directed to join with plain-clothes police and gangs of paid thugs – the *baltagiyya* – in attacks on demonstrators.[9] Soha Abdelaty, deputy director of the Egyptian Initiative for Personal Rights, which had for years monitored conditions in Egyptian prisons, noted: 'clear instructions from the Interior Ministry, specifically its central Prisons Department, to instigate some sort of chaos' (Abouzeid 2011). In a series of savage confrontations, notably during the 'Battle of the Camel' in Cairo on 2 February 2011, gangs together with plain-clothes police failed to see off protestors. As Tahrir Square and other city centres became, for the first time, zones for open political expression the number of participants grew exponentially. The barrier of fear upon which autocracy had depended for decades had been breached. El-Ghobashy comments:

> Mubarak's structures of dominion were thought to be foolproof, and for 30 years they were. What shifted the balance away from the regime

were four continuous days of street fighting, January 25–28, that pitted the people against police all over the country. That battle converted a familiar, predictable episode into a revolutionary situation.

(El-Ghobashy 2011)

Streets and workers

A striking feature of the events was the increasing involvement of working-class people. Media coverage of the protests, especially outside Egypt, focused upon middle-class youth – the 'Facebook generation'. According to the *New York Times*, the key role in the protests was played by young professionals, mostly doctors and lawyers who, 'wired and shrewd', were said to have touched off and then guided the revolt (Kirkpatrick 2011a). Often available for interview in European languages, these activists became the voices and faces of Tahrir on transnational media. Presented as 'a generation changing the world' (*Time* 2001), they were in fact a small minority of participants. Most of those consistently in the streets and in the front line of confrontations with police and the *baltagiyya* were manual and clerical workers, and people from poor families with part-time employment or without regular jobs. Alexander and Bassiouny (2014: 198) note the preponderance of working-class victims among those killed in battles with police and thugs during the January demonstrations in Cairo, and the concentration of deaths among people from the poorest areas of the city. As we shall see (Chapter 2), Egypt's workers and urban poor had a pressing interest in both political and social change, their deepening involvement in the uprising shaping its most radical agendas.

On 6 February, the movement of the streets was complemented by a movement of the workplaces, as mass strikes began in Cairo and cities of the Nile Delta. The key demands of the streets had been formulated on 25 January. In Tahrir they were agreed at an open meeting in the square, quickly organised by activists who rushed to copy centres to make tens of thousands of leaflets for distribution among people flooding to the city centre.[10] These called for the removal of Mubarak; an end to the Emergency Law; freedom; justice; a new non-military government representing the interests of the people; and 'efficient' (non-corrupt) mobilisation of Egypt's resources. As the movement swept Egypt debates entered every workplace, generalising the demands of the streets and adding to them or reformulating them in the context of collective discussion and experience. Mass strikes began, initially among transport workers, health workers, refuse collectors, postal workers, textile workers, steel workers and workers in a range of occupations on the Suez Canal. They called for better pay and job security; many also raised demands for *taṭhir* ('cleansing'/'purification') of corrupt or autocratic owners and managers. Some strikers – initially a minority – engaged directly with protestors in city squares. In Cairo, representatives of workers in the Public Transport Authority went to Tahrir Square to distribute leaflets announcing their decision. There was no co-ordinating centre, however, and no formal relationship among activists in these workplaces. Rather, the strike movement grew organically as part of an uprising in which millions of people were experiencing a surge of confidence in their ability to bring about change.

On 10 February, public transport workers in Cairo closed bus garages, making a demonstrative impact upon the whole city. Strikes spread nationwide, from Alexandria in the north to Aswan in the far south. Some 300,000 workers were now involved, including large numbers in strategically important sectors: in a further significant development, strikes affected military factories under the authority of the armed forces command. On 11 February, demonstrations were on an unprecedented scale: among Egypt's population of some 80 million, over 15 million were said to be on the streets, including many on the brink of further collective action across industry (Naguib 2011a: 27). These developments marked a turning point and in an address delivered on state television Vice-President Omar Suleiman announced abruptly that Mubarak had resigned, passing his authority as head of state to the Supreme Council of the Armed Forces (SCAF).

On the psychological and symbolic level, observed Fawaz Gerges, this was 'a shattering moment' (Petersen 2011). Mubarak – 'the public face of political authoritarianism in the Arab world' – and architect of one of its most feared security machines, had fallen to an unarmed mass movement (Petersen 2011). Amid jubilation, the movement now passed through an important phase. It became broader, deeper and more radical in aspiration and in action; at the same time, some of its early supporters began to express their anxieties and their wish to contain the agenda for change.

Creative activity filled streets the people now claimed as their own. Participants in the '18 Days' of protest in Tahrir (between 25 January and 11 February) describe a festive atmosphere, even during bitter fighting with police and armed gangs. For Keraitim and Mehrez, Tahrir had 'acquired a symbolic life of its own that [became] the sign and language of an ongoing revolution' (2012: 28). In the carnivalesque atmosphere of the Square, they identify traditions of the *mulid*, a popular festival celebrated in Egypt for centuries and familiar to the mass of the population, especially to the working class, urban poor and peasantry, as a rare opportunity for self-expression vis-à-vis the suffocating power of the state (see Chapter 2).[11] The square had become a stage for song, poetry, dance and theatre; on buildings nearby popular artists commented on events with graffiti and paintings. When after early confrontations city centres became safer, children attended in huge numbers. Swing parks appeared, together with stalls selling toys and sweets usually associated with the holiday atmosphere of Eid[12] or with the *mulid*.

This surge in confidence was expressed in all manner of collective actions. During the most bloody confrontations of January and in the context of pervasive threats from plain-clothes police, the *baltagiyya* and prisoners freed by the regime to join the gangs, neighbourhood committees were established widely to ensure local security. El-Meehy quotes a founding member of a group in a poor neighbourhood of Cairo: 'Committees were everywhere in villages and cities. They became the heartbeat of Egyptian society – locally rooted and flexibly organized, informal and voluntary' (2012). Although their experiences were to prove uneven, these groups played an important role in transmitting the collective confidence of city squares into local communities. Of most lasting significance, however, was a further intensive burst of strike action affecting industry, transport and services, and embracing historic centres of labour struggle such as the Misr Spinning and Weaving Company in the Delta city of Mehalla al-Kubra, Egypt's largest workplace with some 25,000 employees. Campaigning journalist Hossam El-Hamalawy observed that the fall of Mubarak had been associated directly with entry into the mass movement of organised labour:

Mubarak managed to alienate all social classes in society. In Tahrir Square, you found sons and daughters of the Egyptian elite, together with the workers, middle-class citizens and the urban poor. But remember that it's only when the mass strikes started [...] that the regime started crumbling and the army had to force Mubarak to resign because the system was about to collapse.

(El-Hamalawy 2011a)

Workers had been emboldened by the overthrow of Mubarak, said El-Hamalawy, and they were 'not going home anytime soon' (El-Hamalawy 2011a). Mehalla workers now demanded a minimum monthly wage of LE1,200 (some $215) and the removal of the company's chief executive, Fuad al-Alim, widely viewed as being part of the Mubarak regime's nepotistic networks. One worker representative told Al-Ahram: 'Corruption at Misr [Spinning and Weaving Company] mirrors the corruption within the country. The plant is a microcosm of what has happened across Egypt' (Rady 2011). Similar demands were raised in another historic centre of labour struggles, the Egyptian Iron and Steel Company in Helwan south of Cairo, and at banks, cement works, chemical and pharmaceutical plants, transport depots and transport hubs including Cairo airport. During February there were 489 strikes (Beinin 2012: 8), many calling for improved wages and conditions and demanding removal of public sector managers appointed by the regime or private sector owners alleged to have obtained their companies by illicit means. In a new development, some workers – notably a large group at the Mehalla mill – declared that they would disaffiliate from the state-controlled Egyptian Trade Union Federation (ETUF) and join the Egyptian Federation of Independent Trade Unions (EFITU), set up only days earlier (Shahid 2011). If the epicentre of the movement had been in city centres, it now moved to industrial zones and to sites of strategic importance for the state itself, notably to transportation depots, military factories and to the Suez Canal. On 19 February 2011, 40 workers' leaders and labour activists associated with EFITU met to adopt a statement on 'Demands of the Workers in the Revolution'. They declared for 'Revolution, Freedom, Social Justice':

O heroes of the 25 January revolution! We, workers and trade unionists from different workplaces which have seen strikes, occupations and demonstrations by hundreds of thousands of workers across Egypt during the current period, feel it is right to unite the demands of striking workers that they may become an integral part of the goals of our revolution, which the people of Egypt made, and for which the martyrs shed their blood.

(Abu-Eita et al. 2011)

Activists from a range of industries, including military factories, identified a 'social aspect of this revolution' and their determination 'to prevent the revolution being taken away from those at its base who should be its beneficiaries' (Egyptian workers' declaration 2011). Their demands included the right to form independent unions, the right to strike, the introduction of a minimum wage and a maximum wage, and a call to dissolve the state-controlled union federation ETUF. They asserted,

> It is our opinion that if this revolution does not lead to the fair distribution of wealth it is not worth anything. Freedoms are not complete without social freedoms. The right to vote is naturally dependent on the right to a loaf of bread.

(Abu-Eita et al. 2011)

Broader and deeper

These workers, and thousands who surged into the independent unions, saw the movement of January and February as means of securing 'social freedoms' as well as political reforms guaranteeing basic rights. The aspiration for fundamental change was unmistakeable.

A discourse of 'revolution' – *thawra* – was pervasive. Most participants in demonstrations, rallies and city centre occupations viewed the movement itself as *al-thawra* and their involvement as *thawri* – 'revo-lutionary' – a means to end autocracy, remove the regime and to bring further change. This was asserted continuously in slogans such as '*thawra, thawra, thawra*' and '*thawra hatta'l nasr!*' ('Revolution until victory!'). Young activists, workers and urban poor were initiators of the uprising and its most energetic and expectant agents, identified by Carapico as: 'Diverse, raucous forces [that] appropriated public civic realms and proclaimed ownership of the commons', making 'a kind of civic revolution' (Carapico 2012: 221). The novelist Ahdaf Soueif spoke for many who, for the first time, experienced the power of a mass movement and the possibility of achieving further radical change. 'Beware of caution and embrace the unknown; we're in a revolution', she wrote, 'Put aside calculations and hold onto the dream; we're in a revolution' (Soueif 2012: 191).

During the 18 Days, the movement appeared unified around demands for the removal of Mubarak and his regime. Researchers at The American University in Cairo filmed hours of demonstrations in and around Tahrir Square; they also collected notices, leaflets and statements, together with images of posters, banners and graffiti. These expressive tools were used by participants: 'as a means of responding to and challenging dominant narratives, relating to one another and galvanizing support'; they reflected: 'conscious participation in a specific culture of resistance', making the aims of the revolution 'an ever-present, explicit call for action' (Gribbon and Hawas 2012: 104). Initially, a few hastily made banners called for 'Bread, liberty and human dignity' (*'aysh, huriyya, karama insaniyya'*). As protests developed, a mass of placards and notices appeared, many directed to Mubarak: 'Go [leave/get out]' (*'irhal'*). Others called for 'true reform'; an end to corruption; freedom for political prisoners; trials for Mubarak and his family; revenge for the martyrs (*shuhuda* – those killed by police and gangs during the protests); and for an end to the regime: 'The people want [will/intend] the fall of the regime' (*'al-sha'ab yurid isqat al-nizam'*) (Gribbon and Hawas 2012: 103–42).

These expectations of change were not shared by all those who entered the streets, however. As the movement grew, it also attracted people with different understandings of 'revolutionary' change, notably members of the middle class with grievances vis-à-vis the autocracy but who, with a stake in the status quo, were less intent on securing the social freedoms embraced by many workers and the urban poor. When the president fell on 11 February celebrations attracted every established political current, including Islamist, liberal and nationalist parties with histories that reached back to the colonial period and which had at various points been represented in government, including under Mubarak. One outcome, given added meaning by the presence of the army in the streets, was an expression of national unity, evident in the proliferation of Egyptian flags and of slogans celebrating Egyptian identity. In this context, 'revolution' could be identified with traditions of nationalist resistance vis-à-vis the colonial powers of the past and with historic interventions of the armed forces in the name of the people. Shokr comments that 'liberation' took on more complex meanings, including those associated with patriotism and what he calls 'a jubilee of national pride' (2011 45).

Mariz Tadros observes that for many months activists spoke of Egypt as being 'in a state of ongoing revolution' (Tadros, M. 2012: 1), anticipating that they would be able to remove Mubarak loyalists from centres of power and governance, oust security officers who had blood on their hands and end brutality and repression At the same time, she noted, the movement had engaged 'a variety of stakeholders' (Tadros, M. 2012: 1). It contained people of diverse political persuasions, including those for whom continuing radical change was uncongenial and even threatening. In this respect, the movement was not unique. A century earlier, Vladimir Lenin (1964 [1916]: 355–56) had observed that revolutionary movements engaged 'all and sundry oppressed and discontented elements'. Political activists who anticipated a 'pure' revolution, in which participants were unified in demands for fundamental social change, 'will never live to see it', he suggested, for included in mass political upheavals were those with 'prejudices, reactionary fantasies, weaknesses and errors' (Lenin 1964: 356). For revolutionary Marxists such as Lenin the key issue was the capacity of those who wished for fundamental change to unite the movement around the aim of 'social revolution' (Lenin 1964 [1916]: 355). In the case of Egypt in 2011, radical aspirations were to be asserted again and again, raising questions about the need for just such social transformation. As with other upheavals past and present the movement was not homogenous, however: it embraced those who aspired to establish a new social order, those who desired reform, and those fearful of further challenges to the status quo. These very different currents were to engage in prolonged conflict over the outcome of the uprising.

'Revolution'

Did the mass movement of January and February 2011 initiate a revolutionary process? Most participants viewed it in this light but their assessments were shaped by differing views of Egyptian history and of social change. As we shall see in Chapters 4 and 9, there were to be many claims to revolutionary legitimacy, including among those who in July 2013 enacted a military coup, launching a retributive campaign against the activists of 2011.

On some accounts, the movement of 2011 was far from a revolution; rather, it was a protest that facilitated brief changes in power relations among Egypt's rulers. This was the view favoured by strategic analyst

George Friedman, an early commentator on the events who days after the removal of Mubarak, observed, 'What happened was not a revolution. The demonstrators never brought down Mubarak, let alone the regime' (Friedman 2011). He continued:

> What happened was a military coup that used the cover of protests to force Mubarak out of office in order to preserve the regime. When it became clear Feb. 10 that Mubarak would not voluntarily step down, the military staged what amounted to a coup to force his resignation. Once he was forced out of office, the military took over the existing regime by creating a military council and taking control of critical ministries. The regime was always centered on the military. What happened on Feb. 11 was that the military took direct control.
>
> (Friedman 2011)

A similar view is expressed by Egyptian academic Hazem Kandil. If the military had not sided with the people, he suggested, it was doubtful that the revolt could have lasted long enough to convince Mubarak to step down (Kandil 2011: 229). The army had been the main player in the uprising, he argued, seizing its opportunity to settle scores with rivals within the regime. The role of the mass movement had been to trigger decisive action by the military command; it had no further significant part to play in Egyptian politics.

Neither of these accounts, nor those of many media analysts who predicted a swift end to the protests, addressed the continuing events in the streets, on campuses, in neighbourhoods and workplaces. For over two years Egyptian society was deeply affected by further mass demonstrations, some larger even than protests that preceded the fall of Mubarak. Hundreds of thousands of workers took strike action; countless community protests addressed matters of local dispute; political parties proliferated; and new independent media were established. Egyptian society was in a state of ferment as the mass of people sought solutions to their predicaments and greater control over their lives. These developments recalled mass movements of the twentieth century in which huge demonstrations in other states were accompanied by strikes and community actions – the Iraqi Revolution of 1958–63, the Chilean events of 1970–73, the Portuguese Revolution of 1974–75 and the Iranian Revolution of 1977–79. In all these cases, the movement was uneven, with changing fortunes for those seeking further change and those intent on containing or destroying its radical potential. What marked them out as revolutionary episodes was entry onto the scene of a mass of people intent on challenging socio-political arrangements that constrained their lives. It was this that had distinguished earlier revolutions, including upheavals of the eighteenth, nineteenth and early twentieth centuries. Leon Trotsky observed that, 'The most indubitable fact of a revolution is the direct interference of the masses in historic events' (1967: 16), further:

> [A]t those crucial moments when the old order becomes no longer endurable to the masses, they break over the barriers excluding them from the political arena, sweep aside their traditional representatives, and create by their own interference the initial groundwork for a new regime [...] The history of a revolution is for us first of all a history of the forcible entry of the masses into the realm of rulership over their own destiny.
>
> (Trotsky 1967: 16)

Events in Egypt in January and February 2011 both broke the barriers imposed by decades of repression and took initial steps towards establishing new arrangements congenial to the mass of people. They initiated 'a revolutionary process characterized by demands for radical social and political transformation' (Abdelrahman 2015: 79). The process has not been concluded, despite its forceful interruption by the military. The purpose of this book is to consider how contending classes and political currents have addressed these challenges and how they have prepared to face the struggles to come.

2

The Streets

The drama of the 18 Days, televised worldwide, produced diverse reactions. The energy and determination of protestors stimulated much admiration, with many expressions of international solidarity. When Mubarak fell, the implications for the wider Middle East gave political leaders worldwide pause for thought. Mubarak's most important ally, US President Barak Obama, declared: 'we have the privilege to witness history taking place [...] The people of Egypt have spoken, their voices have been heard, and Egypt will never be the same' (Obama 2011). Invoking the legacies of Gandhi and Martin Luther King, he acknowledged 'the power of human dignity':

> The word Tahrir means liberation. It is a word that speaks to that something in our souls that cries out for freedom. And forevermore it will remind us of the Egyptian people – of what they did, of the things that they stood for, and how they changed their country, and in doing so changed the world.
>
> (Obama 2011)

These laudatory comments, carefully calculated, sought a response among Egyptian politicians whom the United States hoped to court as events proceeded. Anxious to avoid a repeat of developments in Iran in 1979, when a movement that deposed the Shah targeted the United States as its main enemy, Obama presented the events as admirable, progressive and democratic in character. Most political leaders in Europe, also hitherto linked closely with Mubarak, followed suit. Other voices, however, expressed deep mistrust of the protest movement, invoking the threat of incoherent, disorderly and dangerous movements said to be typical of 'the Arab street'. According to American commentator Stanley Kurtz, events in Cairo recalled protests that preceded the fall of the Egyptian monarchy in 1952, when thousands of young protestors sparked 'mayhem and fires' (Kurtz 2011). He continued:

> This is why we speak of an 'Arab Street'. At critical junctures in Egypt's history, monarchs and politicians have stood by helplessly as the fate of their regimes was determined by mass outpourings on the streets of Cairo. Those crowds may have ratified and given birth to popular autocracies, but liberal democracy is not what they were about – except insofar as Egypt's single experiment in liberal democracy was abolished on its streets. So have we been witnessing an Arab Spring, or merely a new iteration of illiberal regime change via the Arab Street instead?
>
> (Kurtz 2011)

Although protestors might resemble European democratic revolutionaries of the past, he observed, they were 'weak', with alarming signs of Islamist influence, concluding that the events drew on the 'illiberal well-springs' of the Arab street (Kurtz 2011). Similar views were expressed by conservative commentators and politicians, notably in Israel, where Prime Minister Netanyahu declared that, 'The Arab street has awoken', expressing his suspicion of 'the raging masses' (Netanyahu 2011). Egyptian protestors were part of an 'Islamic, anti-Western, anti-liberal, anti-Israeli and anti-democratic wave', he said; the Arab world was 'moving not forward, but backward' (Ravid 2011).

The 'Arab street' had been used for decades as an epithet for public politics in general in the Arab world. Women and men of the region had long been viewed as objects of the political process who appeared in short-lived protests that might disturb the political order but were inadequate to assert participants' presence as genuine political actors. Both media and academic accounts viewed those involved as abnormal or dysfunctional. Bayat notes that participants in public protest were routinely described as 'angry', as likely to participate in 'mobs, riots, revolts' and to threaten those in authority, notably governments linked to the United States and its allies (Bayat 2003). These approaches reflect long-standing scepticism about independent political action by the mass of people in the region. They complement the views of those comfortable with the status quo and for whom authoritarian rule is the preferred option. Cultures of the region, it is argued, are characterised by embedded values that inhibit political progress: above all, it is Islam that accounts for a deficit in participatory politics and a tendency to sudden, violent and irrational expressions of distress. Having failed to develop institutions through which politics can be conducted in an orderly fashion, the mass of people require to be ruled; to the extent that democracy can be of benefit, it should be introduced by benevolent external forces.

This approach has been embedded in colonial ideology. In Egypt, occupied by British forces in 1882, the colonial administration combined suspicion of the mass of people with a conviction that they lacked capacities to modify both their material circumstances and their subordinate political status. According to the British administrator Alfred (later Viscount) Milner, the people of Egypt were 'docile and good tempered'; they were 'a nation of submissive slaves, not only bereft of any vestige of liberal institutions but devoid of any spark of the spirit of liberty' (Milner 2002 [1892]: 178). At the same time, they were 'in the grip of a religion the most intolerant and fanatical' (Milner 2002 [1892]: 2). Egyptians required European rule and reform: British military occupation, Milner suggested, had succeeded in bringing a 'revolution' to their lives in the form of new institutions of administration and justice (Milner 2002 [1892]: 5). These comments were part of a discourse of denial. Milner wrote just ten years after the 'Urabi Uprising – an attempt by Egyptian army officers and their supporters to reduce foreign influence. The 'revolt' was crushed by the British, who organised a naval bombardment of Alexandria followed by an invasion and the establishment of a military regime that lasted for over 70 years. Far from being 'docile', Egyptians had initiated one of the early nationalist responses to colonial rule in the Middle East, prompting a particularly violent European intervention. The twin notion of cultural inadequacy and of passivity that required Europeans to exert benign influence was nonetheless a legitimising theme for successive colonial administrations. Evelyn Baring, Lord Cromer (Controller-General and later Consul-General of Egypt), asserted that: 'Islam as a social system has been a complete failure' (Baring 2000 [1908]: 134). Egyptians were inhibited by the many shortcomings of Islamic culture, he proposed: to experience progress they required the imposition of European values and techniques. Baring observed:

> We need not always enquire too closely into what these people, who are, nationally speaking, more or less *in statu pupillari*, themselves think is best in their own interests, although this is a point which deserves serious consideration [sic]. But it is essential that each special issue should be decided mainly with reference to what, by the light of Western knowledge and experience tempered by local consideration, we consciously think is best for the subject race.
>
> (Cromer 1913: 13)

Political mobilisation by Egyptians violated this approach. For the British authorities, Egyptian self-activity in the political arena was incoherent and irrational; it was often described as 'mad'. During the nationalist uprising of 1919, demonstrations were invariably described by British officials as the work of 'mobs' and 'toughs' who attracted 'rabble'.[1] The streets were places of extreme danger, of 'mob violence', 'pillaging' and 'frenzy' (Seth 1966: 148). Police chief Sir Thomas Russell described Cairenes who protested against the violence of British troops as 'a howling mob of the most horrible looking roughs I have ever seen' (Seth 1966: 144). The 'whole mob was shrieking and yelling', he said: 'If you can imagine a drawing by Hogarth of a scene made up by Dante's Inferno and the French Revolution, add to that mad oriental fanaticism – and you have something like this mob' (Seth 1966: 144).

Edward Said notes the persistence of such attitudes throughout the colonial period and the means by which they were integrated into popular culture in Europe. In the case of Britain, terms such as 'street Arab' entered daily discourse as synonyms for 'riff-raff [...] the kind of unimportant flotsam and jetsam of a society which is basically made up of barbarians and subhuman people' (Barsamian 2003: 170). Said comments: 'I think it's not an accident that this term ["Arab street"] is always used to talk about Arab public opinion' (Barsamian 2003: 170).

'Muslim mind'

In the 1950s one strand of academic opinion fused these ideas with Islamophobic notions of a 'Muslim mind'. Against the background of sustained anti-colonial mobilisations across the Middle East, Bernard Lewis – originator of the theory of a 'clash of civilisations' – depicted people of the region as helpless in the face of technological and social progress.[2] Over the next 30 years he elaborated the notion of a perverse and irrational popular politics expressed in sudden outbursts of distress and of helpless fury – 'an explosive mixture of rage and hatred' (Lewis 1990). The Muslim masses, argued Lewis, existed in conditions of 'aimless and formless resentment and anger' (1990): unable to articulate their aspirations or to organise for effective change they must be assisted by external forces. If they could not be induced to accept models preferred by 'the West', there could be explosive consequences, he argued. Invoking an apocalyptic vision of confrontation between the civilising West and the incoherent but – paradoxically – deadly forces of the East, he argued for continued external intervention in the region, for 'Either we bring them freedom or they destroy us' (Lewis 2006: 7).[3]

These ideas were accepted enthusiastically by neo-conservatives who dominated American policy-making for a generation from the early 1990s. Daniel Pipes, an outspoken representative of the neo-conservative current, was contemptuous of 'the so-called "Street"' (Pipes 2002: 57). He asserted: 'It rises up with much noise but without much consequence, unable to force governments to take its preferred actions. It dies down when its favourite causes perform poorly' (Pipes 2002: 57). In 2002, Robert Satloff told American officials that: 'The Arab "Street" poses no real threat to [the] U.S.':

> The record of the past two decades suggests with unusual clarity that the United States should not adopt policies on the presumption that Arab or other Muslim popular action – mobs, riots, revolts – will either threaten friendly local rulers or target U.S. interests.
>
> (Satloff 2002)

The alleged incapacity of the mass of people to undertake meaningful political action was used to endorse the neo-liberal agenda, becoming part of doctrines of prosperity (the 'trickle down' process/meritocracy/ the new middle class) that accompanied deregulation, privatisation and assaults on the developmental state of the post-colonial era. Partisans of this approach viewed Arabs/Muslims as incapable of sustained political initiative. They required the liberating influences of the market; at the same time their passivity could be read as acquiescence.

Writing in 2003, Marc Lynch – another American analyst – offered a partial corrective to these approaches. He suggested that important changes were under way, notably those brought by mass media and their increased sensitivity to public opinion. He observed: 'Those analysts who argue that the Arab street can be safely ignored, or cowed into submission by the exercise of power, dramatically and dangerously misread the real significance of these transformations in the Arab public sphere' (Lynch 2003: 85). The 'street' remained the key frame of analysis, however. Politics pursued in other contexts, both formal and informal, remained invisible to many academics and foreign policy analysts in Europe and North America. One outcome, as Gause admitted, was that they 'missed the Arab Spring' (2011).

'Passive people'

For decades the mass of Egyptians had been encouraged to believe not only that engagement in politics was futile but that it was inconsistent with national culture and society. In the 1930s, striking workers at the Misr Spinning and Weaving Company in Mehalla al-Kubra were arrested and taken before a judge who told them that strikes 'have nothing to do with Egyptian workers':

> The workers [...] must cooperate with the company for production and sacrifice every personal interest in order to serve the fatherland [...] These acts [strikes] are completely repulsive to them [the workers] by virtue of their education, their circumstances and their religion, which is based on forgiveness, cooperation and nobility of character.[4]

The Egyptian historian Khalid Fahmy comments: 'We were taught in schools that we were a patient and passive people, and for generations we accepted facile sayings about the genius of Egypt, its tranquil landscape, its gentle river and undemanding people' (Fahmy 2013). The regimes' fear of the mass of people was displaced onto the wider society as a conviction that unauthorised public politics was perverse and destructive: those who engaged in protest violated Egyptian norms, threatening social order and harmony. This Egyptian account of 'the street' was a continuous feature of ideologies of control developed under regimes of the post-colonial era. It shaped official attitudes within the education system and in state-controlled mass media, among which evidence of self-activity among the mass of people was almost completely absent. Writing in 2009, Rabab El-Mahdi noted that Egyptian media ignored compelling evidence of effective opposition to the Mubarak regime. The democracy movement that grew swiftly in 2004, she observed, was seen as 'mysterious – as having emerged without warning and as disappearing without trace' (El-Mahdi 2009: 87). For El-Mahdi the movement was one link 'in a chain of continuous currents of protest'; part of 'a cycle of contestation' in which successive waves of protest against the Mubarak regime stimulated further forms of action (El-Mahdi 2009: 87, 95). These included an extensive campaign of solidarity with the Palestinian intifada of 2000, the anti-war protests of 2003, action against land seizures, and a workers' movement that from 2006 spread widely across Egyptian industry. There were many manifestations of political agency, including lobbies, rallies, demonstrations, strikes, land occupations and countless community initiatives. Reflecting on the scale of protest in 2008, *Al-Ahram Weekly* (an English language publication that often evaded the censors) identified a rising tide of public action, with a record number of events and incidents; 2008, suggested the newspaper, was the year when demonstrations and strikes 'became the norm' (*Al-Ahram Weekly* 2009a).[5]

Intervention by the police and security agencies under Emergency Laws in force for over 30 years meant that many episodes of protest against the Mubarak regime were short-lived. Networks of activism were nonetheless consolidating, using both formal and informal arenas of protest. Millions of people could give testimony to the scale of activity, though state officials and mass media continued to ignore it. In a rare departure from denials of the state and of establishment politicians, in 2008 liberal parliamentarian Mona Makram-Ebeid warned against those who dismissed protest as politically irrelevant or who viewed 'the street' as ready to rise in revolts that would lead to chaos (Makram-Ebeid 2009). State-controlled media had been successful in moulding public opinion, she observed, but should awaken to changes under way. As repression intensified, the Mubarak regime closed even the modest spaces it had permitted within the parliamentary system, forbidding independent activity at election time, restricting electoral lists, initiating violence at polling stations and blatantly rigging results, so that the general election of 2010 was a charade even by Mubarak's standards. In this situation the mass of people, as Bayat observed, 'were damned if they did [protest] and damned if they didn't' (2012: 75). For many academic experts in Europe and North America the 'Arab street' remained the dominant paradigm for addressing public politics, as those involved in demonstrations were depicted as '"irrational" and "aggressive"', while those unable to participate or who were forcefully excluded were '"apathetic" and "dead"' (Bayat 2012: 75).

The uprising of January–February 2011 compelled reassessment. The movement of the 18 Days was not only massive and energetic but also creative, participatory and overwhelmingly non-violent. As global media reported events in Cairo in real time, hundreds of millions of people worldwide identified with the struggles that aspired to freedom and social justice. The US government, for almost 40 years an enthusiastic supporter of authoritarian rule in Egypt, felt obliged to keep its options open. Cook observes that the Obama administration, 'hamstrung between the uncertainties of political change and American interests' (2012: 256), hesitated over its public policy. When Mubarak resigned on 11 February, the US president eventually declared for the mass movement:

> This is the power of human dignity, and it can never be denied. Egyptians have inspired us, and they've done so by putting the lie to the idea that justice is best gained through violence [...] Today belongs to the people of Egypt [...]
>
> (Obama 2011)

Washington's academic advisers had spent decades caricaturing popular politics in the region. Gerges (2014: 24) observes that political scientists in particular long viewed Arab society through a distorted lens and were ill-prepared for 'a revolutionary moment of political emancipation and self-determination' (Gerges 2014: 1). Now they witnessed 'bottom-up politics, workers, ordinary people, social movements, public space and resistance, the decay of hegemony, the crisis of authority and the role of agency in general [...]' (Gerges 2014: 1).

'Facebook revolution'

The uprising and sustained mobilisations that followed were a powerful assertion of agency. Although many academics and others were to return to analyses set within the comfort zone of the 'Arab street', the effect of mass protest was to compel unprecedented interest in the participants. Egyptians who stood outside the networks of privilege and structures of institutional politics finally came into focus. Initial assessments identified youthful, middle-class activists mobilised primarily through social media. For many journalists 'the Facebook revolution' provided a simple frame for complex and tumultuous events. El-Mahdi (2009) had observed that the democracy movement of 2004 proved 'mysterious' for most analysts in the mass media; the uprising of 2011 was also perplexing, erupting at a moment when the Mubarak regime appeared solidly in control, backed by powerful allies and with 'the street' apparently quiescent. A common journalistic response asserted that events were driven by hitherto unknown cyber-activists. For the American television network CNN, 'young, anonymous, internet-powered dissidents' were at the centre of events (Sutter 2011) – an approach that provided intriguing headlines[6] and an alibi for the absence of informed analysis of the movement. Some activists understandably encouraged this approach, seeing their particular form of political engagement as the driving force for change. Reporting for the *New York Times* live from Tahrir Square, the novelist Mansoura Ez-Eldin suggested that, 'In the blink of an eye, the Twitter and Facebook generation had successfully rallied hundreds of thousands to its cause.' (Ez-Eldin 2011). Writing in 2012, Wael Ghonim – a Google executive who had been active in establishing Facebook as a campaigning tool in Egypt – argued that social media had shaped the movement. His memoir of the uprising, *Revolution 2.0*, maintained that online initiatives set the agenda, asserting: 'The youth of Egypt made history – they scheduled a revolution' (Ghonim 2012). On some accounts, social media had the determinative role. For Denis Campbell, digital networks had 'unshackled' the system: the 140 characters of a Twitter message, he declared, had removed a dictator in 18 days (Campbell 2011: 1).

Hossam El-Hamalawy, a leading exponent of digital networking in Egypt, had a different view. Recognising the value of Twitter in disseminating news about dissent to large audiences, he nonetheless refuted the notion that social media was the key mobilising force:

I saw Twitter helping to exaggerate the power and strength of some activists and/or groups giving a false impression about their abilities [...] Some [people] are under the illusion that it's enough to have a Twitter account with a big number of followers to 'instigate the masses into action,' which is of course a farce.

(El-Hamalawy 2012b)

Linda Herrera, also a close observer of events in Egypt, makes a similar point. Political and social movements, she insists, 'belong to people and not to communication tools and technologies' (Herrera 2011). Facebook, like cell phones, the Internet and Twitter, does not have agency nor a moral universe and is not predisposed to particular ideological or political orientations; rather, she observes, social media 'are what people make of them' (Herrera 2011). Between January and March 2011 Miriyam Aouragh and Anne Alexander interviewed activists in Cairo and made close observations of social media, assessing the 'Sense and Nonsense of the Internet Revolution' (Aouragh and Alexander 2011). Most of their respondents were critical of analyses that attributed 'magical powers' to Internet technology: 'By repeatedly putting the Internet corporations – Facebook, Twitter, and the like – at the center, it seemed as if particular Western characteristics were artificially being inserted into a genuine popular Arab revolution', they observed (Aouragh and Alexander 2011: 1346), concluding:

It is precisely because [Internet activism] *looked* like it was a new, youth-oriented, non-ideological, online, horizontal movement that it gained attention [...] We think there is also a general problem among journalists and researchers: projecting their own experience with the Internet on other phenomena, and their inability to understand what is discussed between the lines in Arabic. This double bias contributes to sketching a deformed image of the role of the Internet [emphasis in original].

(Aouragh and Alexander 2011: 1355)

Participants

Social media played an important facilitating role during the uprising. Internet activists did not, however, constitute the majority of participants in the protests, nor were they responsible for mobilising the vast numbers involved. Who then was in the streets and city squares, and why did they choose these sites of protest?

A striking feature of media coverage and academic analysis of events in Egypt is the focus on protest in public spaces. Countless protest movements worldwide have made demonstrative statements by rallying in public squares. These have been particularly important in the context of authoritarian political systems in which means of repression and symbols of subordination play key roles in assertion of power and of regime legitimacy. The armed forces, police and security agencies are often stationed in monumental buildings or spaces associated with the state, alongside iconic representations such as statues and inscriptions, and with flags and banners that celebrate individual or collective authority – the monarch, the president, the party leadership (Wedeen 1999). The use of public space for the performance of state authority, often involving spectacle – the mass rally, the military parade, the review of troops and weapons – has been a routine means of asserting control. Movements of protest have often entered these spaces of symbolic importance to challenge state authorities: hence the importance of Wenceslas Square in Prague during demonstrations against Soviet invasion in 1968 and 1969, of Tianahmen Square in Beijing in 1989, of Independence Square in Kiev in 2001 and 2004. In the case of the Middle East, however, mass protests have been addressed by external analysts less in the context of universal practices of protest than as the work of the 'Arab street' – as if entry into public space was the main or even sole means of expressing discontent. In Egypt, urban spaces have long been closely controlled by both colonial and post-colonial regimes. Under Mubarak, city centres were policed continuously by the CSF: demonstrations such as those supporting the Palestinian intifada of 2000, the anti-war movement of 2003, and the marches and rallies of Kifaya in 2004 and 2005 were met with massive force. When the uprising of 2011 began, it was understood that, as elsewhere, the contest for the streets would be a decisive test for the movement. As we shall see in Chapter 3, however, public spaces were not the only sites of protest.

What distinguished the mass engagement of Egyptians with public politics was not an atavistic reflex of people constituted as 'the street' but the vast scale and continuous mobilisations of the movement. The numbers involved, and the drama and danger of many episodes during the 18 Days, made systematic enquiry about participants extraordinarily difficult. Rigorous methods of enquiry that might have established the status and motivation of those involved were out of the question – indeed, the movement defied such approaches. One academic research project has nonetheless made detailed claims about the socio-economic status of participants. Mark Beissinger, Amaney Jamal and Kevin Mazur (2013: 4) propose that participants were 'disproportionately middle-aged, middle class, professional, and religious', 'the poorest segments of society were among the least likely to participate', 'the working class did not play a predominant role' and 'the Egyptian Revolution did indeed represent a middle class revolution' (Beissinger *et al.* 2013: 14, 17, 15). Mobilising disputed theories of political action, including much-criticised 'modernisation' theses, they examined data supplied by the Arab Barometer – a polling organisation that surveyed some 1,200 Egyptians in the months after the fall of Mubarak. Polling data in Egypt is notoriously unreliable because of the reluctance of many people to respond to intrusive questioning (in the context of their experience of the authoritarian state) and due to the difficulty of obtaining a meaningful sample. The sample mobilised by Beissinger, Jamal and Mazur in addition included a majority of rural respondents (52 per cent of the total), making it almost useless as a means of assessing an overwhelmingly urban movement (Arab Barometer Project 2011: 4). The conclusions reached are almost certainly false and have not been widely referenced as a basis for understanding the early phases of the movement. Evidence from other sources, together with the testimony of activists with long experience of social mobilisation in Egypt, offers a different picture.

The demonstrations in Cairo evidenced a very wide range of participants. In a well-informed report of 24 February 2011, the International Crisis Group (ICG) observed that disinterested assessment of the composition of public protests was complicated not only by the fact that attendance was uneven and changing over the course of each day and over the 18 Days but also because the assessments themselves became 'something of a Rorschach test: people found in the mass of protesters what they wanted' and the conclusion reached by many that crowds were a microcosm of Egyptian society 'was itself a political statement' (ICG 2011: 10). The ICG nonetheless observes that at an early stage of the uprising working class and poor people were present in large numbers and that during traumatic confrontations with the CSF 'members of the lower economic classes played a vital role on the frontlines' (ICG 2011: 22). As confrontations continued many who depended on daily wages returned to work but later, as strikes spread, 'scarcely anyone stood back' (ICG 2011: 22). Ibrahim, a veteran activist, observes that protests in Cairo involved increasing numbers of working-class and poor people, while in other cities from the beginning they were a majority of participants. He says:

> The uprising was a popular movement in that it drew in people from across the social spectrum – the middle class, the workers, the poor and even some of the wealthy. The only people missing early on were the peasants. The composition of marches during the 18 Days depended on where they started. In Cairo a march from Muhandeseen was mainly middle class but a march from an old working-class area like Shubra contained many workers – and those demonstrations that passed from more prosperous areas through poor quarters were sometimes transformed by the participation of local people.
>
> More and more people came to the city centre from outlying areas that are neighbourhoods of workers and the poor. By the time Mubarak fell, these people were in the majority – and in cities like Mehalla, Kafr al-Shaikh, Port Said and Suez the workers dominated almost from day one. These are industrial cities, and these were mainly workers' protests.[7]

Strikers joined demonstrations in cities including Alexandria, Mansoura, Damietta and Mehalla al-Kubra. In the three main urban centres of the Suez Canal area – Port Said, Ismailiyya and Suez – there were also large workers' protests (Shadid 2011). Radical activists who participated in front-line battles in Cairo with police and with the *baltagiyya* testify to the presence of workers on the streets. Mohamed said:

> I found that alongside me were many working-class youth – especially young men with a real hatred for the regime, often because of how they'd suffered at the hands of the police. They fought with tremendous courage and without them we might not have survived the battles. They brought others – the movement was built by word of mouth, as families, friends from work, neighbourhoods joined in. Where were they from? Most, I think, from working-class areas close to the centre like Shubra, and then from places like Imbaba, Bulaq [Bulaq

al-Dakrur], Dar al-Salam, al-Marg, Shubra al-Khayma – the so-called *'ashwa'iyyat*.[8]

Working-class protestors proved particularly effective in street battles: Bauer and Schweitzer note that these participants had learned over many years 'how to play games of cat-and-mouse with the police' and how to deal with the latter's violence (2012: 11). Rabab El-Mahdi points to a history of 'clear class confrontations' in which police and security officials focused attention on working-class youth, notably the Ultras – football fans targeted because of their defiance of authority (Bilal 2011). She observes:

> Since the Ultras were created, they were always targeted by state security. They are seen as a mob or as hooligans [...] So they developed skills that none of the middle class was forced to develop. Plus they come from backgrounds where such skills are needed on a daily basis just as survival mechanisms.
>
> (Bilal 2011)

These assessments are given added weight by evidence from NGOs that compiled data on those killed and injured during the events. The Arab Network for Human Rights (ANHRI) recorded 841 deaths.[9] Although the occupations of victims were not noted systematically, they included industrial workers and clerical workers as well as students, teachers and doctors. The Egyptian Journalists' Union collected more detailed information: among records of 279 dead, they included occupational data on 120, of whom 74 were workers – the rest were listed as students or professionals. The Society of Heroes and Victims of the Revolution recorded 4,500 injured, of whom 70 per cent were said to be workers without educational qualifications, 12 per cent were workers with intermediate qualifications, 11 per cent were school students and 7 per cent held higher qualifications (Alexander and Bassiouny 2014: 198). In Cairo, large concentrations of deaths and injuries were among people from poor areas at the fringes of the city. Alexander and Bassiouny note the clusters of victims in Zawiya al-Hamra, Dar al-Salam and Basatin, as well as in 'mixed' areas of wealth and poverty such as Ma'adi (2014: 198–99). They conclude that the presence of workers, urban poor and members of the lower middle class 'as insurgent citizens in the streets' dramatically shifted the balance of forces in the battle between the people and the regime (Alexander and Bassiouny 2014: 199).

'Special interests'

Battlegrounds such as Tahrir Square took on a special status as sites of death and self-sacrifice. In the square families and friends of the dead established a memorial to the victims as *shuhada* ('witnesses' – martyrs). When military police attacked and destroyed the memorial it was promptly rebuilt, with photographs, posters and poems to the dead (later it was to become the site of a *mathaf al-thawra*, Museum of the Revolution, in which the martyrs had special prominence). The square became a *mazar* – a revered place that should be visited in homage to those who had died. For some Egyptians it had become a *haram* – a sanctuary that should be defended against those who brought violence and violated the memory of the dead. A network of local groups, Families of the Martyrs, set up camp in the square, bringing to the city centre relatives and neighbours from all over Greater Cairo and especially from poorer quarters.

Tahrir and other city squares were invested with special significance as places of memory and loss; at the same time they were sites for public celebration, for festivals in the mode of the *mulid*. These carnivalesque occasions had special significance for the mass of people. Keraitim and Mehrez note that traditionally *mawalid* 'reinvent and invert the game of power' as the downtrodden and dispossessed 'seize control of public space, unsettling, even if momentarily, hegemonic religious practices and discourses, as well as oppressive political power and structures' (2012: 45). As sites such as Tahrir were secured by the protest movement, vast numbers of people participated in 'jubilant creativity', with song, dance, food, poetry, graffiti and street art (Keraitim and Mehrez 2012: 45). The mood of collective confidence gave evidence of a 'cultural revolution', reported the *New York Times*: festive protests had become 'a window into what Egypt might look and sound like without the regime of Hosni Mubarak' (Creswell 2011). Participants also engaged in intensive debate, as political currents old and new argued their case from makeshift platforms and distributed leaflets and tracts. Here was a complex mix of influences: students and youth activists encamped in the *mayadin* addressed members of the 'popular classes'. At the same time, workers and urban poor brought experiences of collective struggle and of organisation that for decades had operated underground or on the fringes of formal politics: they too grappled with the challenge of addressing a mass audience.

Strikes that had begun on 7 February surged after the fall of Mubarak, combining economic demands with calls for *taṭhir* and for establishment of independent trade unions, posing a growing challenge to the new SCAF government. A week after it had seized presidential powers, SCAF declared:

> Some groups, prioritising their own demands, have organised [work] stoppages and protests that paralyse [various] interests and inhibit the speed of production [...] Some elements have prevented state workers from carrying out their labour, thereby burdening the work flow and leading to the paralysis of production and consequent losses [...] The Supreme Council for the Armed Forces will not permit these illegitimate actions, which pose a grave danger to the nation.
>
> (ICG 2011: 15)

This was recognition of the impact of labour actions, especially in military factories. If the movement had begun with marches in suburban areas, drawing strength from its concentration in city centres, it had now sprung to the workplaces, which were to remain a focus of militancy until the military coup of 2013. Much foreign media coverage and academic analysis ignored these developments, continuing to describe a movement dominated by youth activists whose successes could be attributed to Internet activism. El-Mahdi criticises both the construction of 'a new imaginary homogenous structure called "youth"' and the complementary assertion that class and class politics – associated with change from below – were entirely absent (2012: 133). The mass movement had compelled new interest in Egyptians as political actors but there was still reluctance to accept that they might challenge the economic order and the structures of the state.

After the fall of Mubarak strikes spread nationwide, together with a new movement for independent trade union organisation. There were soon allegations that workers were pursuing *ihtijajat fi'awiyya* – 'group interests', or special interests. In March 2011, SCAF approved a law banning protests, assemblies and strikes said to impede private and public business, providing for long prison sentences and heavy fines. In April, Egypt's grand mufti, 'Ali Gum'a (a state appointee), declared that 'instigators of *fi'awi* [special interest] demonstrations violate the teachings of God' (Sallam 2011). The military command was now involved in a long struggle to protect both the core institutions of the state and its own interests in the Egyptian economy (see Chapter 8). It drew support from members of the middle class, especially those who had found the Mubarak order disagreeable but were unwilling to concede to sustained demands from below. Their distaste for the vulgar methods of the regime and the venality of the Mubarak family was greatly exceeded by fear of a self-confident movement from below – and in particular anxiety about the entry into public politics of people from the poorest neighbourhoods. David Sims (2010: 15) observes that for over 20 years there had been complaints that people living in the 'new slums' of Cairo brought threatening, alien values to the city. Most were assumed to be rural migrants unsuited to urban life. As one commentator wrote in the journal *al-Ahram al-Iqtisadi* in 1990:

> All the neighbouring villages have become part of the capital, and instead of inculcating them with city ways and civilisation, the capital has become sick with all the backward diseases of the Egyptian villages. It has become a greater village instead of a greater Cairo.
>
> (Sims 2010: 15)

Growth of the informal zones or *'ashwa'iyyat* had been spectacular: in 1960, 15 per cent of people in Greater Cairo lived in informal areas; by 2009, the total had risen to 63 per cent (Sims 2010: 83). For at least 20 years before the events of 2011, however, growth had been driven less by migration from the countryside than by endogamous factors. In 2000, over 80 per cent of the population of Cairo consisted of people born in the city, and over 80 per cent of migrants to the city came from other urban centres (Bayat and Denis 2000: 197). Many had bought land and constructed houses financed by earnings abroad – remittances transferred by millions of Egyptians who worked in states of the Gulf or in Libya.[10] The *'ashwa'iyyat* and nearby 'urban villages' had grown organically as part of the city, home to millions of people embedded in the urban economy and who occupied jobs in all areas of industry, transport and services in both public and private sectors.

Egypt's nouveau riche and some members of the large middle class (small business owners, professionals, managers in state employment) were meanwhile also on the move – to new, gated communities built mainly on the desert fringes to the east and west of the old city. Here California-style estates such as Dreamland, Utopia, Beverley Hills and Lakeside (sic) were established alongside shopping malls, hypermarkets, multiplex cinemas and the campuses of private universities. For the first time, the wealthy and privileged could live much of their lives entirely apart from the great unwashed. Separation reflected global developments in the era of neo-liberalism – the withdrawal of those with money and influence to securitised zones in which they could be isolated from the mass of the urban population. This was associated with practices of displacement among the wealthy and the middle class of their own fears onto people of the poorer quarters. In the case of Egypt, there was increasingly general disdain of the countryside and in particular of the urban 'ashwa'iyyat:

> Some see ashwaiyyat as 'unnatural' communities which trigger 'social disease' and 'abnormal behaviour' such as lack of privacy, overcrowding and violence [...] The informal cities are perceived by many in Egypt as representing a Hobbesian locus of lawlessness and extremism, producing a 'culture of violence' and an 'abnormal' way of life.
>
> (Bayat and Denis 2000: 185)

In Egypt, such fears were heightened by the association of Islamic activism with informal housing zones (especially after clashes in 1992 between the CSF and Islamist activists in the Cairo neighbourhood of Imbaba: see Chapter 5). Residents of informal areas were viewed increasingly as members of 'outsider' communities who required special measures of control. During the heady 18 Days of 2011, these anxieties were somewhat subdued. When, after the fall of Mubarak, demands for social justice were pursued with more and more vigour, the poor and allegedly semi-rural neighbourhoods were again viewed as a locus of poverty, crime and political violence, requiring state intervention and control.

The influence of these ideas can be seen in the analysis of Hazem Kandil, an Egyptian academic who expressed deep concern about people of the *'ashwa'iyyat*. They were 'the poorest of the poor [...] people living in subhuman conditions', he said (Kandil 2011: 25). Many had moved recently from the countryside and were living 'in tragic isolation' from the rest of society amid widespread fear that they might one day stage 'an Egyptian *jacquerie*' (Kandil 2011: 25). Fortunately, he declared, 'this menacing human mass was entirely absent from the [2011] revolt' (Kandil 2011: 26). Millions of Egyptians from 'the dark world' of the *ashwaiyyat* (Kandil 2011: 25) were leading participants in mass protests and strikes: now they were being reviled as a threat to the whole society. Pressing questions were emerging. Who really had made the uprising? What were their aims and hopes? Who was to be included and who excluded from the agenda for change?

3

The Workers and the Movement

'Unknown soldiers'

In early 2011 the *midan* seemed for many activists to express the revolution itself. Tahrir (Arabic – 'liberation') was the place in which liberation/freedom was to be secured. Already, however, the movement for change had moved beyond the streets: most importantly, it now embraced concerted workplace struggles.

The workers and the urban poor were the 'unknown soldiers' of the uprising.[1] Workers organised collectively but did not take the lead in launching events: they were nonetheless key participants in the streets and soon the initiators of strikes that were decisive in prompting the fall of the president. During the 1980s and 1990s, Egyptian governments had described strikes as conspiracies organised by a 'subversive minority' against the will of the 'great majority of conscious workers'.[2] They were said to express a sectional interest and, according to the president, showed a 'lack of nationalist responsibility'.[3] The same claims were made by members of the SCAF government that replaced Mubarak in February 2011. They also attacked the 'economic' demands and 'sectional' interests of striking workers, juxtaposing 'the selfless motives of Tahrir' with '*fi'awi* [special interest] protests that put particular agendas ahead of the greater good' (Sallam 2011). According to the columnist Khalid Muntasir, strikes were a 'contagion':

> Tahrir demonstrations raised a political slogan, 'The people want to bring down the regime.' All the slogans revolved around the meaning of freedom, as demonstrators set aside their *fi'awi* demands and summoned forth the spring of liberty. They did not ask for a raise or a bonus. They looked at the wider context and at the nation as a whole. The contagion of narrow viewpoints did not spread among them, as it

did among those who engaged in continuous, hysterical and vengeful *fi'awi* demonstrations.[4]

Writing as events unfolded, Sameh Naguib described the 'barrages of articles, television shows, army announcements, and interviews with ministers all talking about the new stage of the revolution relying on restarting the "wheel of production"' (Naguib 2011b). The message to the Egyptian working class from the bourgeoisie and its intellectuals was, he said: 'Thank you very much, you helped us get rid of Mubarak, but now go back to work and shut up' (Naguib 2011b).

In March 2011, SCAF approved a law banning protests, assemblies and strikes that impeded private or public business, providing for penalties of up to a year in prison and fines of LE500,000 ($85,000). A determined effort was under way to suppress workers' initiatives, accompanied by efforts to rewrite the brief history of the revolution: the purpose, suggested Hesham Sallam, was to sideline 'both pressing socio-economic problems and the millions of Egyptians who suffer from them' (Sallam 2011). The ideological offensive was ineffective: in the days following Mubarak's fall there were 40 to 60 disputes per day; by the end of February there had been almost 500 episodes of strike action or other forms of collective protest.[5] The issues raised included wages, job security, working conditions and bullying by management. Many disputes also raised the issue of *tathir* – the removal from workplaces and enterprises of corrupt practices and the removal of employers, managers, security officers and trade union officials complicit with the Mubarak regime. This echoed demands of the wider movement to settle accounts with *feloul* – 'remnants' of the Mubarak order – but with the added effectiveness brought by collective action in the workplace. In March 2011, there were demands for *tathir* in hospitals, sugar refineries, textile mills, government ministries, the postal service, schools and universities. These were also given impetus by the movement to establish independent unions. The Egyptian Federation of Independent Trade Unions (EFITU) had been founded on 30 January 2011 by teachers, health workers and tax officers. Independent union groups were soon established across Egypt in a surge of self-organising that produced liaisons across workplaces and regions. Many independent groups demanded cleansing of managers and of ETUF officials; some promptly established elected committees to run their workplaces.[6] Beinin comments that the establishment of the EFITU was 'a revolutionary act' (2012: 7). By violating the legal monopoly on labour organisation enjoyed by state-run unions since 1957, workers asserted democracy from below – a development, he suggested, in which 'a crime becomes the basis for a new legality' (Beinin 2012: 7). The founders of the EFITU were soon joined by unions in the textile industry, pharmaceuticals, chemicals, iron and steel, vehicle manufacturing and by retired workers. Affiliated organisations appeared in both traditional centres of working-class militancy such as public-sector textile mills and in hitherto unorganised private enterprises in new industrial cities. Consistent with demands for *taṭhir*, the EFITU demanded the replacement of Isma'il Ibrahim Fahmi, treasurer of the official Egyptian Federation of Trade Unions (ETUF), who had been appointed by SCAF as minister of manpower and migration. The independent unions instead nominated Ahmad Hasan al-Bura'i, an academic known to favour reform of labour law in the interests of workers: Fahmi was promptly withdrawn by SCAF and Bura'i installed. The new minister undertook to negotiate new labour laws with the EFITU and its component groups, giving a huge boost to independent organisation and entering into the national debates about change issues of workers' collective rights and of democracy exercised from below.

Industrial disputes continued throughout the spring, surging in September 2011, when some 500,000 workers participated. Independent organisation expanded to embrace much of the state sector – ministries, hospitals, the postal service and university campuses, at which for the first time cleaners, cooks and administrative staff joined new unions. Schoolteachers participated in local strikes and demonstrations, many groups sending delegations to Cairo on 24 September 2011 for an unprecedented national protest. This demanded dismissal of the Mubarak-appointed minister of education, investment in schools and books, security of contracts for part-time teachers and a minimum wage of LE1,200 a month. In an important development, large numbers of women participated. As their delegations arrived from provincial cities, thousands marched through central Cairo to join demonstrators at the Cabinet Office in Qasr al-Aini street. One explained:

> I am here to say 'get out' to the minister of education. We have come from all over Egypt to send this message – we want the government to understand that we, the teachers, must be treated with respect. We

removed Mubarak and now we want a new minister who understands that teachers can't go on living on this [low] pay and without means to help the children properly. This is my first demonstration – look at all the women![7]

The blogger Hossam El-Hamalawy commented on the dismay among some activists that strikes had continued to spread. As early as February 2011, he noted, certain 'middle class activists' had urged Egyptians to suspend their protests and return to work, joining in 'ridiculous lullabies about "let's build new Egypt", "Let's work harder than even before"' (El-Hamalawy 2011). In fact, he said, the interests of striking workers did not differ from those of the wider population:

> It's not the workers' fault that you were not paying attention to their news. Every single day over the past three years there was a strike in some factory whether it's in Cairo or the provinces. These strikes were not just economic, they were also political in nature.
>
> (El-Hamalawy 2011b)

This was also the message of leaders in the EFITU, who played a key role in formulating the 'Demands of the Workers in the Revolution', issued on 19 February, asserting that in Egypt's upheaval economic, social and political issues were closely linked: 'If this revolution does not lead to the fair distribution of wealth it is not worth anything', they suggested: 'Freedoms are not complete without social freedoms.' (Abu-Eita *et al.* 2011).

Histories of struggle

At a meeting held in the Rawabet Theatre in downtown Cairo in June 2011, an audience of several hundred activists discussed 'the roots of the revolution'. Many assumed that the uprising had been initiated abruptly by the demonstrations of 25 January, expressing surprise at platform speakers who gave testimony to years of struggle conducted out of public view in workplaces, meeting rooms, on campuses and in prison cells. In a striking contribution, one young woman at the event thanked chair Ala'a Abdel-Fattah and speakers Wael Khalil and Hossam El-Hamalawy 'for telling us about our history that has been hidden from us'.[8]

Egypt has had a particularly rich record of working-class struggles, though for many decades this had been undocumented. During the first phase of industrialisation, from the 1920s to the 1940s, Egyptian writers who addressed labour issues had been concerned mainly with economic performance and institutional developments; autobiographical materials and memoires that recorded working lives and/or raised issues of social class were rare and when they violated dominant narratives such as Nasserism or mainstream communism, were simply suppressed.[9] It was not until the 1970s, when the Sadat regime relaxed official attitudes to Nasserism, that some materials by worker-writers began to appear.[10] Abroad, Soviet scholars produced formulaic accounts that aimed to align workers' interests with Moscow's foreign policy. In Europe and North America, 'exceptionalism' shaped perspectives on Egyptian society as a whole, with religion, sect and 'tribe' the key issues: Lockman observes that 'class was at best irrelevant and at worst distorting when used as a category of analysis for Middle East societies past or present' (1994: xii). This approach, Lockman suggests, 'helped stifle the development of Middle Eastern working-class history' (Lockman 1994: xii). During the 1980s, academic researchers in North America influenced by the practice of 'history from below' adopted a different approach, using archival materials and oral testimony to focus on Egyptian workers' lives and on working-class history. Intensive research by labour historians including Joel Beinin, Eric Davis, Ellis Goldberg, Zachary Lockman and Marsha Pripstein Posusney produced a wealth of material; Beinin and Lockman's *Workers on the Nile*, published in 1987 and translated into Arabic, was soon recognised as one of the most comprehensive analyses of workers' struggles in the Global South. Meanwhile worker activists in Egypt, notably members of the *Sawt al-Amil* ('Worker's Voice') group, began to produce their own records of struggles past and present.

These new accounts demonstrated not only that workers had played a leading role in anti-colonial movements of the 1930s and 1940s but also that they had developed their own radical agendas. In some workplaces these had reached an advanced level: Beinin and Lockman (1987: 280) compare the textile workers of Shubra al-Khayma near Cairo, a centre of worker militancy in the late 1940s, with the steel workers of the city of Petrograd, St. Petersburg – the epicentre of revolutionary activity in Russia in 1917. The nationalist regime that came to power in Egypt in 1952 after a military coup led by Gamal Abdel-Nasser tackled worker militancy as a priority: one of its first initiatives was an assault on strikers in Kafr al-Dawwar and the symbolic hanging of two leading trade unionists.[11] The regime suppressed the workers' movement and jailed thousands of activists. In 1957 it established the Egyptian Trade Union Federation (ETUF) as a means of integrating workers' organisa-tions into the structures of the state. The regime declared that unions should no longer be 'groupings for the seizing of rights of defence of interests in opposition to employers'; now they were to be 'centres of revolutionary radiation [sic] and instruments for pushing forward the wheels of production'.[12] Trade unions were to be means of social control operating alongside the sole legal political party, Nasser's Arab Socialist Union (ASU).

In most academic assessments of Egyptian politics published during the Sadat and Mubarak eras workers were said to have been incorporated into the project of national development or to have discovered their own stake in 'authoritarian populism' (Hinnebusch 1985: 39). Many workplaces in fact retained traditions of local organisation and of vigorous defence of their interests. Strikes undertaken in defiance of ETUF officials included a succession of major actions during the Sadat regime's early programme of marketisation (the *infitah* or 'opening' introduced in 1974)[13] and mass involvement of workers in the 'intifada of bread' in 1977. This national uprising, in protest against IMF-inspired measures to reduce food subsidies, was initiated by workers in Helwan near Cairo. It had an insurrectionary character: strikers cut rail lines and attacked police stations, prompting the regime to mobilise the army and to order frontal assaults on demonstrators (Beinin 1994; El-Hamalawy 2009 [2000]). Despite a ferocious campaign of retribution against worker activists there were further major disputes in public-sector enterprises. In 1984 a dispute at Misr Fine Spinning and Weaving in Kafr al-Dawwar ended only after the intervention of the CSF and three days of battles that engulfed the city and surrounding villages (El Shafei 1995: 24). In 1985, there were at least 50 strikes (Beinin 1994: 262) and in the following year a major stoppage took place on the railway system. In 1989, an occupation at the Egyptian Iron and Steel Company in Helwan involved some 16,000 workers (El Shafei 1995: 35). This dispute revealed the influence of rank-and-file militants organised around the local *Sanay'iyya* group. Like those who organised through publications such as *Sawt al-Amil* and *'Ummal Shubra al-Khayma* ('Shubra al-Khayma Workers') these activists sought to assert an independent presence, challenging state-appointed managers and ETUF officials, and placing their efforts consciously within the history of Egyptian workers' struggles.

Solidarity networks

Mubarak's strategy of violent confrontation in industrial disputes of the 1980s stimulated local and national solidarity with those affected. According to Ibrahim, a veteran activist:

> During each of the big strikes we built up good support [for those in dispute]. We established links all over Egypt: on the railways, for example [during the national strike of 1986], we set up support groups in several cities that raised money for the strikers and sent messages and delegations to them. The links between activists grew stronger, so that in 1989 when a big struggle took place in Helwan [the steelworks] we could move quickly.[14]

During the railways dispute of 1986 a national committee was formed representing all sections of the workforce and a solidarity campaign mobilised lawyers to defend those arrested. The detainees were eventually freed and most of the strikers' demands were met (El Shafei 1995: 31). The scale of the initiative was modest but solidarity networks remained active around successive strikes and were reinforced in 1989 during successive occupations of the Helwan steelworks in support of wage demands and against victimisation of shop-floor activists. Riot police stormed the plant, killing one worker and injuring hundreds. The Interior Minister Zaki Badr, notorious for brutal attacks on workers and on the Islamist opposition, declared that he would use all force to crush local resistance,[15] while the state-controlled press attacked strikers with allegations that they wanted to destroy the whole industrial area of Helwan.[16] Alexander and Bassiouny (2014: 110) comment that the regime's priority had been geographical containment of major disputes: its use of violence and victimisation of activists, however, now had the effect of generalising resistance. Textile workers in Mehalla al-Kubra took strike action in solidarity with those sacked at the steel plant and support was organised in local workplaces in Helwan and among lawyers and human rights activists, some of whom were also arrested (Rady

2008). Collective interests 'had begun to spawn processes of reciprocal action between economic and political struggles perceived as deeply threatening to the existing political order' (Alexander and Bassiouny 2014: 110).

The Egyptian Organization for Human Rights (EOHR) had been founded in 1985 by liberal academics and left-wing activists, supported by Amnesty International.[17] It addressed issues such as workplace organisation and the right to strike in the context of basic freedoms, seeing workers' struggles as part of wider claims for justice. After the Helwan steel dispute there were further initiatives: Joe Stork of Human Rights Watch comments that the strike 'broadened human rights activism beyond the EOHR' (Stork 2013: 114). In 1990, one of the former Helwan militants, Kemal Abbas, founded the Center for Trade Union and Workers Services (CTUWS). In 1993, radical activists founded the El Nadim Center for the Management and Rehabilitation of Victims of Violence and in 1994 established the Office of Legal Aid for Human Rights.[18] Each facilitated links between centres of resistance, notably industrial workplaces, and a growing human rights network.

Neo-liberalism and resistance

In 1991, the government committed to wholesale privatisation of industry, land and commerce, signing an Economic Reform and Structural Adjustment Programme (ERSAP) with the World Bank, the International Monetary Fund (IMF) and the European Economic Community (EEC – now the European Union). In exchange for a debt write-off and new loans, the regime was to impose huge cuts in public spending. When in 1994 it attempted to double workers' contributions to health and pension plans, workers in Kafr al-Dawwar organised strikes in several textile plants. During three days of fighting, police fired directly into crowds of workers and townspeople: four were killed and hundreds injured (Weiss and Wurzel 1998: 151). Omar El Shafei observed prophetically that the dispute marked the beginning of a new wave of protest. Sacrifices demanded from workers and others, he suggested, made 'genuine liberalization' a real danger for the regime (El Shafei 1995: 39).

Husni Mubarak, installed as president after the assassination of his predecessor Anwar Sadat in 1981, had long been favourable to private business. Like Sadat, he rejected the state-centred development policies of the Nasser era. Like Sadat, he intended to integrate Egypt into the world market and to enrich his own family, its business networks and Egypt's officer elite. During the 1980s, the progress of 'marketisation' had been slow. Under growing pressure from creditors and the international financial agencies Mubarak signed the ERSAP agreement, committing to an accelerated programme of privatisation, cuts in subsidies of staple foods and of fuel, and foreign trade liberalisation. State spending on food subsidies, a Nasserist measure that had given the mass of the population access to basic staples, fell sharply.[19] In 1980–81, it had amounted to 14 per cent of government spending; by 1996–97 the figure had fallen to 5.6 per cent (Ahmed *et al.* 2001: xi). After the ERSAP agreement, the regime radically reduced the number of subsided foods to four – *baladi* bread,[20] *baladi* flour, cooking oil and sugar – and prepared for further cuts, inhibited only by fear of 'food riots' like those of 1977. Meanwhile Mubarak revised the tax system in favour of private capital, reducing the highest rate of corporation tax from 78 per cent to 48 per cent: it was later slashed to 20 per cent (Hanieh 2013: 70). A key element in the programme was a reduction in the public-sector labour force. Managers of state enterprises were instructed to implement mass redundancies before companies were presented for sale through the expanded and newly automated stock exchange (later designated the Egyptian Exchange, or EGX). Among the mass of Egyptians employment in the public sector was highly prized, with long waiting lists for many jobs. Although pay rates were low, employment was relatively secure and most workers could expect pensions: by the 1990s, with 500,000 young adults joining the labour market each year, these jobs had become increasingly important (Cook 2012: 176). Twenty years earlier millions of Egyptians had moved to the states of the Gulf or to Libya to work in the expanding oil economies. Following the defeat of Iraq in the Gulf War of 1991, there had been a surge of return migrations to a country in which employment opportunities were contracting and a sense of general insecurity was increasing. A twin development was also under way: as the regime advanced neo-liberal reform (notionally focused upon withdrawal of the state from economic affairs), it also intervened aggressively to support privatisation and in labour affairs, bolstering the position of ETUF officials by guaranteeing their security in office and sending worker activists to military courts empowered under the Emergency Laws.

'Economic liberalisation', noted Weiss and Wurzel, was 'accompanied by tighter authoritarian rule' (1998: 157).

A human rights lawyer described the reaction in industry: according to Hisham Mubarak, resistance to privatisation was accompanied by growing independent action in the labour force,

> Workers have to deal with their managers, the police, sometimes the army – and their trade union leaders. They are forced to be more independent. We can see people organising their own groups and challenging the labour laws. These workers are fighting for rights such as freedom of association and the right to strike, and they are opposing Emergency Law. These are struggles for all Egyptians.[21]

Law 203 of 1991 had provided for over 300 state-owned companies to be privatised. As the process gathered speed in the mid-1990s the regime announced a 'one-company-per-week' plan to dispose of state assets,[22] agreeing sales at token prices that encouraged new owners to re-enter the market and make huge profits. By 2004, USAID (the US development agency) had recorded 199 privatisations (PIP 2004: 12–13). Some companies were closed outright and workers were dismissed as the new owners sold the land for development or cleared sites that remained empty while they speculated on the property market. Even the Privatization Co-ordination Support Unit (PCSU), established by US officials to facilitate the break-up of the state sector, noted the impact on Egyptian workers:

> The attitudes of the typical Egyptian worker to the concept of privatization seems to be at best ambivalent, though more often it [sic] remains skeptical or negative. Although the government points to its publicity campaigns to placate labor anxiety about the impact of privatization, most workers still tend to associate privatization with retrenchment and loss of workplace benefits.
>
> (PCSU 2002: 44)

In 2004, Mubarak appointed a new cabinet under one of his family's close associates, Ahmed Nazif. This was said to be a 'dream team' of leading businessmen focused upon 'privatization in earnest' (Cook 2012: 176). Over the next five years a further 191 public companies were sold (Cook 2012: 176). According to Badr El-Din (2014), in 75 per cent of privatisations employment fell; Cook (2012: 176) estimates that over 400,000 workers lost their jobs directly, noting (like PCSU) the widespread perception among workers that they paid the heaviest price. By 2006–07, official figures showed unemployment at 10 per cent: the reality, suggested El-Naggar (2009: 42), was a rate of some 26 per cent; in the age group 15–29, it was over three times that figure. Meanwhile average pay had decreased significantly: in the period 1980–84, the average industrial wage had been $2,210; by 1995–96, it was $1,863.[23] Assessing the impacts of neo-liberal policy over the course of 20 years, labour lawyer Khaled Ali concluded that, 'Privatisation has stolen Egypt from its people':

> Egyptian workers who spent their lives building factories and public sector institutions, with a degree of job security and decent labour relations, and who gained some financial and social entitlements – those workers became vulnerable to arbitrary dismissal. Their rights, and many of their jobs, were soon lost.
>
> (Muhamadeen 2015)

Neo-liberal reform continued on other fronts. Consistent with efforts worldwide to 'deregulate' labour, more and more workers had been employed on temporary contracts: in 2010 an estimated 3 million Egyptians were employed under arrangements that gave employers the option to dismiss them at any moment (Sallam 2011): one widespread practice involved new employees signing a 'resignation letter' that could be invoked at the whim of the employer. The neo-liberal programme aimed to drive workers from secure employment into a deregulated labour market; at the same time it set out to remove from the land large numbers of *fellaheen* ('tillers'/peasants) who under reforms of 1952 and 1961 had enjoyed new rights to cultivate the land. Under Law 96 of 1992 on 'desequestration', landowning families of the colonial era could assert their title to estates nationalised under the Nasser reforms and which had been distributed to peasants with rights of cultivation in perpetuity.[24] When the law was fully implemented in the late 1990s, thousands of villages were affected. Figures recorded by the Land Center for Human Rights (LCHR) show that in one eight-month period alone during 1997–98, 17 people died, 533 were wounded and 1,588 were arrested for alleged offences in disputes between landlords and tenants (LCHR 2002). According to Adel William of the LCHR, by 2008 a million peasant families had been evicted: 'That accordingly meant that at least 7 million people – the families of the expelled tenant farmers – have been suffering the double onslaught of unemployment and poverty in villages nationwide' (Shahine 2008). The impact was especially severe in 'urban villages' that had mushroomed around major cities. Millions of workers and peasants alike were facing crises of survival in which issues of job security, income and welfare were associated with struggles for basic freedoms – for freedom of expression, freedom of association, freedom of assembly, the right to strike and access to the land.

Strikes and protests

'Economic' issues are always bound into wider questions of political self-expression and social justice. As Egyptian workers sought new means to contest unemployment, falling wages and general insecurity, they confronted a ruling class committed to both privatisation of remaining public assets and tighter control of the political process. In 2000, the president appointed his son and heir-apparent Gamal Mubarak as general-secretary of the ruling NDP. Gamal's personal icon was the British politician Margaret Thatcher, whom he was determined to emulate. As an investment banker in London, Gamal Mubarak had observed Thatcher's privatisation strategy and her mobilisation of the state against workers' resistance: the result, he said, was an 'incredible metamorphosis' in Britain (*Middle East Quarterly* 2009). 'We need audacious leaders [like Thatcher]', insisted Mubarak Junior:

> [Leaders] able to prepare their country for the future and implement some reforms even when they are unpopular. Such a leader must be brave enough to remain faithful to his [sic] convictions, despite all opposition. He must not let public opinion or those who favor shortsighted opinions dictate his choices.
>
> (Middle East Quarterly 2009)

In 2003, new labour laws were enacted, permitting strike action only when approved by ETUF officials: in effect, all strikes were to be illegal. The Nazif government appointed the following year was committed to advance Gamal Mubarak's philosophy of 'New Thinking' – an aggressive pursuit of neo-liberal reforms. The economist Wael Gamal observed that adoption of this approach 'was not just a matter of a technical economic decision'; rather, he said, it expressed commitment to 'a political project that redistributed wealth in favour of the rich. It also extended the reach of local and international firms [at the expense of] union movements, civil society and the marginalised' (Gamal 2013). Nazif arranged new privatisations, including the sale of industrial plants, banks and insurance companies, and of huge areas of land made over to property developers and agribusiness entrepreneurs at a fraction of market prices.[25] In industry, workers responded assertively. In 2003, there had been 86 workers' protests (including strikes, occupations and demonstrations); in 2004, the number of episodes rose to 266, the vast majority after the Nazif government had taken office (Alexander and Bassiouny 2014: 108). Most major disputes were in the textile sector – still a key target for privatisation – but increasing numbers now took place in private-sector enterprises, including those in new industrial cities such as 6th October City, 10th Ramadan City and Sadat City that had been largely unorganised by the official trade unions. In December 2006, a strike by 24,000 workers at Misr Spinning and Weaving in Mehalla al-Kubra focused on management's refusal to pay an agreed bonus. Successful after three days, it prompted similar action across cities of the Delta among both public-sector and private establishments in the textile sector. Within weeks there were also strikes and demonstrations in mining, manufacturing and transport, and among teachers and local authority employees. By the end of the 2007, every sector of the economy had been affected by over 600 episodes of collective action – the most intensive phase of collective action in industry for some 60 years.

In most cases, the regime did not order police intervention – an indication of its anxiety about growing problems of political opposition. Since 2000, a series of overlapping movements had challenged the ban on public protest. In September 2000, a nationwide campaign of solidarity with the Palestinian *intifada* engaged very large numbers of students and school pupils. Ashraf, a witness to events in Giza, describes the unprecedented involvement of young women:

My flat overlooks the main street and I was amazed to see hundreds of young girls – teenagers – leave their school and demonstrate outside, where they shouted slogans of solidarity with the Palestinians. There were a few police who looked astonished and no one tried to stop the girls. Later I discovered that there had been similar demonstrations all over the country. It was strange to see this in Giza. It was the start of something, I think.[26]

A national solidarity organisation was established, the Egyptian Popular Committee in Solidarity with the Intifada (EPCSI), formed by ten leading NGOs including several human rights organisations. In September 2001, it successfully called a demonstration of over 1,000 people who marched through Tahrir Square in protest at US support for Israel. Sit-ins and hunger strikes were called in the offices of professional unions, schools and NGOs protesting against Israeli brutality and 'Arab acquiescence', and local solidarity committees established. When Israeli forces assaulted the city of Jenin in 2002 there were further demonstrations and after police killed a student in Alexandria and injured hundreds of others the movement was dubbed an 'Egyptian intifada' (*Al-Ahram Weekly* 2005). In May 2002, demonstrators gathered in Tahrir Square to mark Nakba Day, commemorating the expulsion of Palestinians in 1948: their slogans included 'Revolution, revolution, till victory, from Egypt to Palestine' (Howeidy 2002). Hossam El-Hamalawy recalls the first time he heard demonstrators use Mubarak's name, when in skirmishes with the CSF at Cairo University protestors chanted: 'Hosni Mubarak is just like [Ariel] Sharon' (El-Hamalawy 2011c).

'Cycles of protest'

The solidarity movement was creating space for public protest unseen in Egypt for decades. Some demonstrations were attacked with the usual violence; others went relatively undisturbed as the regime, aware of the contagious nature of Palestinian resistance and its impacts across the Arab states, hesitated to create Egyptian martyrs for the Palestinian cause. On 20 March 2003, activists opposed to the US-led invasion of Iraq called a remarkable demonstration in central Cairo. Over 30,000 people occupied the main square – a 'Tahrir intifada' that was a breakthrough moment for radical activists. Leila, a member of EPCSI, described her experiences:

At first there was the usual group of protestors and we were surrounded by police. Then something special happened. Thousands and thousands more came from all directions: from Azhar and Bab al-Luq, and from Garden City and along the Corniche. We could hardly believe what we were seeing. There were speeches and then songs: we stayed for hours, just to experience this event. It was a moment of anger about war but also of happiness that at last we'd shown ourselves – and we'd survived.[27]

Inspired by this success, activists formed a 20 March Popular Campaign for Change, adopting the slogan '*la lil-tawrith, la lil-tamdid*' ('no to inheritance, no to extension' [of the presidential period in office]). In 2004, they established the Egyptian Movement for Change, known by its slogan 'Kifaya' ('Enough!'), as a campaign for democratic reform. For two years Kifaya mobilised street meetings, campus rallies and marches. Most were on a modest scale but succeeded in bringing together veteran activists and new, youthful protestors. Among the former were dissident lawyers, academics, journalists and industrial militants, some of whom had decades of experience in clandestine opposition and in solidarity networks. Younger activists introduced blogs, online networks and novel means of organising through SMS/texting and activist websites. El-Mahdi identified the movement as part of 'continuous cycles of protest' (2009: 88) that since 2000 had focused upon different but complementary initiatives including Palestine, opposition to war in Iraq and domestic reform. 'A cycle of contestation had emerged,' she proposed, 'in which each phase of activity was related to earlier actions and to the responses of the state' (El-Mahdi 2009: 96). This affected even core institutions of government. In 2005, over 1,200 judges threatened to abstain from supervising presidential and parliamentary elections (a legal requirement) unless they were given full control over every stage of the process. The Alexandria Judges' Association declared for 'a truly independent judiciary through which we can protect freedoms and rights'; its general secretary insisted: 'elections should either be wholly supervised by the judiciary, or else by whoever wants to forge their results' (El-Nahas 2005).[28]

Public protests were now taking place regularly, involving small but vocal groups including Youth for Change, Students for Change, Journalists for Change, Doctors for Change, the 9 March Movement for the Independence of Universities (university lecturers/professors) and Workers for Change. They attracted close attention from Egyptian security services and from intelligence agencies in the United States, which commissioned the RAND National Defense Research Institute to report on Kifaya and its affiliates. RAND concluded that the emergence of Kiyafa was 'historic', emphasising that collaboration between groups with widely differing agendas was highly significant for the political process in Egypt (Oweidat *et al.* 2008: 11). Linkages between democracy activism and the workers' movement were becoming more effective. The spokesman of Workers for Change was Kemal Abu-Eita, a leading member of the illegal Karama Party, a radical nationalist organisation in the Nasserist tradition. In 2005, he declared that Workers for Change aimed to establish an independent union to represent government employees (*Al-Ahram Weekly* 2005). Other supporters of Kifaya with long experience in the workers' movement had also argued for independent organisation, notably Kemal Abbas of CTUWS, the labour lawyer Khalid 'Ali and the veteran solidarity activist Kemal Khalil. Two years later, Abu-Eita was a leading figure in successful efforts by workers in the Property Tax Authority (PTA) to secure wage parity within the organisation, including a ten-day sit-in in central Cairo involving some 8,000 workers and undertaken without CSF intervention. Thousands of PTA workers subsequently left the ETUF to join a new Real Estate Tax Authority Union (Retau), soon to be one of the founding organisations of the independent federation EFITU.

By 2007, protests organised through Kifaya were less vigorous. The organisation had established a bridgehead for protest but had not succeeded in establishing a mass base. Strikes and other forms of workplace actions continued unabated, however. Beinin and El-Hamalawy commented that these now represented 'the most substantial and broad-based kind of resistance to the regime' (2007). In February 2008, textile workers in Mehalla al-Kubra demanded a statutory national minimum wage of LE1,200 a month (then about $190 or £120). They resolved to pursue the claim with a strike on 6 April 2008, a date soon taken up by activist networks across the country with calls for a general strike. In the event, on 6 April the CSF returned to Mehalla al-Kubra in large numbers, attacking strikers and demonstrators. Detachments of CSF also appeared in industrial centres across the country, patrolling assembly points for local demonstrations: one Cairo newspaper observed that organising a protest 'became the equivalent of mission impossible' (Shehab 2008). The regime boasted that its authority was unchallenged: the leading NDP official Maged El-Sherbini declared that activists had been exposed 'as having neither the tools nor the ability to mobilise the masses' (Shehab 2008). The general strike had not materialised, disappointing activists who hoped to open a broad front against the regime in which 'economic' demands were part of an agenda for radical political change. Kemal El-Fayoumi, a veteran workers' leader at Ghazl el-Mehalla (the Mehalla textile mill), later observed, 'If a few more major cities like Suez or Alexandria rose up with us, the Mubarak regime would've fell [sic] then and there [in 2008]' (El-Sharnoubi 2013).

The workers' movement had advanced rapidly but its progress was uneven and lacked coordination. Links that had developed among solidarity activists in the 1980s and 1990s were inadequate to deal with fast-changing events and with strikes on a large scale. Alaa', a journalist who monitored workers' struggles throughout this period, comments that state repression limited options to share experiences and establish formal links:

> The active people did all they could to support workers' struggles but as Mubarak had prohibited politics in general it was almost impossible to create actual organisations that could really serve the workers. And then of course we had the problem of very bad traditions on the Left within our movement, including collaboration between some left-wing parties and the state's own unions. It was just too difficult to close the gap.[29]

In 2007, Joel Beinin and Hossam El-Hamalawy commented on the absence of coordination between workplaces. Following a successful strike in Kafr al-Dawwar that year, they noted, a statement signed by 'Workers for Change in Kafr al-Dawwar' was circulated at the plant calling for 'expanding coordination between workers in companies that went on strike with us, to create the necessary solidarity links and exchange experiences' (Beinin and El-Hamalawy 2007: 17). The initiative was not successful and the lack of effective links was later to prove a profound difficulty for the whole movement (see Chapter 10). Meanwhile, however, both local and sectoral struggles continued. During 2008, there were over 600 strikes, sit-ins and demonstrations –

another historic high – and postal workers, health workers and teachers formed new independent union groups (Alexander and Bassiouny 2014: 108). Over the next two years, the number of strikes and protests at workplaces decreased to some 70 per cent of the 2008 level; at the same time, key demands of the movement were generalised, notably by the issue of a national minimum wage. On 1 May 2010, hundreds of workers demonstrated in front of the Cabinet Office, the same site at which employees of the PTA had successfully held a sit-in three years earlier. The protest demanded: 'A minimum fair wage, or let this government get out of here', 'Raise prices more and more. Tomorrow the country will be in flames', 'Down with Mubarak and all those who raise prices!' (Atallah 2010). The Labour lawyer Khalid 'Ali spoke at the rally on behalf of demonstrators: 'We call for the resignation of [Prime Minister] Ahmad Nazif's government because it works only for businessmen and ignores social justice' (Atallah 2010).

Democratic agendas

In February 2011, strikes were critical in forcing the hand of the military command and removing Mubarak. They were not 'spontaneous' in the sense that they occurred without focused effort at the local and national levels. On the contrary, activist networks – albeit fragmented and poorly coordinated – played a key role in calling industrial action. Khalid, a labour journalist with years of experience, described how he and others disseminated the call for a general strike against Mubarak during the second week of February:

> You have to remember that half the working class was already on the streets against Mubarak and when people went back to work they took all their experiences with them: there was no 'wall' between the streets and places of work. We knew many local activists: we targeted them and others who'd already been involved in strikes against Mubarak in cities like Kafr al-Dawwar, Mehalla, Port Said, Suez, Helwan and Cairo. We believe that this call made a big difference and played an important role in the fall of Mubarak.[30]

The initiative was consistent with efforts by Egypt's most militant workers to combine demands for job security and improved wages and conditions with the insistence on the right to organise, the right to public assembly and the right to strike. For 20 years, 'economic' issues had been combined more and more closely with attempts to expand Egypt's democratic space. Since 2006, workers had achieved more in this respect than all the efforts of political parties and of NGOs. Joel Beinin, a close observer of labour struggles in Egypt since the 1970s, concluded that with over 2 million workers involved in some 3,400 strikes and collective actions between 1998 and 2010, Egypt had witnessed the largest social movement in the Arab world since the Algerian War of Independence:

> Economic gains won through strikes and other actions taught many Egyptians a crucial lesson: Engaging in collective action, previously regarded as a losing game by all but committed middle-class activists, could achieve something of value […] in an autocracy like Mubarak's Egypt, the capacity to organize large numbers of people to do anything is a potential political challenge to the regime. Workers electing strike committees and debating whether or not to accept strike settlement terms was one of the most democratic public activities during the Mubarak era.
>
> (Beinin 2011)

Far from being *fi'awi* protests, the industrial actions of 2011 were at the heart of struggles for change that drew on decades of contestation of neo-liberalism and repression. The uprising of 2011 was made in city squares and in countless workshops, offices, docks, mills and depots. The relationship between these two focal points of the movement – the streets and the workplaces – was to prove central to the fate of the revolution.

4

Crises and Confrontations

During the 18 Days millions of people declared their intention to bring down 'the order' (*al-nizam*) – the structures of privilege that sustained Mubarak and the institutions that intruded into their lives. What was the effect on the Egyptian state – and how did those in power respond?

Friedrich Engels describes the modern state as based upon 'public power', most importantly upon armed men and 'material adjuncts, prisons, and institutions of coercion of all kinds' (1968 [1884]: 577). In the case of Egypt, core institutions of the state had been consolidated by successive regimes to the extent that they dominated all aspects of public life. The armed forces and security services were bloated even by world standards. In 2011, the armed forces mobilised 835,000 men and women: only six states worldwide had larger combined forces (World Bank 2014). At the age of 18, all young men were subject to conscription, serving from one to three years in the army or in paramilitary corps.[1] Although Egypt had not been involved in significant inter-state conflict for almost 40 years, the army had been mobilised in domestic crises, most importantly against major strikes and mass protests. The regime's main instruments of coercion, however, were police and security agencies whose personnel by 2011 outnumbered military forces by a ratio of three to one (Dunne and Revkin 2011). The Ministry of Interior employed 850,000 regular police, 450,000 riot police of the *Amn al-Markazi* (Central Security, CSF) and 400,000 officers of *Mubahath Amn al-Dawla* (the General Directorate of State Security Investigations, or SSI) (Dunne and Revkin 2011). The security apparatus also included staff of *Jihaz Amn al-Dawla* (State Security Service) *Mukhabarat al-Aama* (General Intelligence and Security Service), *Mukhabarat al-Harbeya* (Military Intelligence Service) and *Jihaz al-Amn al-Qawmi* (National Security Service), as well as vast numbers of civilian informers.

In 1981, Mubarak had reintroduced Emergency Laws promulgated during the Nasser era and briefly suspended by President Sadat. These prohibited strikes, demonstrations and public meetings of more than ten individuals; provided for censorship and closure of newspapers and other publications; and gave security officers powers to arrest and detain without court orders or trials and to refer civilians to military courts at which there was no right of appeal. Both police and security agencies operated with impunity: one outcome had been the spread across Egypt of harassment, torture and abuse. In 2002, Amnesty International warned that: 'In Egypt everyone taken into detention is at risk of torture' (2002: 1). Workers, urban poor and peasants were particularly vulnerable. Those arrested for petty offences, for purposes of extortion or on the whim of police officers were often tortured as a matter of routine: when women and children were involved, sexual abuse was common (Seif El-Dawla 2009). The Egyptian Association Against Torture (EAAT), founded in 2003, described: 'an organized, systematic and ongoing policy used against citizens'; police and security agencies, said EAAT, used torture 'to terrorize citizens and to ensure complete submission of the people to the policies of those authorities' (EAAT 2003).

The uprising of 2011 inflicted serious damage on both police and security agencies, disrupting the regime of intimidation and fear. On 25 January, regular police and CSF troops failed to contain the first dem-onstrations against Mubarak and within hours activists had attacked a police station in Suez, freeing prisoners and setting the building ablaze (*Al Jazeera* 2011a). On 28 January, the 'Day of Rage' on which protestors successfully confronted a nationwide mobilisation of the CSF, there were attacks on police stations in scores of cities. In Alexandria, many police stations were burned down; in Cairo, protestors torched the headquarters of the ruling NDP, with police helpless to intervene. At this point, most regular police and CSF troops were withdrawn from city centres.

Bauer and Schweitzer (2012) observe that the number of casualties in Egypt was low in comparison to those during uprisings in 2011 in Tunisia, Syria, Libya and Yemen.[2] In many incidents, officers deserted units of the riot police. This reflected the massive and effective character of protest in Egypt and the rapid retreat of the state's frontline forces. Adam and Carr (2012) provide testimony from members of the CSF engaged in efforts to contain demonstrators in Cairo. One recalled: 'My commanders, who always said to me "Be a man, be a man", ran away and left us' (Adam and Carr 2012). For the first time since its establishment in 1977, the CSF was absent from the streets. According to Abdel-Latif

El-Menawy, head of news for official television and radio networks, by 28 January the regime had lost the city: 'There were no police, the curfew was totally ignored, the city was lawless' (El-Menawy 2012: 118). When the Interior Minister Habib al-Adly was later interrogated by state prosecutors, he said that CSF units had been exhausted: outnumbered and unprepared, he said, troops had panicked.[3] Adly and other officials were acutely aware of the history of the CSF, which had fractured in 1986 when a national uprising of conscripts was contained only by use of the army. In 2011, the prospect of disintegration of the force soon brought orders to remove all troops to barracks. In a desperate attempt to contain the demonstrations, officials ordered prisons to be opened and summoned the *baltagiyya* to assault protestors alongside plain-clothes police. They were unable to contain the movement.

The SSI was also seriously affected by the uprising. The agency was notorious for its brutality. For decades it had seized all manner of people viewed as 'suspects', raiding homes and workplaces and snatching victims in the street to effect 'disappearances' that often resulted in torture or death at SSI centres or incarceration in military prisons. In early March 2011, protestors surrounded SSI centres in several areas of Cairo, including the organisation's headquarters compound in Medinet Nasr. Despite the presence of military police, they stormed buildings, opening cells and detention rooms in which they found equipment used for torture and files on thousands of 'suspects'. Ali said:

I went into the very cell in which I had been held and where I was beaten. I saw piles of reports on people like me. This time the building was empty of the torturers – it was one of the greatest moments of our revolution.[4]

Protestors seized garbage bags full of shredded paper, taking computers, hard drives and printed records including lists of SSI officers and of the agency's informers, and posting photographs and videos of the events on social media.[5] In similar episodes activists entered SSI compounds across Egypt, retrieving the records of decades of repression. A former senior army officer interviewed by the Egyptian media the following day described 'the elimination, yesterday, of the state security apparatus';[6] the official newspaper *Al-Ahram* headlined, 'The fall of the state of state security'.[7] In an assessment of the implications for the mass movement,

Omar Ashour concluded: 'With the fall of the SSI, Egypt seems quite close to completing phase one of its inspirational struggle for democracy – the removal of its dictator and his coercive apparatus' (2011).

Revolutionary process

The importance of these developments has often been understated in analyses of the 2011 events. There has been an assumption among some academics, foreign policy strategists and media commentators that survival of core institutions in the shape of the armed forces, together with the assertion by the military command (SCAF) of its authority to rule by decree, meant that no meaningful changes were taking place: most importantly that Egypt was not experiencing 'revolution'. The widely quoted American strategic analyst George Friedman of STRATFOR observed after the fall of Mubarak that: 'Power rests with the regime [the SCAF] not with the crowds. In our view, the crowds never had nearly as much power as many have claimed' (Friedman 2011). The scale of events was more modest than activists suggested, Friedman maintained, suggesting that demonstrations were much smaller than during the Eastern European revolutions of 1989 or the Iranian revolution of 1979: 'Those were massive social convulsions in which millions came out onto the streets. The crowd in Cairo never swelled to the point that it involved a substantial portion of the city' (Friedman 2011). He continued:

> What happened was not a revolution. The demonstrators never brought down Mubarak, let alone the regime. What happened was a military coup that used the cover of protests to force Mubarak out of office in order to preserve the regime [...] the military staged what amounted to a coup to force his resignation.
>
> (Friedman 2011)

The Egyptian academic Hazem Kandil shares some of this analysis. Reflecting on the events of 2011, he concludes that the resignation of Mubarak 'was brought forth by a military that saw in the popular uprising an opportunity for retribution' (Kandil 2012: 232). Here the fall of the dictator was precipitated by his own appointees in an army command infuriated by the president's nepotism and the favours he distributed within civilian networks of influence. The emphasis is important: the mass movement, suggests Kandil, created options for the real decision makers but did not effect change. A further reflection on the events comes from Talal Asad, an acute and sympathetic observer of popular movements in the Middle East. Writing in 2015, he observed:

> Some years later, well after the July 3rd military coup, looking back at the January uprising, it becomes apparent that there never was a 'revolution' because there was no new foundation. There was a moment of enthusiasm in the uprising, as in all major protests and rebellions, but the solidarity it generated was evanescent.
>
> (Asad 2015)

Both contemporaneous comments and later analyses misjudge the situation: most importantly, they understate the dynamism of the mass movement and its impact on the old order and the apparatus of state. By April 2011, the Mubarak regime had lost its figurehead, with the president under house arrest facing charges of: 'intentional murder, attempted killing of some demonstrators [...] misuse of influence and deliberately wasting public funds and unlawfully making private financial gains and profits' (Saleh and Ziad 2011). Two of Mubarak's sons, his interior minister, the heads of the CSF and SSI, heads of security in five governorates, and a clutch of senior officers were in prison, also charged with capital offences. The key means of state repression, Engels's 'institutions of coercion', were in disarray – Albrecht describes 'a meltdown of political institutions and policing capacities' (2012: 260). The army command hesitated to confront the movements of the streets, in industry and among community activists organised in hundreds of local committees. Equally important were changes in morale among the mass of people. The anthropologist Samuli Schielke (2015: 172) observes how societal demoralisation associated with decades of repression had been replaced by anger and by the realisation that change was within reach. As events unfolded in 2011, he suggests, there developed awareness that 'it was possible, after all, to face the system head-on'; fear had been replaced by defiance, a sense of powerlessness by 'acts of doing' (Schielke 2015: 80). City centres nationwide had become places of public engagement and celebration, rather than forbidden zones. Independent media were flourishing, encouraged by citizen journalists and bloggers. New political parties and networks were proliferating and scores of independent trade unions were in formation, even among those earlier viewed as immune to collective organisation such as doctors, craftworkers, fishermen and microbus drivers. Demands for *taṭhir* were intensifying, especially in places of work, where they were associated with dramatic shifts in the 'frontier of control' vis-à-vis owners, management and the state itself (Alexander and Bassiouny 2014: 237). This marked a heightened phase of the uprising: '[Cleansing] opened up new ways of thinking for hundreds of thousands of Egyptians, who imagined and acted as if they could remake the state according to the principles of the popular revolution' (Alexander and Bassiouny 2014: 291).

People confident that they had removed a dictator believed they could displace *feloul*, owners and managers, police chiefs and corrupt officials. This reflected the dynamics of a movement attempting to increase the influence of the mass of people over their own lives, opening democratic space and expanding means of self-expression. It challenged both the state and class relations at the local and national levels. It is in this sense that the movement from below was less a 'moment of enthusiasm' than part of a *revolutionary process* – one with the potential to pursue further change.

'Not one hand'

The process was complex. It included significant changes in popular opinion over short periods of time, the making and unmaking of coalitions and alliances, and advances and retreats among the main contending forces. This was especially clear during the first 12 months of the revolution as the armed forces attempted to secure the state against the movement from below.

The uprising brought new confidence to people long excluded from formal politics – what Schielke calls: 'a new kind of political subjectivity' (2015: 191). Millions of people, self-identified as 'revolutionaries', engaged in the process of radical change. *Thawra* has the Arabic root *thara* (th/r/a), with implications of upheaval, rebellion and revolt. This could be interpreted in many ways: in the Spring of 2011, however, *thawra* was associated very widely with action for further change. Observing events as they unfolded in Cairo, Talal Asad noted: 'when Egyptian activists talk positively of "the revolution" they look forward to an entire power structure being destroyed (*ashsha'b yurid isqat an-nizam*, "The people wants to bring down the system!")'; he added: 'there is less discussion in detail about what is to take its place' (Asad 2012: 277). In this respect, the Egyptian experience was not different from other historic upheavals. Activists of the French Revolution of 1789 aspired broadly to 'Liberty, Equality, Fraternity' and Russian activists of 1917 to 'Bread, Peace and Land'. Egyptians initially demanded: 'Bread, Freedom, Social Justice' (sometimes 'Bread, Dignity, Social Justice') – an embracing approach that expressed the hopes of millions.

Social Movement Theory (SMT) has often failed to capture the dynamics of political upheaval. In the case of the Egyptian events, however, Sarah Anne Rennick has drawn on SMT to explain the effectiveness of the movement during its initial phases. Activists' slogans were not merely 'catchphrases chanted by protestors', she observes, but represented collective action frames that served specific purposes of mobilisation, both delegitimising opponents and facilitating a shared sense of purpose (Rennick 2013). The demand for social justice was central, acting as an umbrella term that encompassed values of respect, tolerance and equality. It was synonymous with broader demands for dignity that included freedom from discrimination and abuse, as well as improved standards of living:

> The demand is thus for a reconceptualization of the state as an institution in the service of its citizens that includes not only the guarantee of quality of life but also the erasure of social classifications and divisions, and the absence of corruption. As such, the demands for social justice of the revolutionary forces presupposed the redistribution of wealth, mechanisms of accountability, and the institutionalization of equality.
>
> (Rennick 2013)

This agenda, anticipating a continued challenge to the state and to class relations in Egypt, posed profound problems for the armed forces command. When in February 2011 troops entered city squares, they had been greeted with anger, then embraced and neutralised by protestors asserting that, 'The army and the people are one hand'. This was a honeymoon period for SCAF; soon, however, its efforts to control the streets, its denunciation of strikes and its reluctance to bring Mubarak and his circle to trial, brought a change in approach among activists. On

1 April 2011, mass protests took place in many cities on a 'Friday to Save the Revolution'. *Ahram Online* summarised the issues at stake:

> Mubarak has not been put on trial. The NDP is still at work. The local councils and governors appointed by the old regime have not been replaced, editors of all the national papers hired by the old regime remain in their positions. Members of the old regime still dominate most workers' unions and public companies while the emergency law has not been lifted and most political detainees remain in captivity.
>
> (*Ahram Online* 2011a)

An online group with 300,000 web supporters called for new mobilisations to demand trials of key figures of the Mubarak regime. It asserted: 'The counter-revolution is attempting to abort our demands by claiming that with the mere fall of the president and the dissolution of parliament, the people's demands have been accomplished' (Werr and Zayed 2011). Protestors in Tahrir Square chanted: 'The people want to purify the country' and 'Marshal, Marshal [SCAF leader Field Marshal Hussein Tantawi], legitimacy stems from Tahrir.'[8] The issue of legitimacy had become a theme of the mass movement. During the events of 25 January Mubarak had been declared *batil* – illegitimate or false.[9] By April, SCAF's claims to legitimacy were also in question. On 8 April, a 'Day of Cleansing and Trial' was joined in Tahrir Square by army officers who called for workers' rights, a minimum wage and the trial of Mubarak. In effect they declared for the people against the state, asserting that legitimacy lay with the protest movement – that Tahrir (a synonym for the movement) was the originator of the uprising and represented the aspirations of its participants. That night military police attacked activists in Tahrir Square, killing one protestor and injuring many, and seizing the dissident officers.[10] The following day demonstrators raised a new slogan: 'The army and people are not one hand', SCAF responding with a declaration that those who continued to stage sit-ins in the square after a military-imposed curfew would be viewed as 'outlaws' (Ibrahim, I. 2012).

Hostility to SCAF became more general. Hazem Kandil's accounts of events minimise the impact of activism; he nonetheless notes the importance of a change in public mood, observing:

Those who chanted 'The People and the Military Are One Hand!' began to cry furiously 'The People Demand the Execution of the Field Marshal!': [...] Praise for the patriotism and integrity of the armed forces has turned into sour denunciation by activists of the corrupt and complacent officer corps. Even non-assuming citizens who have not yet warmed up to the revolt [sic] have come to view the military with suspicion [...] the public image of the armed forces has deteriorated from an esteemed partner in the revolution to the avowed leader of the counterrevolution.

(Kandil 2012: 234)

SCAF wished to contain and passify the mass movement but lacked confidence to intervene with full force. Its approach was piecemeal and – at this stage – hesitant. Its greatest fear was of further fraternisation between troops and protestors, so that rather than risk rank-and-file conscripts in major confrontations with demonstrators, the army command ordered military police to seize individual activists: from April 2011 many were taken to military prisons. At the same time, SCAF made important concessions. Key figures of the Mubarak regime were arrested, including Ahmed Nazif of the 'dreamteam' government appointed in 2006; Safwat El-Sherif, general secretary of the NDP; and former speaker of parliament Fathi Suroor. In mid-April, Husni Mubarak's sons, Gamal and Alaa' Mubarak, were also arrested and sent to Tura Prison near Cairo, long a place of incarceration of political dissidents. In mid-April, the Higher Administrative Court met a further demand of activists, dissolving the NDP and ordering the surrender of its funds and property to the state.

Omar, a member of the Revolutionary Socialists interviewed in May 2011, described an increasingly complex relationship between the army and the movement:

The revolution is still very energetic. It's spreading wide and deep among the population, so that a massive counter-revolution of the proportions of 1848 [in Europe] would be needed to reverse the situation.

But there are real dangers. We have serious enemies, because in any revolution the class that loses some of its power will try to regain it. The old leaders of the NDP and the millionaires who benefited from it want to turn back the revolution. The police and State Security have been humiliated and now their officers are furious and want revenge. SCAF wants to be seen as a 'protector of the nation' but Tantawi is also trying to hold back the tide of struggle, sending troops [military police] to attack us when he can. We have to be vigilant.[11]

'Transition' and political reform

Most Egyptians anticipated prompt democratic reform. They expected new guarantees of rights including the right to association, and elections free of the violence, vote-rigging and fraud of the Mubarak era. The dissolution of the NDP seemed to indicate progress on this front and in April and May 2011 scores of new parties were established. Some were no more than 'shell' organisations: fiefdoms for leaders who took advantage of changed circumstances to extend their personal influence on the basis of old models of clientism. Many, however, expressed the interests of existing groups denied a voice by the former regime or were new formations encouraged by the uprising to enter public politics. These were ranged across the political spectrum: they included liberal capitalists such as the New Wafd Party, the Conference Party and the Free Egyptians Party of billionaire and media mogul Naguib Sawiris. Parties identifying as 'centre ground' emerged around a novel current in Egyptian politics – social democracy – loosely based on European models of gradualist change and including the Egyptian Social Democratic Party and the Destour (Constitution) Party. On the left new organisations included the Socialist Popular Alliance of reformists and Marxists, and the Workers Party, which hoped to coalesce industrial militants. Islamist organisations included the Freedom and Justice Party (FJP) established by the Muslim Brotherhood, the Wasat (Centre) Party, an earlier split from the Brotherhood, and a clutch of Salafi groups, notably the Nour (Light) Party.

Much was expected by Mubarak's former allies abroad of the most assertively capitalist organisations, usually described as 'liberals'. Roger Owen (2014: 264) suggests that during the events of January and February 2011 Tantawi had received a stream of phone calls from US President Obama and his secretary of state Hillary Clinton, and on the fall of Mubarak, says Steven Cook, 'Washington was abuzz with a renewed interest in democracy promotion' (Cook 2012: 302). The USA was focused on 'transition' – a process of reform that would lead Egypt towards economic and political models adopted in Eastern Europe after the fall of the Soviet Union and the 'colour revolutions' a decade later. The USA had long supported Mubarak, rejecting Egyptian lobbyists who called for support similar to that provided earlier in Europe and in the Caucasus. In Serbia, Ukraine and Georgia, Washington had directly funded the 'liberal' opposition, assisting the rise of politicians committed (at least formally) to free-market economics and to closer links with the USA and the EU (Hamid 2011: 21). The new parties of the Egyptian right were also candidates to pursue change acceptable to Washington – 'transition' that would introduce political change while minimising disruption to Mubarak's neo-liberal agenda. The nature of the uprising presented problems, however. Michele Dunne and Mara Revkin, in an analysis for the Carnegie think-tank, pointed to Egyptians': 'fierce deter-mination to dismantle the old regime and everything associated with it, including neoliberal economic reforms'; the uprising, they said, had: 'turned the logic of prioritizing economic over political reforms on its head' (Dunne and Revkin 2011).

This was also the central problem for SCAF. The military command was embedded in the structures of Egyptian capitalism: it had no intention of surrendering its political authority or its economic interests (see Chapter 8). How should the generals proceed with political change that did not facilitate further struggles for social justice, with their implications for the whole economic order? SCAF's strategy was to inhibit public discussion about reform and to seek an alliance with those who shared its aim of controlling the mass movement and facilitating business as usual. This brought the generals into an accommodation with the Muslim Brotherhood, a key target of the security agencies for over 40 years. Each now struggled to maximise the benefits of a relationship fraught with tension and mutual suspicion.

Constitutional chaos

The generals intended to maintain the integrity of the state and of their positions within it: the Muslim Brotherhood wished to fulfil an historic ambition by gaining access to positions of influence and shaping the state in line with a specific vision of the Islamic order. Many participants in the mass movement had aspirations that threatened the interests of both.

Two days after the fall of Mubarak SCAF suspended the constitution and appointed a team of legal experts to formulate new constitutional arrangements. Within ten days a set of amendments had been proposed, including a limit of eight years on the period a president could serve in office, new electoral procedures, a modification to arrangements for Emergency Law and a ban on parties that represented religious constituencies – a measure that targeted the Muslim Brotherhood. SCAF rushed forward a referendum, and within a month had obtained a large 'Yes' vote (77 per cent), albeit on a modest national turnout (41 per cent).[12] Many activists including liberals and social democrats argued for a 'No' vote, among them Mohamed ElBaradei, founder of the Destour Party and widely seen as the embodiment of cautious middle-class reformism. The Brotherhood meanwhile enthusiastically backed the proposals, for reasons that soon became clear. On 30 March, a revised 'Provisional Constitutional Declaration' was issued by SCAF as a working arrangement until the drafting of a full new constitution. This contradicted amendments put to the vote in the referendum days earlier. Both the amendments and the Declaration had been drawn up in secret by SCAF with selected 'experts', including Subhi Saleh, a prominent member of the Brotherhood. Radical activists suspected that, under intense pressure from the mass movement, the generals were reluctantly seeking an accommodation with the Brotherhood – a key reason that many declared the provisional constitution to be illegitimate (*batil*). Their fears were realized when SCAF also issued the draft of a new Parties Law and the Brotherhood promptly declared the establishment of a Freedom and Justice Party (FJP).

SCAF urgently needed allies: the Brotherhood was not merely an option but the only plausible choice for Tantawi and his colleagues. Its leaders held authority in the sole organisation possessing the attributes of a national political party, together with significant mass support. They had initially opposed the uprising; they had also joined SCAF in opposing strikes, accusing workers of engaging in *fi'awi* protests that undermined national consensus: one of the Brotherhood's most prominent figures, Essam El-Erian, had expressed 'understanding' for the army's point of view (Sallam 2011). Observing the emerging alliance, Elijah Zarwan of the International Crisis Group said: 'It makes sense if you are the military – you want stability and people off the street. The Brotherhood is one address where you can go to get 100,000 people off the street' (Slackman 2011).

When the Provisional Constitutional Declaration appeared on 30 March it revealed a new accommodation between SCAF and Brotherhood leaders. There was no reference to the ban on parties representing sectarian, geographic or religious constituencies that had appeared in the initial amendments to the constitution (and that had already been approved in the referendum). Owen describes the Declaration as 'an incoherent and deeply problematic document' that caused confusion among the public (2014: 265). Amid this uncertainty, SCAF established working relations with its new ally. The Brotherhood offered the means to control a mass movement with increasingly radical demands: the quid pro quo was agreement by SCAF to a Parties Law that soon produced the FJP and to an accelerated electoral process favouring the latter vis-à-vis a host of organisations still emerging and which had hoped for time to build their constituencies and to formulate their strategies. By April 2011, the Brotherhood's leaders believed they were in pole position for forthcoming parliamentary elections and for the presidential election to follow.

Renewed struggles

Following the fall of Mubarak, the Brotherhood's leaders had issued a series of assurances about their ambitions. According to Essam El-Erian: 'we [the Brotherhood] are not a party [...] we are an organization, institution, group working for the people in all aspects of life' (2011: 95). He continued:

> We are not going to run in the presidential elections with a candidate. We are not targeting to have a majority in the coming parliament. We are not speaking on behalf of the people. Our demands are the same demands of the people. We don't have a special agenda. We are not going to negotiate anything for our own interests.
>
> (El-Erian 2011)

Establishment of the FJP, led by key figures of the Brotherhood, told a different story. The Brotherhood prepared for parliamentary elections initially scheduled by SCAF for June 2011, to be followed in August by presidential elections. These were soon delayed by the generals, who were increasingly preoccupied by problems of public order and by labour disputes. Renewed protests expressed increasing public impatience with the military command, which at first responded hesitantly – a reflection of the strength of the movement and of the officers' reluctance to risk major confrontations. In Tahrir Square successive occupations demanded the trials of Mubarak and *feloul*, and immediate political reform – military police observed from a distance. In May, however, police attacked protestors at the Israeli embassy and the following month they assaulted demonstrators supporting the families of the martyrs (those killed earlier by state forces). In July, soldiers, police and the *baltagiyya* assaulted a large march from Tahrir Square to the headquarters of SCAF called to protest that demands of the movement had been ignored. During this episode, the Abbasiya protest,[13] tanks blocked marchers who were then attacked by military police, CSF troops and plain-clothes thugs, resulting in one death and almost 300 injuries (*Ahram Online* 2011d). Hossam El-Hamalawy, a participant, wrote on his blog:

> As soon as we reached the Nour Mosque, we found rows of army soldiers and officers, with the interior ministry's Central Security Forces lined behind them. We stood our ground, demanding we pass. We were refused. Chants started immediately against Tantawi. The attack started. Young men carrying swords and knives flocked to our right, while others were stoning us from the side streets. Army soldiers kept firing their machine guns into the air, to be followed later by a chopper circulating over our heads. It was a war zone in every sense of the word.
>
> (El-Hamalawy 2011d)

Activists across the political spectrum, including youthful members of the Brotherhood, unified in condemnation of the army, with an unusually broad coalition of organisations endorsing a five-point manifesto: an end to military trials for civilians; justice for the martyrs; swift trials for Mubarak cronies; a minimum wage for workers; and a new treason law to punish those who had corrupted political life under Mubarak (Ali 2011). Huge demonstrations again filled city centres for a 'Friday of the People's

Will and United Front'. Notwithstanding its formal support for a unified protest, the Brotherhood promoted a separate agenda. Its organisers raised slogans including: '*Allahu akbar*' ('God is the greatest'), 'We will sacrifice blood and soul for the sake of Islam' and 'Islamic state, Islamic state' (Ibrahim *et al.* 2011). Brotherhood speakers told the crowds that they fully supported the army and called for swift elections: in effect they used the rally to demand that SCAF should honour promises to facilitate the Brotherhood's political advance. Meanwhile secular demonstrators raised their own slogans: 'Civil state not religious state' and 'The military cheated you, tomorrow they will pull you down' (Ibrahim *et al.* 2011).

If SCAF was comforted by the support of the Brotherhood, it soon faced new challenges. In September, collective action in industry intensified dramatically, with some 500,000 workers involved in strikes and protests (Alexander and Bassiouny 2014: 201). This surge, engaging more workers than at any time since the fall of Mubarak, included postal workers, doctors, transport workers, dockers, sugar workers and teachers in a series of sector-wide protests. There was also a sharp rise in demands for *taṭhir*, with almost 20 per cent of all strikes and protests calling for removal of corrupt owners, managers, union officers or *feloul* (Alexander and Bassiouny 2014: 312–13). The impact was especially clear in education. A national teachers' strike – the first since 1951 – affected thousands of schools. Independent union groups demanded increases in pay, a minimum wage of LE1,200, contracts for part-time teachers and reform of the education system. The mood among strikers was insistent and radical, despite attempts by the Muslim Brotherhood (with its historic base of support among teachers) to moderate demands. At a national demonstration outside the Cabinet Office in Cairo, thousands of strikers abandoned the Brotherhood's slogans – '*Allahu akbar*' and '*Al-Islam huwa al-hal*' ('Islam is the solution') – in favour of demands for the resignation of the minister of education. The most popular slogan was: '*Irhal*' ('Go') – the message directed at Mubarak during the 18 Days.[14] One banner at the Cabinet Office summed up the mood: 'A message to the military council and the government: the minister must resign and increase our pay [...] or no one is going to school' (MENA 2011).

Academic staff at universities meanwhile demanded a purge of presidents, deans and department heads appointed by the Mubarak regime, a commitment initially made by SCAF in May 2011 but which had not been honoured. Some 5,000 professors and faculty members marched in Cairo to insist on their removal, calling for new arrangements to elect senior executives at public universities and threatening a full nationwide strike at the start of the academic year (Zohny 2011). It was in this climate that SCAF finally announced arrangements for parliamentary elections to take place in three rounds between November 2011 and January 2012.

Massacres, elections

The generals may have believed that elections would divert protestors towards the safer terrain of institutional politics. There was soon evidence to the contrary, as within days demonstrators in Tahrir Square demanded an end to Emergency Law and a speedy transfer of power to full civilian government. They were severely beaten by the CSF – the first in a series of attacks directed by SCAF that produced renewed anger vis-à-vis the armed forces. A week later a demonstration by Christians and their Muslim sympathisers marched to the television centre at Maspero in central Cairo to protest against official failures to investigate killings at churches. They were attacked savagely by troops using armed personnel carriers: 15 people were crushed by the vehicles, others were shot. There were at least 27 deaths: a massacre that exceeded in brutality the worst excesses of the Mubarak era (Amnesty International 2012: 6). The generals ploughed on, endorsing an incendiary statement on principles of government produced by Deputy Prime Minister Ali El Selmi. This recognised the military command as guardian of 'constitutional legitimacy', giving the armed forces the authority to decide policy even after election of a civilian parliament and a civilian president; the generals would also be empowered to prevent elected politicians from inspecting details of military budgets, which were to be concealed from the public. A 'Friday of One Demand' produced the largest public protests since July, including many supporters of the Brotherhood furious that the organisation's electoral advance would be rendered meaningless. The government backed down, resolving to suspend discussion on the Selmi principles until after the parliamentary elections. No sooner had one protest ended, however, than another was under way. As Egyptians prepared to vote in the first phase of elections, over 40 activists were killed during prolonged battles in Mohamed Mahmoud Street, near Tahrir Square. The clashes began when security forces attacked a sit-in of Families of the Martyrs who were demanding greater state support. Tens of thousands of activists flocked to Mohamed Mahmoud, where they were confronted by the CSF in battles that continued for five days and nights. Marwa, a doctor who volunteered at a field hospital nearby, described her experience:

> We treated hundreds of people suffering from inhalation of a powerful new tear gas, from traumatic injuries and from police bullets – several people lost eyes to these monsters [CSF snipers]. If anyone had illusions in the armed forces, thinking they would give up power or surrender to a new democracy Mohamed Mahmoud showed something different. Don't forget that no one among the demonstrators had a weapon. The generals were prepared to shoot them off the streets.[15]

In December, as a second phase of polls got under way, more prolonged fighting took place during the 'Cabinet Office clashes'. A three-week sit-in had been under way in protest at the appointment of Mubarak-era politician Kamal El Ganzouri as prime minister following the Mohamed Mahmoud killings. After attacks by police, commando units and paratroopers fighting continued for several days in nearby Qasr al-Aini Street, during which plain-clothes security men and the *baltagiyya* hurled missiles into the crowds: some protestors were killed or severely injured by concrete blocks and sheets of plate glass dropped from the roofs of nearby buildings.[16] According to government officials 17 people died; participants reported a much higher death toll and medical volunteers registered almost 2,000 injuries at field hospitals near Tahrir Square (Amnesty International 2012: 8, 17). Crowds raised the slogan: 'The people demand the execution of the Field Marshal [Tantawi]' (Feteha 2011). Even the Muslim Brotherhood could not restrain its supporters, who joined the protests in large numbers – most reluctant to confront troops, police and thugs but demonstrating their solidarity with those who did.

In an incident that caused further national outrage, military police were seen clubbing a woman protestor, removing her *abaya*[17] and repeatedly kicking her head and stomping on her semi-naked chest. The film of the 'blue bra' attack on social media brought thousands of demonstrators back to the streets in the largest women's protest in Cairo in modern Egyptian history: 'Drag me, strip me, my brothers' blood will cover me!', they chanted: 'Where is the field marshal? The girls [daughters] of Egypt are here' (Kirkpatrick 2011d). In a formal statement, SCAF regretted the attack: 'The Supreme Council of the Armed Forces expresses its utmost sorrow for the great women of Egypt, for the violations that took place during the recent events [...] It stresses its great appreciation for the women of Egypt' (Kirkpatrick 2011d). The generals urged calm, 'until we can reveal the infiltrating and paid agents of thuggery that aim at destruction, sabotage and damaging the revolution and the great Egyptian youth' (Kirkpatrick 2011d).

Throughout the events, said Amnesty International, officials and state media sought to portray protesters as 'troublemakers, criminals, "thugs" or simply as being irresponsible and serving those seeking to undermine the state or serving the interest of "foreign hands"' (2012: 7). The leaders of the Brotherhood endorsed this view. According to Khairat al-Shatir, one of its senior figures, 'groups trying to sow chaos' had attacked police during both the Mohamed Mahmoud and Cabinet Office battles (Salah 2012). At Maspero, said the Brotherhood, clashes were 'the work of domestic and foreign hands endeavouring to abort the revolution and disrupt the march towards freedom, justice and democracy' (Muslim Brotherhood 2011). In an official statement the Brotherhood called on Christians 'not to give the opportunity to the enemies of the nation at home and abroad to stir up discord and unrest', concluding that Israel played the key role in promoting sectarian and social tension and fomenting conflict in Egypt (Muslim Brotherhood 2011). Egyptians should show 'patience and prudence': they should 'wait for a government elected by the people [...] especially on the eve of free elections that we have always sought' (Muslim Brotherhood 2011).

'Down with military rule'

On 21 January 2012, as Egyptians prepared to mark the anniversary of the revolution, results of the country's first free parliamentary election were announced. The Muslim Brotherhood's FJP had won 37 per cent of the vote, followed by the Safalist Nour Party with some 27 per cent. Secular parties of the Egyptian Bloc, including the liberals expected to lead Egypt's 'transition', had failed spectacularly – with some 9 per cent – and the leftist Revolution Continues alliance had registered less than 3 per cent of votes. When the People's Assembly convened two days later,

Islamist parties held over 70 per cent of seats – what Mona El-Ghobashy (2012) called 'an Islamist super-majority' in Egypt's first representative parliament. Brotherhood leaders were jubilant, expressing satisfaction that after 80 years of struggle they had finally been called – 'summoned' – by the Egyptian people to fulfil a historic responsibility.

SCAF had a different view. General Mukhtar al-Mulla had already warned that whatever majority the Brotherhood enjoyed in parliament, 'they won't have the ability to impose anything that the people don't want', adding cryptically: 'The majority of the People's Assembly will not be the only one represented in the constituent assembly' (Kirkpatrick 2011d). Activists of the popular movement expressed their own opposition in protest marches that converged on the People's Assembly. They derided: 'the Sheikhs' Assembly, not the People's Assembly', calling for: 'A revolution against the Brotherhood' and 'Bread, Freedom, Social Justice' (*Ahram Online* 2012a). Two days later, on 25 January 2012, Egyptians marked the first anniversary of the uprising with demonstrations judged to be the largest since the fall of Mubarak (Michael and El Deeb 2012). The leaders of the Muslim Brotherhood had anticipated a mood of public celebration; they were faced instead by crowds expressing anger and intense hostility to SCAF: '*Yasqut, yasqut hukm al-askar*' ('Down, down with military rule') and 'Tantawi, come and kill more revolutionaries, we want your execution' (Michael and El Deeb 2012). Recalling deaths at the hands of both Mubarak and the generals, and in assertion of Muslim–Christian solidarity, demonstrators declared: '*Ti'tl Khaled, ti'tl Mina: kul rosasa bitaweena*' ('Kill Khaled, kill Mina – all the bullets make us stronger').[18] In Tahrir Square Brotherhood speakers struggled to be heard against a repeated chorus: '*Thawra, thawra hatta an-nasr*' ('Revolution, revolution until victory').

A year of upheaval had ended with the mass movement still vigorous and intent on change. It had profoundly affected the institutions of the state: police and security agencies had been compelled to retreat and for the first time in decades most neighbourhoods, workplaces and campuses enjoyed freedom from constant surveillance. Independent unions had proliferated, organising sustained campaigns for improved wages and conditions. The incomes of those in work had risen and the government had reluctantly set a minimum monthly wage. These gains were modest, however, and fell far short of demands raised in countless strikes and protests.[19] The government had enacted political reform – but grudgingly and according to limits established by the armed forces command, which still held power. The dictator had gone but the dictatorship was in place, intent on containing the movement from below. Its ally in this endeavour was the Muslim Brotherhood, beholden to the generals for its electoral opportunity and ready to turn upon the mass movement.

Many assessments saw a revolution already in decline. Writing in the *Washington Post*, Daniel Byman proposed that the hope of the Arab Spring had already been succeeded by the chill of 'Arab winter'. The army was determined to hold onto power and the Muslim Brotherhood was in a position of unprecedented opportunity, he argued, while the mass movement was 'leaderless and loosely organized [...] you cannot govern by flash mob' (Byman 2011). There were many similar analyses. Kandil suggested that 'the old political temple' of the Mubarak era was in ruins (2012: 239). Around it lay 'an incredibly chaotic political scene' dominated by Islamists prepared to collaborate with the armed forces command 'without reservations' (Kandil 2012: 239). The mass of people, though 'seemingly fearless', had failed to accomplish a revolutionary breakthrough (Kandil 2012: 242). The process of change continued, however. Year One of the revolution had moved millions of people towards an acute awareness of their interests vis-à-vis those in power. Year Two was to see further radicalisation – and to test it in new ways.

PART II
THE PAST IN THE PRESENT

5

Islamism and the State

As the second year of the revolution began, the military command and the Muslim Brotherhood found themselves to be both allies and rivals. Their relationship as partners in government, suggests Maha Abdelrahman, amounted to 'a brief intense honeymoon' (2014: 112). It expressed mutual commitments to the Egyptian state, to capitalism in its neo-liberal phase and to control of the revolutionary movement. As historic rivals, the generals and the leaders of the Brotherhood had long viewed one another with suspicion that could amount to deep hostility and even hatred. Their common project during the revolution, however, was that of containment of the movement from below, which each viewed with anxiety and disdain.

The leaders of the Brotherhood at first made determined efforts to prevent their members and supporters from joining the uprising. Essam el-Erian – a member of the organisation's senior body, the Guidance Council – rejected calls to join demonstrations on 25 January, Police Day, on the grounds that the organisation would not violate a national holiday (Fahmy 2011). The youth of the organisation persisted, arguing that abstention would damage the organisation: the leadership nonetheless refused. Two days before the demonstration Mohamed El-Beltagy, also a prominent member of the Guidance Council, said that the organisation had decided to participate 'symbolically' by attending a rally at the Supreme Court but its members would not, he insisted, join street demonstrations (Elyan 2011). Ahmed, a radical activist who had worked closely with the Brotherhood in campaigns for Palestine and in anti-war protests, described the organisation's dilemma:

> They were caught between the state and the people. They'd been attacked so often by the regime that the Brotherhood leaders were frightened of exposing themselves again. They were also on the retreat

from politics in general – but the youth were much closer to the mood of the people and knew they had to be involved.[1]

Within hours of protests beginning on 25 January, the Interior Ministry issued a statement blaming the Brotherhood for fomenting unrest – a claim its leaders promptly denied (*Al Jazeera* 2011b). As it became clear that a massive national uprising was under way, the Guidance Council was compelled to reverse its position and on 28 January, the 'Day of Rage', members of the Brotherhood joined the protests in large numbers – according to one account there were 100,000 Muslim Brothers in the streets of Cairo (Tammam and Haenni 2011). There was an immediate impact in confrontations with the CSF. Ali, a veteran activist of the left, explains:

There were some members of the Brotherhood in the earliest demonstrations but not in an organised way. When they joined us for the Day of Rage we could see that they'd come as organised groups. They made a big difference – they were in disciplined blocs, they knew and trusted one another. They hated the police for years of violence against them – and it showed. They were very effective fighters in the streets and got a lot of respect for it.[2]

The organisation reported that 40 of its members had been killed and its most senior figure, the Murshid ('Guide') Mohamed Badie, accused Mubarak of 'state terrorism' (Tamman and Haenni 2011). Now there was a feeling of 'no return' within the Brotherhood, its members aware that, if the protest movement did not succeed, they would be among the principal victims of the regime. 'Our only card is the mobilisation in Tahrir Square,' said a Brotherhood activist: 'It has become our life insurance against the swing of the pendulum which awaits us if the regime gets back on its feet.'[3] The Guidance Council was under intense pressure. Millions of Egyptians demanded the resignation of Mubarak and immediate political change; Brotherhood leaders nonetheless met Vice-President Omar Suleiman, former head of intelligence and one of the organisation's historic adversaries, for talks about a negotiated end to the crisis. An announcement that agreement had been reached for constitutional change without Mubarak's resignation prompted fury among its members and supporters, with young activists asserting that their commitment to the protest movement was greater than their loyalty to the Guidance Council. As the protests continued, the organisation faced the prospect of unmanageable internal tensions and splits. Its leaders withdrew from talks with Suleiman but within days, following the resignation of Mubarak, they were represented in new discussions convened by SCAF.

Birth of the Brotherhood

These changes in approach, accompanied by tortured debate within the Brotherhood about its aims and principles, are best understood in the context of the long history of relations between the state and the Islamist movement.

The modern state was shaped initially by the reforms of the nine-teenth-century ruler Mohamed Ali, who used military institutions as a key means of centralisation – part of the strategy by which he asserted Egypt's independence of the Ottoman Empire (Fahmy 1997). By the 1870s, army officers were among those most active in advancing proto-nationalist ideas. They found common cause with the earliest Islamist thinkers, notably Jamal al-Din al-Afghani, whose project of Islamic unity embraced the struggle for independence of the colonial powers (Barghouti 2008). Following the 'Urabi Revolt and British occupation in 1882, Egypt's ruler Khedive Mohamed Tawfiq[4] was compelled to surrender the armed forces, announcing days after British invasion that: 'The Egyptian army is suspended' (Baker 1978: 19). When reconstituted under British control, the army was no more than an auxiliary corps of the colonial authorities and for decades it remained a token force alongside the powerful British garrison. In the 1930s, its own com-mander-in-chief observed that the army was 'worthless': according to General Aziz al-Masri, 'It was the British who organised it, and they had their reasons for making a poor thing of it' (Baker 1978: 19).

The rise of the armed forces to new prominence during the 1950s was an outcome of growing resistance to colonial rule. During the previous decade the British authorities and their Egyptian client King Faruq (the last ruler of the Mohamed Ali dynasty) faced sustained struggles including huge public protests and strikes: the historian Robert Stephens describes the late 1940s as a period of 'revolutionary ferment' (Stephens 1971: 63). The working class had emerged as an independent political force on a national scale; though small and fragmented, it had a profound impact in major urban centres, bringing a radical political agenda to anti-British protests. In 1946, a National Committee of Workers and Students organised demonstrations that involved scores of thousands of workers – the most militant expressions of nationalist sentiment since the upheavals that had followed the First World War. At the same time, the Muslim Brotherhood engaged even larger numbers in the first mass-based Islamist movement. This set forth conservative values based on idealised models of the early Muslim community: in the context of decades of British occupation, however, it had a radical appeal. Denying the legitimacy of European rule and the effectiveness of mainstream 'liberal' nationalism, the Brotherhood mobilised large numbers of the middle class, the urban poor and sometimes the working class.

By the late 1940s, there were widespread expectations of a decisive move against the monarchy by the two main opposition currents, the communists and the Brotherhood. Founded in 1928 by Hassan al-Banna, the Society of the Muslim Brothers (*Jama'at al-Ikhwan al-Muslimin* or Muslim Brotherhood) had developed with extraordinary speed to become the first mass organisation in modern Egypt. Banna drew on the ideas of Afghani, who had been a supporter of the 'Urabi movement and of Muslim unity in the face of European occupation. With the growth of Egyptian nationalism and the rise of the Wafd Party, Afghani's ideas and those of co-thinkers in the tradition of the *salaf* ('forefathers' or 'founders' of the early Islamic communities) had weakened. In 1924, the Wafd Party was elected to lead an 'independent' government but its accommodation with the British meant that Egypt remained a colonial state under military control. British officials intervened repeatedly to enforce their preferred policies, with the Wafd Party – committed to cautious bourgeois nationalism – unable to respond and the army powerless. It was in this context, comments Maghraoui, that the Brotherhood emerged as a current that 'refused to play according to the rules of the liberal constitutional regime' (2006: 132).

The organisation's first group was established in Ismailiyya, an administrative centre for the Suez Canal and a garrison town constructed on the model of the British cantonments of colonial India. Richard Mitchell comments on the importance of Banna's own experiences in the city:

Here were not only the British military camps, but, equally hateful to Banna, the Suez Canal Company; complete foreign domination of the public utilities; and the conspicuously luxurious homes of the foreigners overlooking the 'miserable' homes of their workers. Even the street signs in the popular Egyptian quarters, he [Banna] observed, were written in 'the language of the economic occupation'.

(Mitchell 1969: 7)

Banna was hostile to the influence of occupation on Egyptian society and the impact of European culture in general. Like Afghani, he aimed to reassert the principles and values of early Islam, seeing himself as a teacher or counsellor who would awaken commitments to Islamic culture. By 1929, he had founded branches of the Brotherhood in four cities along the Canal, each focused upon a mosque, a school or a welfare project.[5] Mitchell traces the organisation's subsequent growth: 10 branches in 1931; 15 in 1932; 300 in 1938; 500 in 1940; 2,000 in 1949 (1969: 328). At its peak, between 1946 and 1949, the Brotherhood's membership, he suggests, was between 300,000 and 600,000, with another 500,000 sympathisers: during that period (when Egypt's population was less than 20 million) the organisation's claim to be speaking in the name of a million Egyptians 'was not exaggerated' (Mitchell 1969: 328).

This pattern of growth was unparalleled in the modern history of the region. Other Muslim self-help initiatives were undertaken at the same time but it was only Banna's project that succeeded in drawing mass support, principally because of a change of strategy during the mid-1930s. The organisation had at first been explicitly non-political, focusing on study, self-reflection and the implementation of religious codes and personal practices. The catalyst for change was the Palestinian *intifada* of 1936, an uprising against both British rule and Zionist settlement. The Brotherhood undertook demonstrations of solidarity and began raising money for the Palestinian resistance as a means of expressing their support for fellow Muslims in struggle. Increasingly Banna criticised the role of Britain in Palestine and Egypt: he also attacked the record of the Wafd Party, alleging that nationalist leaders were in the service of the occupation, calling for the withdrawal of troops and for a programme of social reform. In 1941, Banna and other leaders of the organisation were imprisoned – a mark of their growing influence and of the nervousness of the regime and the colonial authorities.

The Brotherhood rose to prominence as part of a surge in anti-colonial activism taking place across the Middle East. Its ideology and practices were distinct, however. Banna drew his core principles from Afghani and the *salafiyya* movement. His vision was of a society purged of non-Islamic influence and integrated by a shared commitment to *shari'a* (Islamic legal codes). This would facilitate progress towards unification of the *umma* (the collective of believers) which, he argued, had been divided by notions of nation and race that were alien to Islam. The project attracted mainly educated urban Egyptians, especially teachers, civil servants and students, together with small businessmen and traders. They provided the organisation with a conservative, middle-class leadership strongly attached to Islamic traditions but which also offered a means of reaching broader constituencies, including the peasantry, the urban poor and the working class, whose predicaments Banna placed in the context of a crisis of Western civilisation that he saw as 'bankrupt and in decline':

> Its foundations are crumbling and its institutions and guiding principles are falling apart. Its political foundations are being destroyed by dictatorships, and its economic foundations are being swept away by crises. The millions of its wretched unemployed and hungry offer their testimony against it.
>
> (Wendell 1978: 106)

As an alternative to colonisation and weak national government, the Brotherhood offered activism in the name of Islam. Its slogans were vague and encompassing – 'God is our King; the Quran is our constitution; the Prophet is our leader' and 'Islam is the solution' – but provided a means of attaching people from all sectors of society, articulating widely felt grievances and rising anger.

Towards 'revolution'

According to Anwar al-Sadat, later President of Egypt, Hassan al-Banna had his first meeting with dissident army officers in 1938 (Mitchell 1969: 24–25). They were particularly impressed with Banna's support of the Palestinian cause and the Brotherhood's supply of arms to Palestinian guerrilla groups. Relations continued as the group gradually established a clandestine network, the Free Officers (al-Dubat al-Ahrar), that aimed to purge the army of its ineffective leadership and to assert Egypt's independence. Among the Officers, most of junior and middle rank, some came under the influence of the Brotherhood; others were allied with the left and in particular with the communist movement. Both communists and Islamists participated in mobilisations against the British, each competing for public support and attempting to exert influence within the army. By the late 1940s, opposition to the regime had achieved unprecedented breadth and depth: Joel Beinin and Zachary Lockman comment that, 'Everyone understood that the old regime was dead, but nobody knew precisely how to bury it' (1987: 396–97). After several years of further crisis, the Free Officers broke the deadlock by enacting a carefully prepared coup.

The Free Officers were obsessed by security and secrecy, mistrusting all those beyond a close-knit network of junior-/middle-ranking officers and a handful of more senior colleagues. Their relations with the Brotherhood and the left varied over the years, with the former holding the greatest influence. At one point, the Islamists recruited a significant group of young officers, including activists who later became key figures in Egyptian politics, notably Gamal Abdel-Nasser. The Free Officers remained independent, however, focused upon building within the officer corps and evading periodic purges conducted by the king within the most senior ranks. Its members were disinterested in the common soldiery and hostile to all ideas of public involvement in their project: Raymond Baker comments, 'From its inception the Free Officers movement was elitist' (Baker 1978: 25). On 23 July 1952, it seized power without significant opposition, quickly assuring both the British and Americans that they would not act against their interests.[6] US officials were encouraged: the American ambassador in Cairo reported to Washington that the coup was 'designed to undercut and forestall all the chaos and perhaps outright communist takeover' (Gordon 1992: 166). The Officers also sent reassuring messages to key Egyptian organisations including the Wafd Party, the Muslim Brotherhood and parties of the left, with the result that each backed the coup, expecting that it would favour their own specific interests. Declaring themselves the Executive Committee of 'the command' or 'general command' (known after 1953 as the Revolution Command Council, RCC) they removed Faruq and to general acclaim declared a republic.[7] Within two years, all British troops except for a contingent on the Suez Canal had left and after the Suez war of 1956 all foreign detachments were expelled. The RCC and its leading figure Gamal Abdel-Nasser accumulated enormous prestige as champions of national liberation and in 1956 Nasser became President of Egypt.

In 1947, an Egyptian government newspaper described the Brotherhood as 'not just a party but [...] a state with its armies, hospitals, schools, factories, and companies'.[8] Despite its advanced forms of organisation and an enormous following, the Brotherhood did not attempt to remove Faruq or to pose a direct challenge to his loyalist governments. It was characterised above all by contradiction – its leaders raised expectations of change that they were unable to pursue, for attempts to challenge the regime implied an assault on structures of privilege in which they held their own interests. Leading members came predominantly from the urban middle class: in the early 1950s the Guidance Bureau included senior civil servants, lawyers and professors, while its activist core was dominated by 'an emergent and self-conscious Muslim middle class' (Mitchell 1969: 329, 330). The leadership criticised European control of the economy and those it called 'internal imperialists' who sustained the British occupation (Mitchell 1969: 329). At the same time, Brotherhood leaders were committed to national unity and the integrity of the state, and in most circumstances they opposed independent working class organisation (see Chapter 6). As the mass movement of the 1940s brought increasing pressure from below, the limits of their ambitions became clear. The leadership's 'middle-class conservative reformism' prompted efforts to rescue the state rather than reshape it, while an assault on power was unthinkable (Mitchell 1969: 329).

Banna was fascinated by the monarchy and deferential towards the king. He maintained links with the palace and at times of crisis sent messages of reassurance to Faruq.[9] In return, he was consulted about official appointments and allegedly received favours that may have amounted to financial support.[10] He was loyal to the throne, suggests Mitchell, and 'hoped in fact, to achieve his reforms through it' (1969: 40). The Brotherhood's radical rhetoric was in practice a cautious politics of reform that allowed the regime to survive years of mass opposition. It contributed to the growth of the anti-colonial movement, benefited from it and at the same time failed to fulfil the expectations of those who participated in it. Banna's grand design of an Islamised state could not be realized by an organisation that dare not challenge economic and social structures in which its leaders were embedded. To this extent, the Brotherhood's programme for change was a utopian project (Marfleet 1998).

The 'Great Ordeal'

The Brotherhood welcomed the coup of 1952. Its leaders viewed the Free Officers as a 'wayward faction' of the Brotherhood and anticipated that they would be able to join the group in shaping a new government (Gordon 1992: 53, 98). They proposed political changes and religious reforms including a ban on usury, the establishment of Islamic charitable foundations and the teaching of religion in the armed forces. They backed the Officers' early repression of the workers' movement and did not question their hostility to independent public politics. The Officers meanwhile accommodated the Brotherhood and leading figures of the new regime, including Nasser, spoke at Brotherhood rallies. When in January 1953 the Officers banned all political organisations, they exempted the Brotherhood on the grounds that it was a religious association rather than a party. The Brotherhood's leaders responded by endorsing the Officers' announcement that they were to rule Egypt directly.

The new regime's ban on parties was accompanied by the inauguration of an organisation designed to formalise public support for the army command. The Liberation Rally was to have a presence in workplaces, campuses and neighbourhoods: it was also designed to co-opt senior members of the former Faruq government, the Wafd Party and the Brotherhood, with the implication that the latter was to lose its independence. Brotherhood leaders resisted and in January 1954, following a minor dispute between supporters of the Rally and student members of the Brotherhood, the regime arrested hundreds of its members, issuing a formal ban on the organisation. In March 1954, large public protests demanded democratic change. They were supported by parties of the opposition including the Brotherhood (all were now technically illegal), by much of the labour movement and by many within the armed forces.[11] Nasser, who had been declared 'Commander of the Revolution', suppressed the movement using a combination of tactics: a temporary pact with the Brotherhood, co-option of several trade union leaders, manipulation of the media, and the use of police and of mob violence in the form of the *baltagiyya* (see Chapter 6). The Brotherhood changed tack once more, declaring support for the

RCC, and hundreds of its members were freed from prison. The rapprochement did not last long: an assassination attempt on Nasser was attributed to the Brotherhood and the regime launched a full assault on the Islamists, depicting them as religious zealots and terrorists. Nasser organised a series of public trials – 'a circus side show' (Wheelock 1960: 47) – after which six leading members were executed and some 20,000 arrested (Kandil 2015: 129).

For the Brotherhood, the 1950s and 1960s became years of 'The Ordeal' (*al-Mihna*). Between 1954 and 1970, scores of thousands of members were incarcerated in prison camps under harsh desert conditions; many were tortured. Others fled into exile, most travelling to Saudi Arabia, where they were accommodated by a regime strongly opposed to Nasser's nationalism and his turn in the mid-1950s to the Soviet bloc. In prison, some activists drew radical conclusions. Under the leadership of a prominent Brotherhood member, Sayyid Qutb, they reassessed their experiences of repression in the context of Islamic traditions, concluding that the Nasserist state was no different from societies of the pre-Islamic era: it represented ignorance and barbarism, or *jahiliyya*. A determined struggle against impious rulers such as the Egyptian dictator was required – a modern *jihad* to be led by dedicated Muslims who would form an activist vanguard that, unlike the mainstream of the Brotherhood, would be capable of awakening believers to their task.[12] When the network was discovered, Qutb and two others were tried on charges of plotting to overthrow the regime and were executed in prison. The '1964 Organisation' was crushed and thousands more suspects sent to prison.

Nasser died in 1970 and Sadat, a veteran of the Free Officers group, was installed as president. He faced serious problems of discontent among Egyptians who were shocked and disillusioned by defeat in the 1967 war with Israel, in which the army – the focus of the Nasserist project – had failed dramatically. In 1968, there had been widespread strikes and public protests: the workers' movement was recovering from years of repression and a mood of discontent was spreading. Sadat called for a 'correction of the revolution' of 1952, purging Nasser loyalists and leftists earlier co-opted by the regime and who held senior positions in government institutions. He declared himself the 'Believer President', invoking Islamic values and advancing clerics and Muslim scholars to positions of influence. In 1971, he announced a general amnesty for the Brotherhood and released its members from prison. He encouraged the return of exiles from the Gulf states and the Brotherhood was able to reorganise around its publication, *al-Da'wa* ('The Call'). This was a different organisation from that suppressed in 1954. At its core were returnees who had absorbed the conservative values of Saudi Arabia's state ideology, Wahhabism; some had also had become successful businessmen, especially through their relationships with financial institutions and trading houses. When in 1974 Sadat declared a new economic strategy, the *infitah*, endorsing the role of private capital and abruptly turning Egypt from East to West (from its alliances with Moscow to a rapprochement with the USA and its allies) the organisation was an enthusiastic supporter. In 1976, the Brotherhood won six seats in parliament, encouraging the Da'wa group and its politics of mild piecemeal change focused on introduction of *shari'a* principles to the law.

The Brotherhood also became an important influence in the student movement. The left had re-emerged on campus, campaigning in support of the Palestinian cause, against *infitah* and for democratic change. In 1972–73, there were mass demonstrations involving workers, students and junior officers: Sadat responded by jailing left-wing activists. In 1975, a Club for Progressive Socialist Thought was established within the official Student Union, organising protests that brought together the independent left and young Nasserists (Abdalla 1985: 226–28). Sadat further encouraged the Brotherhood as a countervailing force, providing official backing for its Society of the Youth of Islam. By 1977, the organisation was a dominant force in campus politics, winning successive elections in the Student Union, while radical Islamist groups also developed new influence. Inspired by the work of Qutb and the *jihadi* current, they organised with increasing effectiveness at universities across the country, financed by government officials who provided space on campus specifically to contest the influence of the left.[13] In 1977, however, the state's accommodation with the Islamists was disrupted by Sadat's visit to Israel and his subsequent negotiation of a peace deal with Israel that effectively abandoned the Palestinian national movement. Muslim activists, including the Brotherhood, launched a torrent of criticism and Sadat responded with a crackdown on campus activity. In September 1981 the regime made over 1,500 arrests including Umar al-Tilmisani, the most senior figure in the Brotherhood, and banned *al-Da'wa*. In October 1981, Sadat was assassinated by the Al Jihad group – one of the Islamist currents he had cultivated for almost a decade.

Again repression

Despite its problems during the closing years of the Sadat era, the Brotherhood had found a means to co-exist with the regime. It saw Sadat's embrace of neo-liberalism as congenial, comparing his policies favourably with Nasser's nationalisations of industry and commerce and expropriations of privately held land (see Chapter 6). Tilmisani argued that: 'the era of Gamal Abul Nasser was characterized by evil and wrongdoing' and that 'the communist economy [sic – of Nasser] brought us to these deadly crises' (Baker 1990: 249). The Brotherhood could in effect do business with Sadat and continued to find a means of co-operating with his successor Husni Mubarak. Its prisoners were released by Mubarak and, still technically illegal, the organisation entered elections by placing its own candidates on the lists of parties with official status – first the Wafd Party, later the Socialist Labour Party and the Liberal Party. In 1984, it entered parliament with eight seats; in 1987, it formed an Islamic Alliance campaigning under the slogan: 'Islam is the solution', winning 56 seats of which 36 went to members of the Brotherhood. The organisation had again become the largest force in opposition to a regime facing growing resistance. Its strategy remained one of gradualism – an attempt to advance within parliament and within the professional associations or syndicates (*naqabat*) that represented doctors, dentists, pharmacists, lawyers, journalists, engineers and others. Here the Brotherhood was strikingly successful. For generations it had recruited among middle-class professionals: by the late 1980s it had influence, and in some cases controlling majorities, in several of the associations – an expression of the massive expansion of higher education and the disillusion of young professionals. In less than a decade, suggests Kandil (2015: 134), 21 syndicates with a combined membership of 2.5 million fell under its control.[14]

In the early 1990s, Mubarak ended this phase of accommodation. In 1991, Brotherhood-led syndicates issued a joint statement condemning the military assault on Iraq launched by the USA and its allies including Egypt and the following year the organisation led a public demonstration (called by the doctors' syndicate, under Brotherhood influence) against

Egypt's participation in the Madrid 'peace' talks involving Israel and the Palestinians. The regime responded with arrests of Muslim Brothers it described as 'extremists, terrorists, fanatics and infiltrators' (Campagna 1996: 286–87). In the same year, a major earthquake struck Egypt, causing hundreds of deaths and leaving some 50,000 people homeless. The Brotherhood moved quickly, providing medical assistance, food, blankets and temporary accommodation through clinics and local aid centres festooned with its unmistakeable slogan *al-Islam huwa al-hal* ('Islam is the solution'). Its efforts contrasted with the regime's feeble response: the state appeared disinterested, while the Brotherhood demonstrated that it had a large network of activists and the means to intervene effectively in a national crisis. The Minister of the Interior, Abdel Halim Musa, was alarmed, asking: 'What is going on here? Do we have a state within a state?' (Campagna 1996: 286).

The Brotherhood had undergone a further important change: having been rehabilitated under Sadat, it had continued to grow under Mubarak, developing wide popular appeal by reaching out to constituencies with which it had not engaged systematically since the colonial era, notably the urban poor. As the state focused more intently upon the neo-liberal agenda, withdrawing progressively from welfare provision, the Brotherhood's welfare networks were of increasing importance, especially in provincial cities and in 'urban villages' across the country. When in 1993 Mubarak ordered legal changes to contain Islamist influence in the syndicates, there were large public protests. Capturing popular support in the mode of Brotherhood initiatives of an earlier era, the organisation was again in open confrontation with the regime.

Interviewed in 1996, Maya – a doctor who had been a student activist in the 1970s – described the contradictory nature of the Brotherhood's rising influence:

> I'd always despised the Brothers. They were enemies of the left – and they were against all independent action in the university. They played according to Sadat's rules and then they played according to Mubarak's rules. But now they are back as a national opposition movement and people are moving towards them. They get thousands of people at their rallies, even if they are still 'illegal'. And they are paying a price for standing up to Mubarak.[15]

Reform agenda

During the 1980s, Mubarak had attempted a dual strategy vis-à-vis the Islamists. Unlike Sadat, who initially encouraged each and every Islamist current in order to inhibit opposition from below, Mubarak distinguished between 'radicals' (*jihadis*) and 'moderates' (the Brotherhood and allied groups). He initially suppressed the *jihadis* but by the late 1980s, in the context of growing public despair at his policies, they had re-established their influence, especially in deprived cities of the South (*al-Sa'id* – Upper Egypt) and in the *'ashwa'iyyat* of Greater Cairo. In 1992, the regime launched a massive assault on *jihadi* groups in the Cairo district of Imbaba and in effect declared war on activists in the South. When the lawyers' syndicate protested following the killing by police of one of its members who had defended *jihadi* suspects, the regime held the Brotherhood responsible and the organisation was swept into a general campaign of repression. In 1995, there were widespread arrests of Brotherhood members, who were referred to military courts: for the first time since the Nasser era, Emergency Laws targeted Islamists en masse. For the next 15 years, the Brotherhood was presented by the regime as its chief public enemy. Having finally disposed of the *jihadis* by means of brutal repression, including the use of 'disappearances', death squads and – in rural areas of the South – of scorched-earth policies, Mubarak maintained continuous pressures on the organisation. Thousands of its members were arrested and jailed: even United States officials suggested that in one year, 2005, there were 10,000 detainees (US Department of State 2006). Repression continued relentlessly, with hundreds of leading members of the Brotherhood seized and imprisoned without trial: in 2009 the organisation said that 30,000 members had been incarcerated (*Ahram Weekly* 2009b).

These developments had their impact on policy making within the Brotherhood. On the one hand, its prominence as the sole organisation with a national presence and an agenda for change brought wide support. This strengthened the hand of younger activists who favoured a strategy of engagement with emerging movements of protest. The series of campaigns that began in 2000 – in support of Palestine, against war and for democratisation – followed by mass workers' struggles, encouraged the Brotherhood to launch its own agenda for reform. Wickham observes that this integrated democratic themes into a wider project of Islamic reform, so that many of the organisation's demands 'echoed those of secular opposition groups' (2013: 105). In 2004, it launched a formal programme:

> [This] asserted that the people are the source of all authority and have the right to select their political representative in free and fair elections. It called for the separation of the presidency from any political party and the restriction of the holder of that office to two consecutive terms [...] it called for the lifting of the state of emergency and replacing the country's restrictive party and syndicate laws [...] for a release of political prisoners, an end to torture and limiting [the powers of] the security establishment.
>
> (Wickham 2013: 105)

In 2005, the *murshid*, Mohamed Akef, announced that the Brotherhood's key campaigning slogan 'Islam is the solution' was to be replaced by 'Reform is the solution'. Akef was widely viewed as a relatively liberal figure within the Islamist tradition. He interacted with other organisations of the Egyptian opposition and with secular radicals in the Middle East and beyond.[16] Influenced by the growth of the democracy movement, by young activists within the Brotherhood and by somewhat greater success for the organisation in electoral activity, he attempted to consolidate an orientation on political reform. 'Freedom is a basic part of the Islamic order', he insisted: 'If it is absent then the slogan "Islam is the solution" has no value. It becomes the problem, not the solution.'[17] Until 2010, the organisation maintained a relatively open strategy of involvement in public politics, combining activism with commitments to *da'wa* ('calling', or proselytisation) and consolidation of the Brotherhood as – on the original model of Hassan al-Banna – an expression of collective Muslim interests. Its most publicly active members faced further serious problems however. As Mubarak became increasingly intolerant of movements for change, he closed the limited space available to the Brotherhood through the electoral process. In successive elections, police attacked polling stations in areas where the organisation's candidates enjoyed strong support, using violence that was intense and uninhibited even by the regime's standards. The *baltagiyya* assaulted voters and election officials, stuffed ballot boxes and approved fictitious results, while mass arrests and torture of Brotherhood activists continued. These developments increased the influence within the organisation of conservatives who had long sought to retreat from electoral activity and public politics in general. In January 2010, the Brotherhood elected a new leader, Mohamed Badie, associated with an earlier generation of members who had come to prominence in the Sadat era.[18] His first public statement announced a political retreat: 'We reaffirm that the Brotherhood was not for one day an adversary to the regime', he said, urging members 'to show how the world the true Islam, the Islam of moderation and forgiveness' (Ikhwanweb 2010). Frustrated young activists made public their fears 'that with Badie in charge the youth success and reform push of recent times will be put on hold' (Mayton 2010). In parliamentary elections of November 2010, intimidation and fraud by police and officials was again particularly marked and the Brotherhood withdrew from the second phase of voting. This marked an official retreat from the electoral arena – and it was in this context, with conservative leaders tightening their grip on the organisation – that the Brotherhood faced the challenges of 25 January 2011.

'Cobra and mongoose'

Assessments of the Brotherhood's long political history differ widely – as do analyses of its role in the revolution and its fate in 2013 at the hands of the military command. One influential approach has emphasised the continuity of the organisation and its influence on Egyptian politics. Since the 1940s, suggests Robert Springborg (2012), the Brotherhood has been locked in struggle with the Egyptian state. Each, he says, has sought domination of the other – in the mode of the epic clash between the mongoose (the forces of the state) and the cobra (the Islamists), with the former always winning. On this view, the state encounters the Brotherhood as a long-standing institution of equal standing – a view given weight by Trager (2011: 114), who proposes that the Brotherhood, shaped by generations of struggle under a cohesive and assertive leadership, has for decades been 'unbreakable'. This perspective is consistent with dominant attitudes among academics and media observers in 'the West' in which Islamist movements are seen as homogenous and largely unchanging.

Asef Bayat warns against this view and the tendency 'to reify both Islam as a religion and Islamism as a political project' (2005: 891), overlooking variations over time in religious perceptions, practice and institutions, and changing socio-political circumstances in the wider society. The neo-Orientalist approach has been pervasive, with organisations such as the Brotherhood presented as static, their commitments to 'fundamentalist' values said to shape unchanging policies and practices. Bayat draws attention to the dynamics of change within and outside the Brotherhood, and to the reciprocal effects: 'Social movements [such as the Brotherhood] transform their own environment, their relationships with surrounding social and political forces and institutions, society, their constituency, and the state, which in turn affects their own existence' (2005: 898).

The Muslim Brotherhood in Egypt might be taken as a paradigmatic case of the need to address context and conjuncture when considering the character and impacts of social movements. The cultural association established by Hassan al-Banna in 1928 had within a decade been transformed into a mass organisation of national significance. A generation later, it had been rendered marginal by the Nasser regime and by the 1960s was a shadow of the force that had dominated the anti-colonial movement. Under Sadat the organisation reappeared, advancing policies that differed sharply from those of earlier eras. Under Mubarak it again became a mass organisation, embracing new agendas for change. Naguib (2009: 105) observes that the Brotherhood's history has been full of shifts, contradictions, and both systemic and anti-systemic features. It has been in a constant state of flux, 'as internal contradictions and changes in the social composition of the movement have forced changes in its strategy, tactics, discourse and programmes' (Naguib 2009: 105).

There have nevertheless been two important continuities in the record of the Brotherhood. One has been a continuing presence of leaderships located primarily in the professional and commercial middle classes, weighting the organisation throughout its history towards the 'conservative reformism' identified by Richard Mitchell. The second key feature has been the almost continuous advance of slogans that encompass the range of interests present in a cross-class movement. 'Islam is the solution', 'For the Islamic state' and 'Enforce *sharia*' have been repeated over the generations – but with varying meanings for different audiences and at different periods. As Naguib observes, while an industrial worker joining the Brotherhood might conceptualise an Islamic 'solution' in terms of social justice and equality, a businessman could view the same 'solution' in terms of law, order and economic conservatism (2009: 107). These vague, ambiguous phrases should be understood in relation to societal change and to debates and conflicts within the movement. As general ideological signifiers, they have been integral to the survival of an organisation known continuously as the Muslim Brotherhood but which has undergone repeated, often abrupt changes during its 90-year history.

Towards electoral triumph

The uprising of January 2011 gave new impetus to the Brotherhood's reformist current. The conservative majority in the leadership feared victimisation and further repression, while youth activists demanded engagement with the protests. Writing as the events unfolded, Nabil Abdel Fattah of the Al-Ahram Center for Strategic and Political Studies observed that the organisation was confused by the scale and energy of the new movement. Its leaders lacked strategic vision: 'The Brotherhood is afraid of aggravating security forces against them and are at the same time afraid of missing the opportunity to participate in this widely anticipated protest against the regime,' he said (Fahmy 2011).

Young activists of the organisation entered the streets alongside student networks and the left, dropping their usual slogans in favour of embracing demands for Mubarak to resign, for an end to corruption and for the freeing of political prisoners. Carrie Wickham quotes Ibrahim al-Za'afarani, a prominent member of the Brotherhood's reformist tendency, to the effect that: 'The Guidance Bureau was forced to depend on them [the youth]' (2013: 163). The latter, observes Wickham, 'replaced their elders as the prime movers of events, exhibiting an unprecedented degree of operational authority' (2013: 163).

This sharp turn gave further evidence of the impacts of change on the organisation. It did not transform the Brotherhood, which remained a movement of cautious reform focused upon the state and its stake in the existing order. On the fall of Mubarak, however, the Brotherhood was in a novel position: for the first time it could use its status as

Egypt's sole independent opposition of national standing to bargain for influence. Within weeks it had secured a deal with SCAF that provided an historic electoral advantage. In December 2011 this delivered a parliamentary majority; in June 2012 it produced victory in the presidential election. These successes must also be seen in the context of internal and external developments – most importantly relationships between the Brotherhood, parties of the left and the forces of the state.

6

Fate of the Left

Army commanders who began negotiations with the Muslim Brotherhood in February 2011 faced a deepening crisis. Millions of people were in the streets and strikes were affecting most key areas of industry. The offices of the former ruling party were smoking ruins and core institutions of the state were increasingly ineffectual – in much of the country, police were out of action and the CSF had been withdrawn to barracks. On 10 February 2011, SCAF issued a first public statement:

> Based on the responsibility of the Armed Forces, and its commitment to protect the people, and to oversee their interests and security, and with a view to the safety of the nation and the citizenry, and of the achievements and properties of the great people of Egypt, and in affirmation and support for the legitimate demands of the people, the Supreme Council of the Armed Forces convened today, 10 February 2011, to consider developments to date, and decided to remain in continuous session to consider what procedures and measures that may be taken to protect the nation, and the achievements and aspirations of the great people of Egypt.
>
> (SCAF 2011a)

The following day Omar Suleiman announced the resignation of Mubarak; within a week the generals had suspended the constitution and were urging an end to strikes and protests. A further statement declared:

> Normality has been restored [...] all groups and sectors of society [sh]ould work together to support this positive progress and the efforts of the Supreme Council of the Armed Forces to realized [sic] the ambitions and aspirations of the people.
>
> (SCAF 2011b)

The restoration of 'normality' was an aspiration – an attempt to assert control over people who threatened both the state and class structures within which the military command had for decades been embedded. As strikes spread nationwide, SCAF inveighed against *fi'awi* interests and 'irresponsible persons [who] commit illegitimate acts' (SCAF 2011b). Its threats had no obvious effect: the fall of the president had energised protestors whose demands were more insistent. In this fraught situation, the generals sought urgently for mediators with the mass movement.

Establishing an eight-member committee to propose reforms to the constitution SCAF included Subhi Saleh, a well-known Brotherhood lawyer and former MP – the sole member of the committee who clearly represented an opposition organisation. Members and sympathisers of the Brotherhood who had been jailed, exiled or marginalised by Mubarak were rehabilitated. The Islamist scholar Yusuf al-Qaradawi returned to Egypt from exile in Qatar and was soon speaking to mass rallies in Tahrir Square; members of the Guidance Council who had for years been in prison and had recently escaped or been released appeared on national media. In an important development, Mohamed el-Beltagi, formerly an MP for the Brotherhood, spoke in Tahrir alongside 'Issam Sharaf, the prime minister appointed days earlier by SCAF. Such consideration for the organisation from those in authority in the state had not been seen since the earliest years of the Sadat regime. The Brotherhood had been invited to enter a new liaison with the armed forces and, despite the problems of the past, each moved quickly towards an accommodation. For the majority of the Brotherhood's leaders, a historic achievement appeared within reach. With Mubarak gone and his party in tatters, they anticipated that their organisation would move to its rightful place at the head of Egyptian society. Here, they believed, the leadership would supervise a programme of Islamisation, reforming the legal system, education and cultural life; at the same time, it would secure the interests of those who had remained loyal to Banna's project. Committed to authoritarian perspectives and modes of action, they assumed that this would be achieved through increased influence in institutions of the state: in effect, they aspired to replace the NDP and were ready to align themselves with those who could assist. Kandil comments that the goal determined the strategy: Brotherhood leaders resolved to convince 'the all-powerful coercive institutions' (of the state) that their new partners would not rock the boat; 'Appeasement, therefore, became the order of the day' (Kandil 2015: 138).

Many assessments of the Brotherhood's move to centre-stage in Egyptian politics emphasise the durability of the organisation and its survival through decades of repression. Discipline, coherence and fortitude, it is argued, allowed the Brotherhood to maintain its organisational integrity, so that in 2011 it had unmatched influence among opposition currents. These qualities, suggests Trager, produced an 'unbreakable' organisation with unique capacities to mobilise support (2011: 114, 115). Such accounts overstate the continuity and coherence of the Brotherhood. As we have seen in Chapter 5, it had passed through many developmental phases. During the Mubarak era it had grown rapidly, attracting a large periphery of supporters who exercised their own influence upon the membership. Efforts to advance by electoral means had introduced novel debates about democracy, pluralism and citizenship and resulted in a minor split in the mid-1990s in the form of the Wasat (Centre) Party. In the decade before the uprising of 2011, young members of the Brotherhood engaged with secular radicals while others moved towards ultra-Islamist currents in the form of Salafi groups. Contrary to neo-Orientalist depictions of a homogenous body in which members had unwavering commitment to leaders exercising military discipline on the basis of unchanging religious principles, the Brotherhood was much affected by exogenous pressures. These included, in January 2011, an uprising that compelled the leadership to make an abrupt strategic turn.

The Brotherhood had been shaped by complex developments over many decades. Why had it emerged as the dominant opposition vis-à-vis Mubarak? What was the fate of other currents within the opposition? How had they interacted with the state and what were the implications for the Brotherhood? What political histories influenced the alignment of forces in the crisis of 2011?

Revolution deferred

Sixty years earlier, Egypt's opposition parties had been involved in sustained struggles against the colonial state, with outcomes that were to have a lasting impact on their mutual relations and their capacities to intervene in public politics.

In the late 1940s and early 1950s there were widespread expectations of revolutionary change in Egypt. Years of anti-colonial mobilisation, including mass demonstrations and general strikes, had made the country ungovernable for the colonial authorities; the pro-British Faruq regime, comments the historian Peter Mansfield, 'gave off the smell of death' (1971: 298). Examining in detail relations between the mass movement and the state, Selma Botman observes: '[T]he revolutionary left or the Muslim Brothers could have become the heirs of political power in Egypt. Each was organized, politically conscious and growing in popularity. Yet both groups were unable to capture the moment' (1988: 115).

In the case of the Brotherhood, an interest in and attachment to the state among its leaders ruled out such an initiative. On the left, a number of organisations, notably the Democratic Movement for National Liberation (DMNL), were formally committed to radical change but lacked a means – in the form of a political strategy – for challenging the state. They were focused on the communist orthodoxy of the period – the requirement to search for 'progressive' members of the capitalist class with whom to forge relations aimed at establishing a 'popular front' that could facilitate democratic change. According to principles disseminated among communist parties worldwide since the late 1920s by rulers of the Soviet Union, it was necessary for all nation-states to pass through specific stages of development. Attempts to secure revolutionary change by accomplishing a transformation of social relations must be preceded by a 'democratic' phase – and this was to be secured by a progressive capitalist class encouraged and assisted by subordinate classes and by the communist movement by means of the popular ('people's') front. In the case of Egypt, communists sought an imagined ally in the Wafd Party, long compromised by its relations with the British and which by the 1930s was dominated by large landowners.[1] The effect was to orient the left – and its networks within an energetic trade union movement – towards parties hostile to the mass movement. Gordon comments that even as 'the liberal order' (of the Wafd) disintegrated, the left was unable to take the initiative: 'Ideology, organisational deficiency, and a mind-set that remained reformist precluded serious thoughts of revolution.' (1992: 32).

Several years passed during which a decisive move against the regime was assumed by many Egyptians to be inevitable. The American radical Ed Suvanto recalls the atmosphere in Cairo in 1950:

Every morning I woke up expecting to hear that the socialist revolution had begun. The left was strong, the old regime was rotten and there was support everywhere for independence. Egyptians wanted to remove the king and the British. But somehow nothing ever happened – it was a time of possibilities but also frustrations.[2]

In the early months of 1952, the government's authority finally collapsed. Mainstream parties including the Wafd Party were widely seen as corrupt and compromised, and there were calls for *tathir* and for a purge of political leaders across the board (Gordon 1992: 32–33). Still the left did not act. Botman describes the communist movement as 'internally divided, tentative and insecure'; she also observes that, 'it was not set up to assume political power' (Botman 1988: 115). Searching fruitlessly for 'progressive' allies among nationalist parties, the communists turned their attention to the Free Officers, hoping their links with the group would assure influence from the left. Others, however, also held hopes that the army would take the initiative: 'Disaffected liberals, progressives, communists and Muslim Brothers [all] constructed a new savior myth', each hoping that a military coup would serve their specific interests (Gordon 1992: 38). After months of further crisis, in July 1952 the Officers at last seized power.

Nasser's 'revolution'

The key figure among those allocated the role of 'saviour' was Colonel Gamal Abdel-Nasser of the Free Officers group. He was a complex and contradictory figure. When the Officers seized power in July 1952 Nasser insisted on the prompt deposition of King Faruq and declaration of a republic; within a few years, he had also secured removal of British forces and his economic and social policies were producing tangible benefits for many Egyptians. At the same time, he supervised a reconstruction of Egyptian capitalism and of a regime of repression that alienated supporters left and right.

Nasser and his colleagues were committed to an elitist, authoritarian vision of change. His *Philosophy of the Revolution*, published after several years in power, portrayed the Free Officers as a 'vanguard' failed by the masses (Abdel-Nasser 1955: 33). In 1952, the Officers had 'charged the battlements of tyranny', he said, then 'paused and waited for the serried ranks [of the mass of Egyptians] to come up in their sacred advance':

For a long time [the vanguard] waited. Crowds did eventually come, and they came in endless droves – but how different is the reality from the dream! The masses that came were disunited, divided groups of stragglers [...] We needed order but we found nothing behind us but dissension. We needed work but we found behind us only indolence and sloth.

(Abdel-Nasser 1955: 33–34)

Egyptians were 'disunited, divided', offering a 'dark and ominous' future, he said (Abdel-Nasser 1955: 31) – a reflection of the Officers' dismay when it became clear that the mass movement, so energetic vis-à-vis the British and the monarchy, had further expectations of change. Rather than 'order' as envisaged by the Officers, millions of people wished for access to the land, rights to organise at work, freedom of association and direct involvement in public politics. Nasser had envisaged a 'political revolution' directed by the Officers and focused upon the project of national unity. Other Egyptians had a duty to concentrate on their work, he said: 'Everyone must remain at his post, to which he should dedicate all his efforts' (Abdel-Nasser 1955: 42). In writing a script for the post-colonial era, the Officers had allocated the mass of the people non-speaking parts.

Egyptians were not inclined to silence and passity. Immediately after the 1952 coup (Nasser's 'revolution'), trades unions and parties of the left called for democratic freedoms; in some workplaces strikes were declared in support of the Officers and to demand collective representation.[3] The Officers responded with troops and mass arrests. At Misr Fine Spinning and Weaving in Kafr al-Dawwar they brought capital charges against local union leaders and two activists were executed to demonstrate that the Officers would not tolerate autonomous working-class organisation.[4] In September 1952, the Officers announced a land reform, prompting jubilation among peasants expecting access to private estates. In some villages tenant farmers refused to pay rent to landlords and prepared to occupy lands they cultivated. The Officers were focused upon a limited and closely controlled reform, however, and organised against those said to be disturbing order (Ansari 1987: 80–81).[5]

These episodes captured the contradictory interests and ambitions of Nasser and the Officers. They had enacted a decisive strike against the old regime; at the same time they were hostile to the movement that had facilitated their bid for power. Six months after the coup they suspended the Constitution, dissolved all political parties (except the Muslim Brotherhood) and ordered the arrest of over 100 activists, among whom the largest group came from communist organisations. The message was clear: change would be directed from above; independent organisation was not acceptable; and those with radical agendas would be targets for exemplary punishment. The Officers meanwhile demonstrated their sympathy with private capital. Soon after the coup they introduced Law 430, giving new companies a tax holiday on all profits for seven years. They also reassured foreign investors, issuing a mining law that provided equal rights for local and foreign companies and set out generous conditions for repatriation of profits from Egypt. Gamal Salem, minister of national guidance, told business groups: 'We are not socialist: I think our economy can only prosper under free enterprise' (Baker 1978: 49). Policy continued in this mode for three years, giving the USA confidence that Egypt under the Officers could be a long-term ally with a place in its anti-Soviet alliance in the Middle East. Provisional agreement was reached with Washington for a large aid package, including military supplies, and the American ambassador in Cairo reported to Washington that Egypt's future 'looked brighter than ever' (Gordon 1992: 174).

American arms were not forthcoming, however, and Nasser considered other options for both weaponry and development aid. In 1955, he initiated a change in domestic and foreign strategies, tightening the grip of the regime on the economy and reorienting away from the USA and its allies. He spoke for the first time of a 'socialist' strategy, proposing that, 'The Revolution [the coup of 1952] aims at creating a socialist society without class distinction' (Baker 1978: 65). Now his aim was to establish a 'socialist, democratic and cooperative society, free from political, social and economic exploitation' (Wheelock 1960: 69). In 1956, the Suez Canal Company – the chief symbol of historic European interests in Egypt – was nationalised, prompting invasion by Britain, France and Israel, and Nasser turned sharply towards the Soviet Union and its satellite states to obtain arms, export deals and technical assistance. In 1957, a series of 'Egyptianisation' measures was announced and key foreign banks were placed under state control. Further nationalisations affected much of industry and commerce, and extended the scope of land reform by sequestering large private estates: by the mid-1960s, most of Egypt's economic resources were in the hands of giant public corporations. Nasser was constructing an Egyptian state capitalism under the control of military men and senior bureaucrats among whom most were retired officers.[6] Writing in 1968, the former communist Anouar Abdel-Malek argued that in just 15 years Egypt had become a 'military society' (Abdel-Malek 1968: 367). The people had fallen into the hands of 'a devouring bureaucracy', he said: the military-bureaucratic elite now shaped national politics, the mass of people were present merely 'to supply the manpower':

> [T]he group in power has no socialist roots in its thinking, it resorts to quasi-socialist schemes and formulas in order to attract the masses, which are deeply angered by the dictatorship, and it uses them to cloak what is in reality planning and statism [so] establishing this enormous bureaucratic and security apparatus with all its privileges.
>
> (Abdel-Malek 1968: 367)

Crises and co-options

Egypt's opposition parties had played their own role in consolidating the new ruling class. As we have seen in Chapter 5, the Muslim Brotherhood used its considerable influence to back the coup of 1952 and at first maintained cordial relations with Nasser and his colleagues. The largest faction of the communist movement was the DMNL, which claimed several thousand members and strong influence in the main trade union federation.[7] It had long-standing links to the Free Officers: according to Khaled Muhieddin, a leading member of the Officers who was sympathetic to the left, the DMNL had for years enjoyed relations of trust with the group (Mohi el-Din 1996: 38–39).[8] DMNL considered the Officers to be 'a part of the national movement [...] sharing a communality of aims and aspirations' (Botman 1988: 120).[9]

The coup brought confusion on the left. Official spokesmen in the Soviet Union, most communist parties in the Middle East, and smaller communist groups in Egypt such as the Egyptian Communist Party (ECP), were suspicious of the army but eventually cautiously welcomed the junta. The DMNL was much more positive, applauding the Officers' seizure of power as an expression of the 'national democratic movement' (Beinin 1990: 107) and later – to the astonishment of others on the left – denouncing the Kafr al-Dawwar strikers as 'agents of imperialism and reaction' (Gordon 1992: 95). Following the executions at Kafr al-Dawwar, the ECP asserted that the regime was 'fascist'[10] but the DMNL continued with enthusiastic support until, in January 1953, all parties were banned. The organisation finally distanced itself from the regime, attacking its then most prominent figure Mohamed Naguib, said by the DMNL to have abandoned his commitment to the people – to have 'lift[ed] his veil to reveal a fascistic face' (Gordon 1992: 95). Over the next two years, hundreds of communists were imprisoned, including the entire leadership of the DMNL. Most were tried in secret in military courts and sent to prison camps in remote desert areas. Such was the attraction of the regime to some veteran leaders of the DMNL, however, that in 1953 a group of its leading members in prison responded to a personal appeal by Nasser for their support. Their credulity, comments Gordon, 'stunned' supporters in the workplaces and campuses, where the regime still struggled to contain opposition (1992: 150). During the crisis of 1954 (see Chapter 5), the left was disoriented by Nasser's successful co-option of several trade union leaders who agreed to mobilise their members in support of the RCC, causing a serious split in the labour movement. (Nasser later boasted that he had 'bought the working class for £E4,000' [Gordon 1992: 136]). Having successfully sown divisions and mistrust within the movement, Nasser reneged on promises to free communist prisoners and purged the RCC of leftist sympathisers including Khaled Muhieddin, who was expelled from Egypt. The DMNL now re-asserted its earlier position that Nasser was a traitor: the junta was allied with Britain and the USA, it said, and was committed to 'subjugating our people to American imperialism forever' (Ismael and El Sa'id 1990: 76). In August 1954, the DMNL called for an armed uprising against the RCC (Ismael and El Sa'id 1990: 76).

It was not long before the left took another turn. In the highly charged atmosphere of the Cold War in the mid-1950s, Egypt's international relations were of special importance. The USA was attempting to forge a Middle East alliance that eventually became the Baghdad Pact,[11] while the Soviet Union was courting anti-colonial movements and newly independent states across the region. Nasser attempted to exploit inter-imperialist rivalries – initially he had sought arms and aid from the USA and Western European states. Military supplies were of special importance. Nasser wished to modernise Egypt's armed forces and to guard against the continuous threat presented by Israel. Frustrated

FATE OF THE LEFT

by refusal of the USA and the Europeans to provide the weaponry requested, he turned to the East. Following the Bandung Conference of 1955, organised with the aim of establishing a non-aligned group of Afro-Asian states (and at which Nasser emerged as a key figure), Egypt established relations with the Soviet Union. Arms soon arrived from Czechoslovakia, together with technicians and advisers, and Egyptians began to travel to the Eastern bloc for military instruction.[12] Trade deals also tied Egypt to the Soviet Union and its satellite states, which became a key market for Egyptian cotton and a source of machinery and technical expertise. Nasser now spoke of 'a socialist' strategy for Egypt, announcing that: 'The Revolution aims at creating a socialist society without class distinction' (Baker 1978: 65) and Soviet analysts began to identify Egypt as an important new ally. One of the leading Soviet experts on Arab affairs declared that: 'the national liberation movement is widest in scope in Egypt', lauding 'the very positive element in the foreign policy of Nasser's government'.[13]

In 1956, Soviet President Nikita Krushchev declared:

These countries [of the East], although they do not belong to the socialist world system [the Soviet bloc] can draw on its achievements in building an independent national economy and in raising their peoples' standards. Today they need not go begging to their former oppressors for modern equipment. They can get it in the socialist countries, free from any political or military obligations.[14]

Egypt had in effect become an associate member of the Soviet bloc. Later that year Nasser nationalised the Suez Canal and emerged unscathed from the tripartite invasion of the Suez War, having not only defied Egypt's former occupying powers but also Israeli forces – an important assertion of Arab solidarity vis-à-vis the Palestinians and of Egyptian integrity in relation to the Israeli state, and a matter of satisfaction for Nasser's new allies in Moscow.

These developments had their impact on Egypt's communists, who again revised their assessment of the Nasser regime and moved closer together in the belief that their duty was to combine in its support. Communist currents formally recognised earlier 'errors': they now placed Egypt 'in the category of nations whose national bourgeoisie had moved out of the imperialist orbit and elevated the national struggle to a higher plane' (Agwani 1969: 80). Nasser once more released communist prisoners and provided space for public activities of the left[15] and in 1957 the DMNL and the ECP fused to form the Unified Egyptian Communist Party. In 1958, the small leftist faction Workers Vanguard adhered to the new organisation, which was again renamed as the United Communist Party of Egypt. The organisation did not last long: disoriented by multiple twists and turns of strategy, and by factional rivalries, the party experienced further splits and in 1958, after some groups declared support for the Iraqi revolution (and for Nasser's nationalist rivals in Baghdad) the regime again attacked the left with a campaign of arrests. The mainstream of the party, containing those who remained from the DMNL, now declared establishment of a new Egyptian Communist Party (ECP). There were further arrests, leaving the communist movement reeling from repression and from the disorientation of its political turns and repeated splits. Leading members of the ECP who stood in the traditions of the DMNL were still fixed upon the regime as a 'progressive' force and drew closer to Nasser after he announced further nationalisations and extensions to land reform. In 1964, President Krushchev visited Egypt to inaugurate the Soviet-built High Dam and the regime freed all communists from prison, inviting leading figures of the movement to join the Arab Socialist Union (a revised version of the Liberation Rally) provided they renounced membership of the ECP. Several influential figures defected; in March 1965 remaining members dissolved the party, informing Nasser by telegram of their decision:

> The most beautiful thing we present to you on this historic occasion is the information that the representatives of the Egyptian Communist Party Haditu [the DMNL] in their meeting held today decided to put an end to their independent organization because of their belief in your call for the unity of all the socialist forces in one revolutionary political organization, and that this one party under your leadership is the substitute for our independent organization.[16]

Other factions also disbanded, advising their members to join the Arab Socialist Union (ASU), now said to be 'alone competent to carry out the tasks of the revolution' (Agwani 1969: 86). There was no longer an independent left in Egypt.

The Brothers and the left

For many years, the Brotherhood and the left had competed for support. Banna, comments Richard Mitchell, was 'violently repelled by communist doctrine' (1969: 39). Like others who stood in the tradition of pan-Islam, he maintained that divisions of social class were like those between nations, separating Muslims who shared an underlying bond: the Brotherhood was to proceed on the basis of Afghani's principle that: 'it is only the religious brotherhood which counts' (Moazzam 1983: 24). The organisation inveighed against social and economic radicalism and joined conservative nationalists in attacking the left. In the mid-1940s its publications reported favourably on government repression of communist organisations, even running a daily column titled 'The Fight Against Communism' (Mitchell 1969: 39). At the same time, Banna sought support among large sections of the population he identified as oppressed by colonialism, setting his 'activist reform attitudes' in Islamic terms and making an appeal to audiences also addressed by the communist movement (Mitchell 1969: 39). Paradoxically the Brotherhood identified certain virtues in communism, notably its commitment to 'equality', 'brotherhood' and 'humanitarianism' and its advocacy of 'the abolition of classes, distinctions, and pride in property', while insisting that the approach of the left on these issues was greatly inferior to that of pious Muslims.[17] The Brotherhood even spoke of 'Islamic socialism' based on 'the cardinal points of monotheism and the brotherhood of man' (Mitchell 1969: 225).

These were modifications of Banna's early principles and reflected the increasing influence of anti-colonial struggles and of radical elements in the workers' movement. Beinin and Lockman (1987: 365) observe that the Brotherhood had 'an absolute aversion' to workers' actions it believed would exacerbate class tensions among Egyptians but that this did not prevent engagement with the labour movement:

[To] understand the actual role the Muslim Brothers played in the workers' movement, it is necessary to give primary attention not to the abstract content of their ideas, but to the concrete activities of the Society and its supporters and their relationship to other political forces involved in the workers' movement.

(Beinin and Lockman 1987: 364)

From the late 1930s, the Brotherhood was involved in labour struggles, initially in Shubra al-Khayma near Cairo, where the textile mills were centres of industrial militancy. In the mid-1940s, a Workers' Section of the Brotherhood was established and the organisation intensified its activity, participating in a general strike and engaging in increasingly tense conflict with the left over leadership of the textile workers' union. The Brotherhood was compromised by its relations with employers, conservative nationalists and the palace; it was nonetheless a pole of attraction for many workers, while its own members and supporters came under the influence of the left. One of the seminal figures of the Egyptian labour movement in the 1930s and 1940s, Taha Sa'ad 'Uthman, was for many years a prominent member of the Brotherhood and was encouraged by Banna to undertake union activities.[18] He eventually joined the communist New Dawn group – a trajectory followed by other labour activists, as this testimony from Ahmed, a veteran labour organiser in Helwan, makes clear:

> I was a member of the Brotherhood in the 1940s. I was with Hassan al-Banna, even when he said that strikes were *haram* [impermissible]. Our religion says that we'll be rewarded in paradise but I needed bread for my family – I couldn't wait for the hereafter, so I left the Brothers, I joined the union and became a communist and I'm still a communist today.[19]

Communist organisations were in general hostile to the Brotherhood, which they denounced for its conservatism, its sectarianism – expressed in general hostility to 'foreigners' (a synonym for Christians and Jews) – and its attempts to organise independently in the workers' movement. In a typical attack on the Brotherhood, a statement produced by the NCWS in 1946 accused the organisation of 'spreading intrigues and planning plots [...] in a manner which serves nothing but imperialism' and of using 'fascist methods'.[20]

Relations between Islamists and the left became more fluid, however, largely as an outcome of the increased radicalisation of some sections of the Brotherhood. When the organisation was declared illegal in 1948, many leading members found themselves alongside communist cadres in the regime's prisons: under the latters' influence one wing of the Brotherhood called for collaboration with the communists against imperialism (Botman 1988: 92). In 1950, the DMNL initiated a Movement of Supporters of Peace (Harakat Ansar al-Salam), an Egyptian section of the Soviet-inspired World Peace Council. This sought support from the Wafd Party, liberal nationalists and the Muslim Brotherhood, together with leading figures in Egyptian cultural life. Those the left had earlier dubbed 'fascist' were now welcomed into a movement carefully named by the left to offer space to Islamists (the *ansar* – 'helpers'/ 'supporters' – had special status in Islamic history as associates of the Prophet and members of the first *umma*). The movement established peace committees in towns and villages across Egypt and published a newspaper, *Al-Katib* ('The Scribe'/ 'The Writer') to which members of the Brotherhood regularly contributed articles.

The coup of 1952 initially brought support for the RCC from both the Brotherhood and the DMNL. When communist organisations were banned in 1953, they first sought to join forces with the Wafd Party against a regime they now described fascist; when the Muslim Brotherhood was also declared illegal in 1954, the DMNL appealed to the Islamists to join them against 'the fascist dictatorship' of Nasser and his 'Anglo-American props' (Agwani 1969: 50). According to the communists, the Brothers had a 'mass character' and an 'anti-imperialist programme and propaganda' (Agwani 1969: 50). The clandestine communist journal *Rayat al-Sha'ab* ('People's Flag') announced: 'The resistance to the revolution [the junta] is led by two basic forces, the Communist Party and the Society of the Muslim Brothers', calling for joint action to bring down the regime (Mitchell 1969: 140–41). Attempts to organise joint demonstrations were inhibited by the Brotherhood leadership, although significantly one prominent member, Sayyid Qutb, backed the initiative. These liaisons came to an end when in 1954, following an attempt to assassinate Nasser, the regime ordered the execution of six members of the Brotherhood, jailing thousands of others and opening an offensive on the organisation that was to continue for the next 15 years.

Co-option and retreat

Many members of the Brotherhood left Egypt, most seeking refuge in Saudi Arabia and the Gulf states. The communists meanwhile were adjusting to Nasser's new 'socialist' strategy, moving towards full accommodation with the regime, consummated in 1965 by the dissolution of the ECP. Leading figures of the left were co-opted by Nasser, who placed them in positions of limited authority in government ministries, in the press and in the Arab Socialist Union (ASU). Their formal aim was to influence the ASU from the left but the Union was no more than an organisational shell, without active membership: even Nasser admitted, 'The fact is we have no internal organization, except on the books' (Baker 1978: 96). Like the party bureaucracies of the Soviet bloc, the ASU was a means to subordinate the population at large; it also served to integrate both communists and leaders of the trades unions. In exchange for job security, inflated salaries and other privileges, union leaders became senior bureaucrats in the Egyptian Trade Union Federation (ETUF). Candidates for election within all unions were required to demonstrate membership of the ASU, so that ETUF leaders were in effect part of the apparatus of state. Maye Kassem observes that 'unruly labor activists' were excluded while those favoured by the regime and who took office 'complemented strict state control' (2004: 94).

Nasser's strategy of co-option, enacted together with the former communists, soon proved invaluable to the regime. Following a swift defeat at the hands of Israeli forces in the June 1967 war, disillusion and anger spread across Egyptian society. In 1968, student protests were followed by mass strikes – the most significant since the early 1950s. Students raised all manner of demands: against the secret police on campus, for freedom of expression and of the press, for democracy and accountability (Abdalla 1985: 152). Workers meanwhile demanded wage rises, arguing that they had been made to pay for the bloated and incompetent armed forces. There were several rounds of protest in major cities, during which police stations and government buildings came under attack, and slogans were raised not only against the familiar target of American imperialism but also against Soviet imperialism (Stephens 1971: 537). Nasser blamed 'counter-revolutionaries' (Stephens 1971: 537); at the same time he intervened personally to address strikers;[21] his subsequent promise to meet workers' demands, observes Kassem 'was a strategy to subdue labor' (2004: 95), leaving union officials to police the activists and the president free to tackle further student protests.

The events of 1968 were a harbinger of many episodes during the turbulent 1970s. An upsurge in student protests in 1972 and 1973, and of workers' struggles between 1974 and 1976, climaxed in the 'intifada of bread' of January 1977. This national uprising, eventually brought to an end by the army, was blamed by President Sadat on the communists. The uprising in fact took place despite the left (see below). Although Sadat had purged some former communists incorporated by Nasser, others remained embedded in the machinery of state. The main thrust of communist policy during the 1970s was to celebrate Nasserism, asserting nostalgia for the 1950s and 1960s and for Egypt's association with the Soviet bloc. Together with timorous calls for democratisation, these were the preoccupations of the National Progressive Unionist Party (usually known as al-Tagammu' – 'The Rally'), which emerged in 1975 under the leadership of Khaled Muhieddin after Sadat had agreed to establish a number of tame platforms (*manabir* – 'pulpits') within the ASU.

As the left continued to retreat, the Islamists accomplished a spectacular advance. The dissolution of the ECP in 1965 had coincided with an important development in the Muslim Brotherhood. Sayyid Qutb and his co-thinkers, members in the early 1950s of the radical faction of the organisation, had used their years in prison to produce a new Islamist strategy. They asserted that the Nasser regime was not only repressive but also impious – that it was necessary to confront the state and to replace it with an Islamic order. In order to liberate Egypt's Muslims, they maintained, dedicated activists should prepare for an assault on the structures of power, mobilising their energies as *jihad*. This revised Banna's approach and the policies of accommodation that had ended with repression of the Brotherhood. It soon provided a powerful pole of attraction for young activists.

Dissolution of the ECP had left Egypt's communists 'totally demoralised' (Ismael and El-Sa'id 1990: 127). Those who believed they were to play an active role in Nasser's regime discovered they were to be 'isolated, quarantined, and contained' (Ismael and El-Sa'id 1990: 127): even a hint of reorganisation among the communists was met with pre-emptive action by the *mukhabarat*, with the effect that most remaining activists withdrew from public politics.[22] It was several years before there were hesitant efforts to create Marxist circles. Some groups were attacked by police and their members arrested; others consolidated in great secrecy: in 1975 the largest, Jama'at Bila Ism ('Group with No Name'), declared establishment of a renewed Egyptian Communist Party. To its left, the small Communist Party of Egypt-January 8 and the Communist Workers Party were critical of some aspects of the left's earlier strategies and sought to establish new currents focused upon rising movements of protest on campus and in industry.

The left competed with a revitalised Islamist movement. The Muslim Brotherhood, rehabilitated by Sadat, proceeded cautiously to establish working relations with the regime. The *jihadi*s adopted a different approach, using the space provided by Sadat to polemicise against the state. Organisations such as the Gama'at Islamiyya (Islamic Groups/ Associations) and Al Jihad interpreted the work of Qutb as a call to establish networks of activists committed to a frontal assault on the regime. Sadat was slow to recognise the implications: when he eventually attempted to restrict their growth, the *jihadi*s had already developed momentum that extended their influence nationwide. Young recruits came from the universities, the fast-growing *'ashwa'iyyat*, the cities of the South, and from the armed forces: Khalid Islambouli, who assassinated Sadat in 1981, had organised a cell of Al Jihad in the army. Their success was associated with the despair and anger felt by millions of people in the face of the *infitah*. While Sadat postured as 'The Believer President' his economic policies had increased the sense of insecurity among the mass of Egyptians. Marketisation also produced a nouveau riche of middlemen, commission agents and fixers – the 'Sadat class' identified by the magazine *Rose el-Youssef* as 'the fat cats' (Hirst and Beeson 1981: 217). In an atmosphere of rising tension, insistent mass struggles and general hostility to the regime, the Islamists made rapid progress. Büttner (1979: 66) estimates that the Gama'at Islamiyya recruited some 100,000 members, most on campus but also with groups in poor city quarters and provincial towns. In an important observation about political choices for the mass of Egyptians, Hinnebusch comments that, 'The very dearth of legitimate means of political expression at odds with official policy turned many to the mosque and Islamic associations as outlets for their dissidence' (1985: 207).

The official left in the form of Tagammu' at first recruited many supporters. It drew in former communists and Nasserists and attracted industrial workers and peasants who had benefited from the land reforms of the 1950s and 1960s. Within a few years, the party claimed 150,000 members with core activists numbering some 20,000 (Hinnebusch 1985: 195). The organisation was compromised by its first major challenge, however, failing to support those who undertook the uprising of 1977. The Muslim Brotherhood had joined the regime in declaring the events a 'communist conspiracy' (Harman 1994). Tagammu' disowned the movement, in which millions called for the fall of Sadat. According to its most senior official, the party attempted to stop demonstrations (El-Hamalawy 2009 [2000]: 8); another of its leaders declared:

> Our party neither raised the slogan of overthrowing the regime, nor called for it. Our position on the regime is clear. We are struggling against the *clientalistic wing* inside the regime [...] Our main struggle is focused on the formation of the widest front of patriotic and progressive forces [emphasis in original].[23]

Tagammu' rejected the protest movement in favour of efforts to construct a 'front of electoral activity and patriotic and progressive forces' (El-Hamalawy 2009 [2000]: 9). In elections, however, it faced systematic vote-fixing and the mobilisation by Sadat loyalists of powerful networks of privilege: the four members of parliament elected for Tagammu' in 1976, comments Hinnebusch, could achieve 'little more than a gadfly' (1985: 198). In 1984 and 1987, the party won no seats; it nonetheless persisted in standing in the 1990 election, the only organisation to break an opposition boycott in protest at Mubarak's decision to end judicial monitoring of the electoral process. Winning five seats, the left became the largest 'opposition' group in a parliament of regime loyalists. In 1992, a Nasserist faction departed to form the Arab Democratic Nasserist Party: Tagammu's influence was shrinking, a process accelerated by its insistent support for the regime. The organisation was drawn both by the prospect of electoral advance and by a commitment to support the state's offensive against the Islamists, whom it routinely described as 'fascist'. This term, used and abused by the left for over 50 years, was mobilised initially to justify backing for Mubarak's campaign against *jihadi* groups. The offensive mushroomed into a general assault on dissidents that resulted in scores of thousands of arrests and 'disappearances'. In a culture of impunity the police abused all manner of people, including peasants resisting desequestration of state land, workers protesting privatisation and anti-war activists.

In 2003, a group of lawyers and human rights activists established the Egyptian Association Against Torture. It included activists of Tagammu' who could not longer stomach the party's support for Mubarak. 'Amr said:

I stayed with Tagammu' for years because it gave an opportunity for political action, especially at election time. We worked in campaigns and attended meetings and rallies, and kept in touch with others on the left. But in the end I had to leave because it was impossible to accept the support of Rifa'at El-Said and Amina Shafiq [party leaders] and the others for Mubarak. It was better to be out than in.[24]

The Brotherhood, having integrated the less strident members of the *jihadi* current, had become a champion of democratic rights, calling for political freedoms and an end to the Emergency Laws. Ironically, comments Sameh Naguib (2009: 170), the tactical alliance between the Sadat regime and the Islamists to stem the rise of the left in the 1970s had given way to an alliance between the Mubarak regime and Tagammu' aimed to prevent the Brotherhood making further political gains.

Tagammu' played no meaningful role in social movements that emerged in the decade preceding the uprising of 2011 (see Chapter 2). The independent left, liberals, Nasserists and – intermittently – members of the Brotherhood[25] joined solidarity movements and initiatives such as Kifaya, of which Tagammu' was a strong critic. In 2005, its leader Rifa'at El-Sa'id attacked the movement, criticising its slogans as inappropriate (Arafat 2009: 159). Tagammu' was locked into a relationship with the Mubarak regime – still searching for a 'progressive' ally in a ruling class dedicated to aggressive neo-liberalism. It had become 'the government left' (Abdelrahman 2014: 116). In 2011, El-Sa'id declared that the party would not support the protests of 25 January because these would violate National Police Day. Unlike the Guidance Council of the Brotherhood, which was soon compelled to reverse a similar decision, Tagammu' leaders remained equivocal about the uprising – an index of the party's detachment from the mass of Egyptians. After decades of sustained effort to influence the state it was the communists' historic rivals, the Brothers, who in February 2011 entered discussions with SCAF to form a new working alliance.

PART III
COUNTER-REVOLUTION

7

Egypt Under Mursi

In February 2011, the armed forces command and leaders of the Brotherhood found common cause in defending the state against an insurrectionary movement. Each had a stake in Egyptian capitalism – SCAF with an interest in public resources and private capital, together with command of the coercive bodies of the state, and the Brotherhood with a network of business interests and an orientation on political institutions as a means to secure Islamic reform. In the short term the generals hoped to use the Brotherhood to inhibit the uprising; the Brothers wished to extract concessions from the military command: above all, they wanted access to national decision-making bodies from which for generations they had been excluded.

The energies of the mass movement provided leaders of the Brotherhood with a unique opportunity. The security apparatus had been seriously damaged and the ruling party was in disarray. At the same time, the popular movement lacked formal leadership – its networks of activists were dispersed and in the earliest phases of co-ordination. Liberal and left-wing parties had long been marginal to Egyptian politics: leaders of the Brotherhood held authority in the sole body seen as untainted by open collaboration with the regime and which possessed national reach and influence. They moved quickly to seek alliance with SCAF in a deal they believed would provide novel electoral opportunities. The quid pro quo for the generals was an effective intervention by the Brotherhood to restrain the popular movement.

The military command took an instrumental approach to the Brotherhood. A retired general offered the view from SCAF: 'When you enter a new block, you usually look to see who is the strongest thug with whom you could have an understanding. The SCAF was the newcomer, and the thug was the Muslim Brothers' (ICG 2012: 14). The constitutional referendum of March 2011 was part of a deal between the two under which elections for a new parliament would be held within six months – an arrangement congenial to the Brotherhood, with its mass membership, well-organised internal structures and network of branches. The new parliament was to select a 100-member commission to draft a full constitution – a prospect equally appealing to the Brotherhood, which was confident of securing a large parliamentary majority. In this scenario, the uprising would deliver within months an influence the organisation had not enjoyed during an 80-year history. Neither party to the deal delivered, however: the Brotherhood failed to rein in the popular movement and the generals postponed elections, without any assurance of when they would be held.

The Brotherhood leaders could not contain the activists of the streets and workplaces, who included many of their own members and supporters. In March and April, protestors stormed hundreds of police stations and local security centres, paralysing the intelligence networks; meanwhile strikes spread, independent trade unions established groups nationwide and demands for *tathir* intensified. This radical mood affected the Brotherhood. Although its core structures remained intact, the organisation experienced a series of defections as members of the reformist wing sought alternatives to the conservative agenda of the Guidance Council. Historic figures such as Ibrahim al-Za'afarani, Abdel-Moneim Aboul-Futouh and Mohamed Habib departed soon after the fall of Mubarak, while young activists established a Muslim Brotherhood Youth Revolution current within the organisation, arguing that the leadership was out of touch with what they called the '25 January revolutionary spirit' (Shukrallah 2011a). Many young members had joined youth coalitions. Mohamed Osman, prominent among the Brotherhood's young activists and also a member of the Revolution Youth Coalition, said that some Brotherhood youth had 'a more progressive vision than that of the [Brotherhood] leadership': they had resolved to stay within the organisation, he said, but would maintain an active dialogue with non-Islamist forces (Shukrallah 2011a). In March 2011, activists held a first Muslim Brotherhood Youth Conference – an unofficial meeting that challenged authoritarian structures of the organisation, calling for accountability of the leadership and more involvement of women and youth at all levels. Many speakers contrasted the Brotherhood's calls for democracy and openness in Egypt's political system with the closed regime inside the organisation. Organisers of the March conference were promptly expelled and several hundred members left to establish a new party, the Egyptian Current, also joined by Aboul-Futouh. Mohamed Osman observed: 'reform within the Muslim Brotherhood proved impossible':

> Our analysis is different and so is our vision. The Brotherhood does not believe in revolutionary change only reform and to them the revolution so far has given them all they needed which is legal recognition. We want complete change from below […] from the roots.
>
> (Shukrallah 2011b)

Disquiet among members and supporters focused on long-standing debates about whether the Brotherhood was a 'movement', a 'party' or an expression of the will of Egypt's Muslims, and whether it should enter the electoral arena. In February 2011, days after the fall of Mubarak, Essam el-Erian (a senior figure in the organisation and earlier a member of the reformist wing) asserted that the Brotherhood was not a party:

> What's the role of the party? The role of the party is seeking power, mainly according to Western theories. But here [in Egypt] we are not a party. We are still keeping our mind [open] about our role that we are not only a party. We can practice [sic] politics but we are an organization, institution, group working for the people in all aspects of life, not only politics by the narrow perception.
>
> (El-Erian 2011)

There was much anger when only weeks later the Guidance Council declared the establishment of the FJP, insisting without debate among the wider membership that the organisation must support its decision. Wickham describes the Brotherhood and the FJP as being 'joined at the hip' (2013: 176): they were indeed the same entity. Fatma, a lifelong supporter of the Brotherhood, describes her distress at the decision:

> My whole family has been in the Brotherhood for generations. Several of us have been imprisoned, suffering for our beliefs. But I cannot accept we should be told how to act politically in this revolution – and I was furious when the leaders broke their word by setting up the FJP

and then did all they could to win a national majority for the party. I rejected the Brothers and I will not return to them.[1]

In the face of a mass movement it could not contain, the Brotherhood's approach was soon reduced to 'barefaced support for military and security transgressions' (Kandil 2015: 140). When Ramadan began on 1 August 2011, the pace of events lessened; after the 30 days of fasting, however, protests were renewed with a *millioneyya* (a million-strong march) against military trials. On 10 September, a large demonstration in Cairo attacked the Israeli Embassy, declaring solidarity with the Palestinians and demanding that the border with Gaza should be opened. As if the workers' movement had been drawing breath, a further wave of strikes spread across the country, affecting public services including schools and universities. Exasperated by the generals' broken promises and now ready to exploit opportunities presented by the protests, the Brotherhood finally distanced itself from SCAF: leading member Hassan El-Brence declared: 'In the Brotherhood we were raised on the idea of martyrdom and we are more than happy to offer new martyrs and begin new protests and strikes in Tahrir Square if the will of the people is denied' (*Ahram Online* 2011e). Under relentless pressure, the generals reactivated their deal with the Brothers, announcing that parliamentary elections would begin on 28 November.

Manifesto for reform

A pattern had become clear: as the ICG observed: 'SCAF tended to reach out to the Brothers whenever it perceived its position, core interests or objectives to be in peril' (2012: 13). In October and November, public hostility to the generals intensified after savage assaults by military police on protestors at Maspero and Mohamed Mahmoud in central Cairo. As elections approached, circumstances became more and more favourable to the Brotherhood. Parties established after the fall of Mubarak were still in formation: only the Brothers and Salafi currents tolerated under the former regime were able to prepare effective national campaigns. The FJP launched a manifesto that headlined the key economic and social demands of the uprising. Dedicated to 'the blessed revolution of the great Egyptian people' this undertook to complete 'the demolition of the repressive regime, to purge the country of corruption and to begin a new phase of building and development of Egypt' (FJP 2011). It presented the party as a means to realize aspirations for social justice, promising radical reform in the mode of the more vital currents of European social democracy. The FJP declared:

> The absence of social justice was one of the most important causes of the January 25 revolution and achieving it was one of its most important goals. Thus our election program regards achieving social justice [sic] and ensuring that distribution of revenues from economic activity achieves justice, equality and equal opportunities, some of the most important obligations of the State. In recognition of this responsibility, the most important goals of our election program are addressing the issue of high prices, the elimination of poverty and unemployment, providing basic public services such as education, health care, transportation and other services and facilities, improving living conditions of workers and peasants, finding practical solutions to social problems like spinsterhood [sic], street children and those with special needs, supporting adoptive families, and increasing the incomes of pensioners. In all the above, we will work to bring justice to all citizens, taking into account that the recovery of what has been looted from state funds, reforming the tax system, promoting the Zakat and Waqf (national endowment and charitable trust) systems and combating corruption and deliberate waste and squandering of sovereign resources will provide the resources necessary to achieve the desired social justice among all citizens.
>
> (Muslim Brotherhood 2011)

The Brotherhood was now on familiar territory. It had not engaged with intent in public protest for over 60 years; for most of that time, however, it had participated in electoral activity in parliamentary polls and, with great success, in the syndicates. It had also developed an effective national network of welfare centres. Combining these areas of political practice, the Brothers presented a manifesto for social reform, given credibility by their years of outreach activity in charities, local clinics, schools and youth groups, and through a national network of mosques. Citing its record as the only untainted opposition of the Mubarak era, the organisation was also able to pose as a champion of democratic change. The 'reformist' wing of the Brotherhood, earlier marginalised by the conservative faction and by the defections of 2011, was now – paradoxically – its greatest assert.

As the election campaign gathered momentum, many Egyptians were repelled by SCAF's efforts to entrench the interests of the armed forces by means of the 'Selmi declaration' of November 2011[2] and by the events at Maspero and Mohamed Mahmoud, followed by days of fighting in the Cabinet Office battles. Increasingly the generals were a target for popular anger: '*Yasqut, yasqut hukm al-askar*' ('Down, down with military rule') was heard more and more often at public protests. For months SCAF had spoken of the 'internal and external enemies of the state' seeking to 'create disunity between the army and the people' (Martini and Taylor 2011: 132). In a mark of their increasing alarm, the generals attempted to stoke fears of foreign conspiracy, accusing demonstrators of being inspired and directed by external forces – by 'foreign hands'. Several liberal parties withdrew from the elections in protest at state violence and Tahrir activists announced that they would boycott the polls. In the first free election in Egyptian history, 54 per cent of those eligible nonetheless participated – some 28 million people. The Democratic Alliance dominated by the FJP won 10.1 million votes, 37 per cent of the total, with Salafi parties registering 7.5 million votes, or 28 per cent. The principal non-Islamist ('secular')[3] parties received a combined 20 per cent, with a further 15 per cent being divided among minor parties including organisations led by *feloul*.

The Islamists' success brought alarm among its political opponents and among analysts outside Egypt. Tadros comments that: 'Shock and surprise, both in Cairo and Washington, soon gave way to desperate efforts to explain why the Islamists won' (Tadros, S. 2012). On some accounts, the Brothers and the Salafists were representatives of SCAF, which had secretly backed their campaigns; they were said to have been financed by vast amounts of money injected by regimes in the Gulf; to have engaged in electoral fraud; and to have been beneficiaries of unthinking support by the Muslim masses: 'Egyptians, it was claimed by the non-Islamist elite, are ignorant and illiterate people who were led like sheep by the Islamists' (Tadros, S. 2012). Both the Brotherhood and the Salafis had benefited from specific electoral arrangements put in place by SCAF and from the relatively short period of campaigning;[4] in addition, their religious credentials were important for many voters. These factors, however, do not explain the breadth of support for Islamists in the ballot in all parts of the country – in relatively prosperous neighbourhoods as well as in poor urban and rural areas. The Islamists' main asset was their record, in particular their standing as: '"clean" and "untainted" figures attuned to the daily struggles of the poor' (Wickham 2013: 251).

The presidential election of May–June 2012 would soon emphasise that attachment to Islamic agendas was not enough to guarantee success: rather, public commitment to change, together with a reputation for principled conduct, were key factors. In this context, secular parties suffered badly. New liberal and reformist parties were unknown to most Egyptians and had not had an opportunity to make their mark. The Wafd and Tagammu', however, had long histories and high public profiles. In 1999, Tagammu' leader Rifa'at al-Sa'id had observed that all political parties of the Mubarak era 'represent nothing in Egyptian politics and have no standing whatsoever with the Egyptian people'.[5] He had added:

> Do not believe any person who says that the Nasserite Party is a real party, or that the Progressive Unionist Party [Tagammu'], the National Democratic Party, the Muslim Brothers, nor the Islamic groups are parties in the true sense of the term […] All these are just groupings of individuals floating on the surface of society.
>
> (Hussein *et al.* 1999: 77)

Here El-Sa'id associated with other parties the characteristics of his own. By the 1990s Tagammu' was a shadow of organisations that once represented the radical wing of the anti-colonial movement. Its retreat as the 'official' left had opened space for others prepared to challenge the regime and who bore the brunt of the latter's punitive measures. As the left surrendered ground, the Islamists had advanced. In comparison with the Wafd and Tagammu', the Brotherhood appeared as a champion of popular interests: far from 'floating on the surface of society' it had a mass membership, millions of supporters and tens of thousands of political prisoners whose fortitude inspired others. It was indeed 'a real party' that in January 2012 entered parliament leading a bloc with 235 of the 508 seats in the People's Assembly.

New millionaires

The democratic space to be occupied by Islamist MPs had been created by the movement from below. Many of the movement's activists were hostile to the Brotherhood or at best sceptical about its willingness to follow through on electoral promises. Egypt's electors had nonetheless opted to put the organisation to the test and had high expectations: they were to be disappointed, as the organisation failed to meet both its manifesto commitments and wider challenges of the revolutionary process.

Examining the Brotherhood's economic agenda in the wake of election victory, Nathan Brown observed: 'In terms of general orientation, the Brotherhood has two strong impulses: first, it seeks to protect property rights and a market economy; second, it also feels that the state has a strong obligation to look after its weaker citizens' (2012: 15). From its earliest years, the organisation had drawn in merchants and petty capitalists for whom the mainstream nationalists of the Wafd Party, dominated by large landowners and big business interests, were unattractive (see Chapter 5). During the period of Nasser's repression, Brotherhood members who sought refuge in the Gulf states played a leading role in developing Islamic finance and commerce. They benefited from the huge oil price rises of the early 1970s, investing in Egypt through import–export firms, supermarkets and money-exchange companies that processed the remittances of millions of migrant workers. Returning to Egypt under Sadat, they embraced the opportunities of *infitah*, establishing the country's first generation of Islamic finance houses – companies that offered extravagant returns said to be untainted by interest-bearing transactions (usury being *haram* – impermissible – in Islam). When the Mubarak regime accelerated the process of privatisation, they participated enthusiastically. Kandil records the Brothers' investments in construction, luxury housing, car dealerships, electronics, Islamic schools, media and tourism (mainly pilgrimage, a multi-million-dollar business): 'a new breed of Brotherhood businessman was born', he comments (Kandil 2015: 78). Leading figures included Youssef Nada, founder of Al Taqwa Bank; Hassan Malek, with investments in textile manufacturing, electrical supplies and trade fairs; Khairat al-Shatir, with diverse investments including IT, pharmaceuticals and textiles; Abdel-Rahman Seoudi, owner of a supermarket chain and agricultural export company; Safwan Thabet of the Juhayna group, the largest processor and distributor in Egypt of dairy products and with investments in livestock and land reclamation; and Mohamed Moamen of Mo'men Group, Egypt's largest fast-food chain, with branches across

North Africa and the Gulf. Some of the wealthiest Brothers held high office in the organisation and were prominent in its activities outside Egypt.

Hassan al-Banna had insisted that all had a right to private property – one that should be exercised in accordance with Islamic principles of 'general welfare' based on good conduct including selfless commitment to other Muslims (Mitchell 1969: 252–53). This approach drew on important historic traditions in which the mosque and the marketplace were closely linked (Engineer 1980); it also echoed European experiences of early capitalism and the 'muscular Christianity' of reformist Prot-estantism.[6] The Brotherhood had at first been strongly influenced by the radicalism of the anti-colonial movement; later, however, its businessmen of the 'new breed' prospered under post-colonial regimes intolerant of all opposition. They embraced free-market principles modified from the 1990s by criticism of the Mubarak state for its retreat from welfare provision, especially from public support for the poor (Naguib 2009).[7] The Brotherhood was also critical of Mubarak's 'crony' networks, although it was unclear whether this was a matter of principle or an expression of frustration at the exclusion of prominent Islamists from deals brokered by Mubarak and his associates to favour private capitalists including senior officers of the armed forces (see Chapter 8).

Despite their new-found wealth, the Brotherhood's businessmen remained a small fraction of the Egyptian bourgeoisie – a grouping that wished to increase its status vis-à-vis the state and corporate interests. When Mubarak fell they saw opportunities to advance, favouring strategies pursued for a decade in Turkey by a sister organisation, the Justice and Development Party (AKP). The organisation faced two major problems, however: the obstacles presented by SCAF and the expectations of the mass movement, eager to see the delivery of radical reforms to which the Brotherhood had made a public commitment.

Brotherhood and presidency

In February 2011, the Brotherhood set out its approach to the popular movement as one of 'participation not domination'. Essam El-Erian insisted: 'We are working with the people. Our target is the people. Not the power [...] Participate, not dominate' (El-Erian 2011). Soon however the organisation was working to secure electoral arrangements that would win for the Brothers a dominant influence in Egyptian politics. Parliamentary elections established a bridgehead from which to advance upon this goal: the next target was the presidency.

Interviewed days after the fall of Mubarak, El-Erian had insisted that the Brothers would not seek Egypt's highest political office. 'We are not going to have a candidate [for president], neither men, neither Muslim, neither women. We are not going to have a candidate now, at all', he said (El-Erian 2011). In March 2012, the Brothers nonetheless nominated Khairat al-Shatir, causing a public outcry and open dissent within the organisation. The Brotherhood had already expelled a leading 'reformist' member, Abdel-Moneim Aboul-Futouh, for declaring his wish to stand for the presidency: now it nominated one of its most controversial members, a leading conservative widely seen as the organisation's 'fixer', for the same post. Shatir was one of the wealthiest men in the organisation – a successful businessman with investments in Egypt and abroad in IT, furniture, fabrics, tractors, car manufacturing, chemicals and management consultancy (Howeidy 2012). He had been jailed several times under Mubarak. When released from prison in the 1990s, he had been appointed deputy general guide; jailed again in 2006, he was finally freed in March 2011 and immediately resumed a senior role in the Guidance Council. His nomination was an eloquent statement of the leadership's intentions: having won an election victory on a programme of radical change designed to appeal to the mass of Egyptians, it now proposed for president one of the 'new breed' of multi-millionaire capitalists.

Shatir was said by Brotherhood insiders to exercise de facto control over the organisation's finances. He was reported to have devised the means to expand his personal wealth together with that of the Brotherhood, so that there was 'ever greater overlap between his own business interests and the Brotherhood's finances' (Howeidy 2012). *Al-Ahram Weekly* described his priorities after leaving prison in 2011:

> He's been roaming Asia and Gulf to talk about investment, and finds the economic successes of Turkey, South Korea, Brazil, Singapore and Malaysia admirable [...] he's been meeting with senior officials and ex-officials in the industrial and investment sectors, clearly to prepare for the Brotherhood's near future role in the government.
>
> (Howeidy 2012)

Shatir's nomination was given added significance by SCAF's refusal, following the parliamentary elections, to appoint a new prime minister and cabinet. The generals used the constitutional agreement of 2011 to retain for the president the right to make such appointments. In effect, SCAF would control the government until a new president was elected: military rule was to continue. If the Brotherhood hoped that the nomination of a leading businessman would soften the generals' stance, they were soon frustrated by the news that a SCAF-controlled committee had disqualified Shatir on the basis of an 'irregularity' – his convictions during the Mubarak era.[8] Faced with this rebuke, the Brotherhood meekly brought forward another candidate – a low-profile technocrat with a reputation for dutiful service to the organisation. Much mocked by activists of the mass movement, Mohamed Mursi was said to be the Brotherhood's 'spare tyre' nominee for an election eventually scheduled for May–June 2012.

The Brotherhood appeared to be fixated on the presidency and its relationship with the generals. It gave little thought to economic and social reforms anticipated by the majority of the electorate, still less to the expectations of the streets and workplaces, where hostility to both SCAF and the Brotherhood had been intensifying. On 16 December 2011, military police and the *baltagiyya* had moved into Tahrir Square at dawn, killing at least 14 people and injuring hundreds: their assaults on women demonstrators had included the notorious 'blue bra' attack (see Chapter 3). According to SCAF's newly appointed prime minister, Kamal El-Ganzoury, protestors were to blame for the violence: 'Events taking place in the streets aren't a revolution,' he said. 'They're an attack on the revolution' (Kirkpatrick 2011b and 2011c). On 25 January 2012, Egyptians marked the first anniversary of the uprising. Millions headed for city squares: in central Cairo 10 marches moved towards Tahrir, where the Brotherhood had erected a stage and a large banner that announced: 'Our presence in Tahrir is to celebrate the 25 January Revolution and declare that we support all its goals' (Montasser 2012). Brotherhood speakers congratulated the people on their achievements and introduced patriotic songs. It soon became clear, however, that they had misjudged the mood. Demonstrators were not celebrating; rather they demanded: 'Freedom, justice, social equality', insisting that the people's goals had not been fulfilled and that the revolution must continue. Two days later, on the anniversary of the 'Day of Rage' when in 2011 the CSF had killed hundreds of protestors, large sections of the crowd in Tahrir again howled down Brotherhood speakers, chanting, 'Get off the stage!'. In a vast demonstration, scores of thousands chanted: 'The army, the police – one filthy hand!', 'The people demand the fall of the Field Marshal [SCAF leader Tantawi]', 'We, the people, are the red line [that cannot be crossed]' and 'The people demand the fall of the Field Marshal'.[9] They insisted that the movement was still in mourning for those killed by the police and the army, that their murderers must be brought to justice, and that the struggles would continue until SCAF stepped down or was removed. Protestors demanded, 'We want civilian, not military [government]' – a challenge to Brotherhood leaders as well as to the generals.

Hostility towards SCAF increased when within days a tragic episode in Port Said resulted in over 70 deaths at a football match between the local team and Cairo's Al-Ahly. Police blamed fan rivalry; those attending testified that police and thugs had assaulted supporters of Al-Ahly, allegedly in revenge for the latters' involvement in street protests. In demonstrations of solidarity, SCAF was again a target, with Ultras of both Cairo clubs, Ahly and Zamalek, protesting that, 'Police are the thugs' and 'Down, down with military rule' (Trew 2012). The incident brought to a head months of confrontation with the *baltagiyya* and military police, intensifying hostility towards the generals. In Cairo, the city centre had again become a no-go area for police and security agencies. Tahrir was an encampment at which youth groups, cultural associations, political parties and revolutionary currents maintained a permanent presence. In the absence of police, young activists directed traffic and in nearby streets traders once excluded from the area established informal markets. Impromptu meetings took place across the Square: on Fridays large numbers of people attended street meetings and debates. In the centre of the *midan* the Museum of the Revolution had been extended, with posters, hand-written testimonies of the uprising and photographs of the martyrs. For some activists, the Square was still the heart of the revolution and the key task at hand was to revive the Tahrir Republic of January–February 2011 (see Chapter 10).

The workers' movement had continued to advance, albeit unevenly. A year after its establishment, the independent trade union federation EFITU claimed a membership of 200 unions and 2 million blue- and white-collar workers (Beinin 2012: 12). Its most important affiliates were the property tax workers' union Retau, independent unions of teachers, and workers in the Cairo Public Transport Authority, Egypt Telecom, the postal system and aviation. The federation had made a breakthrough in new industrial cities, notably 6 October and Sadat City, where most private sector enterprises had hitherto been unorganised by official unions. During the first six months of 2012, there were strikes in the postal service, Cairo public transport, the Railway Authority, court and prosecution services, and the ports of Alexandria and 'Ain Sukhna: a survey conducted by the Egyptian Center for Social and Economic Rights during two two-week periods in April and May noted 258 collective actions by workers (Beinin 2012: 20). The movement faced problems of disunity and bureaucratisation (see Chapter 10) but continued to pose pressing problems for SCAF. Failing to head off disputes in the transport sector, the generals attempted strike-breaking. In February and March 2012, they ordered the army to replace buses usually operated by drivers of the Delta Bus Company. Delta strikers had demanded a host of changes: improved wages, rights to organise in an independent trade union, transfer of employment to the Transportation Ministry, an efficient supply of spare parts for vehicles, proper maintenance of buses, and *taṭhir* – the removal of corrupt administrative officials (Charbel 2012a). Warned that they were breaking SCAF's Law 34/2011, which criminalised strikes and protests said to harm the economy, the workers argued that they were protecting the public: 'We strike not only for our interests, but for the interest of the commuters – for the sake of improving our company, and improving state-owned transport services' (Charbel 2012a). The strike ended inconclusively but at a high risk to the government: using troops to break strikes exposed rank-and-file conscripts to subversive influence. The bus dispute also highlighted a growing disillusion with the Muslim Brotherhood. A striker told the journalist Jano Charbel: 'the [Muslim] Brotherhood and Salafi MPs who we voted for in Port Said have ignored our demands [...] They're not defending our rights or the rights of commuters' (Charbel 2012a).

Parliament had failed to bring forward a Trade Union Liberties Law proposed in 2011 by Minister of Manpower Ahmad Hassan al-Bura'i after discussions with the independent unions. SCAF had postponed this legislation until, said the generals, it could be placed before a parliament. Following the election of November–December 2011, the FJP proposed an alternative bill formulated without consulting independent union groups. Drawn up by MPs associated with the official labour federation

ETUF, this prohibited workers organising more than one union within any enterprise, providing for the dissolution of unrecognised unions and seizure of their funds. Khaled Azhari, a senior ETUF official and the FJP MP who proposed the bill, said: 'Our main target is just to protect the Egyptian economy in this transitional period; we need stability in the workplace' (Dale 2012). The ETUF had been formally dissolved in August 2011 but remained under 'caretaker' leadership, continuing operations in key areas of the public sector. The Brotherhood's bill aimed to roll back the gains of the independent unions in favour of the official federation, which for over 50 years had operated as a wing of the state and part of the apparatus of repression. Abdel-Hafiz Tayel, vice-president of the Independent School Teachers Union, with 80,000 members, saw the bill as part of a strategy to force workers back into old union structures; it should be contested, he said: 'Laws are there to be broken. A bad law shouldn't be followed. The people of Egypt struggled hard for the right to organize. Hundreds of people were killed for this right, and we are ready to fight again' (Dale 2012).

For Ibrahim, a veteran union activist, the new bill contradicted the FJP's manifesto, which had promised freedom of association:

The Freedom and Justice Party – that means the Brotherhood – promised in its election manifesto to protect trade union freedoms. It tried to win support as a defender of our revolution. But even before they won the election they'd planned to attack the workers' movement. We're going to see many battles, not just with SCAF but with the Brotherhood too.[10]

'The president is in the Square!'

The first round of the presidential election on 24 May 2012 produced a startling result. Widely seen as a two-horse race between SCAF's Ahmed Shafiq, a former minister and Mubarak loyalist, and Mohamed Mursi of the Brotherhood, it turned into a tight three-way contest with Hamdeen Sabbahi, a Nasserist who had emerged as candidate of the popular movement. On a 44 per cent turnout, Mursi received 25.3 per cent of the vote, Shafiq 23.7 per cent, Sabbahi 21.6 per cent, Aboul-Futouh 17.9 per cent, and *feloul* candidate 'Amr Moussa 10.9 per cent (*Ahram Online* 2012b and 2012c).

Sabbahi had none of the resources mobilised behind the two favourites: he had been written off, noted *Al Jazeera* (Hill 2012a), as 'the classic no-chance candidate'. His campaign slogans – 'One of us' and 'Bread, freedom, dignity and social justice' – had however aligned him with the people against the generals and against an Islamist parliament seen as increasingly hostile to the mass movement. Sabbahi had been a member of the Arab Democratic Nasserist Party that split from Tagammu' in 1992; in 1998, he been a founding member of the radical nationalist Karama (Dignity) Party, and in 2004 of the democracy coalition Kifaya. He had gained public attention in 1997 after an arrest for opposing Mubarak's desequestration laws and had subsequently been jailed on several occasions. He had twice been elected as an independent MP and had participated in many of the protests between 2000 and 2011 that challenged the Mubarak regime. His campaign for the presidency included commitments to the implementation of the mass movement's call for a national minimum wage of LE1,200 a month, which he proposed to fund with a one-off tax on 10 per cent of the income of anyone with assets worth more than LE50 million. He promised to end Egypt's role in the siege of Gaza and to stop the government's deals with Israel for the import of natural gas.

Sabbahi's performance in the first round of the presidential election was viewed by his supporters as a triumph and a marker of the continuing vigour of the revolution. Appearing in Tahrir Square days after the announcement of first-round results, he was greeted by a large demonstration as if the winner – scores of thousands chanted: 'The president is in the Square!'[11] In Cairo a majority of voters had opted for Sabbahi: results across the city showed that he had obtained 34.6 per cent of the vote (followed by 25.9 per cent for Shafiq, 20.1 per cent for Mursi and 19.2 per cent for Aboul-Futouh) (*Ahram Online* 2012b). In many industrial centres of the Delta, he had also been a clear winner. In Alexandria, Egypt's second and most industrialised city, he had scored an emphatic victory, with more than double the votes recorded by Mursi, who had topped the national poll; there were similar emphatic votes in Kafr al-Shaikh and Port Said. Meanwhile, the Brotherhood's vote had halved since the parliamentary elections six months earlier. Then the FJP received some 10.5 million votes; in the first round of the presidential elections Mursi received just 5.7 million votes, concentrated in predominantly rural constituencies. The election suggested a swing away from the Islamists towards Shafiq, as candidate of the SCAF, and to Sabbahi and Aboul-Futouh as candidates of the popular movement, with the latter capturing a significant share of the Islamist constituency. A shift of 3 per cent in the overall vote would have put Sabbahi into the second round in a run-off with Mursi; among Sabbahi's and Aboul-Futouh's supporters there was some regret that they had not stood on a joint ticket for president/vice-president; their combined votes in the first round suggesting that they might have won a commanding victory.

SCAF again

Two days before the second round of the elections, the Supreme Constitutional Court dissolved parliament on the basis that a third of its members had been elected illegally and that the whole body lacked legitimacy. Politicians across the board reacted furiously, declaring that the Court – composed of Mubarak appointees – had enacted a coup on behalf of the military command. The generals intervened again, hours after the polls had closed and before results were announced: state media broadcast a statement declaring that SCAF had taken new powers to make laws and set budgets, that it had decreed a new interim constitution that would remove most of an incoming president's powers, and had empowered military officers to arrest civilians, in effect reinstating Emergency Laws. The election results were not declared for several days as the generals and the Brotherhood apparently haggled over arrangements for a new government, including the allocation of ministries to SCAF loyalists. Mursi was eventually declared the winner, with 51.7 per cent of the votes on a turnout of 52 per cent.

SCAF's declaration was in effect a formalisation of the Selmi Document of November 2011 – an assertion of 'supra-constitutional' principles that entrenched the military command in authority over an elected president and parliament. Brotherhood supporters rallied in central Cairo to declare: 'Down, down with military rule!' – a slogan they had earlier repudiated. Eventually declared president on 30 June, Mursi attempted to use his presidential powers to reinstate parliament: he was soon over-ruled by the Supreme Constitutional Court and turned his attention to a new cabinet, which emerged from prolonged discussions with SCAF. Hisham Qandil, a senior bureaucrat under Mubarak, became prime minister; Hussein Tantawi, leader of SCAF, was retained as minister of defence, a position he had held for years under the former regime; Ahmed Gamal Eddin became interior minister, having supervised police intervention against the mass movement during much of 2011. Other ministers included a clutch of technocrats committed to neo-liberal principles and who had been implicated in many of the most egregious practices of the Mubarak era.

Abdelhadi commented that Mursi 'seems to think that they [the Brotherhood] can rule Egypt without dismantling the old machinery – instead he wants to take command of it' (2012). Struggling to assert his authority among Mubarak loyalists, Mursi soon embraced a new problem, replacing Tantawi as minister of defence and military production with a more junior member of SCAF – Abdel-Fattah Sa'id Hussein Khalil al-Sisi. Introduced by Morsi to 'defend the revolution', he was to prove the new president's nemesis.

8

Brotherhood, People, State

In April 2012, the Muslim Brotherhood organised a delegation to the USA. Its aim, observed the *Washington Post*, was to pursue a 'charm offensive', convincing American officials and policy makers that the organisation could be a 'moderate, centrist' force in Egyptian politics (Wan 2012). The visit suggested emerging priorities on the Brotherhood's agenda. It had hitherto been under suspicion among policy makers in the USA – an outcome of its stance vis-à-vis Mubarak and close relations with other Islamist currents in the region, notably Hamas in Palestine. A strong lobby among the Brothers now wished to persuade the USA that it could be trusted in both domestic and foreign affairs – that in government the Brotherhood would offer continuity with key policies of the former regime.

The fall of Mubarak had opened new opportunities for leading businessmen of the Brotherhood, who resolved to cohere their position and to exert greater influence over the organisation's economic policy (Lübben 2015). Interviewed in April 2012, Hassan Malek, a key figure within the Brothers' business elite, described how Mubarak's security agencies had imposed limits on his activities: they 'allowed me to reach a certain level, but there was a ceiling', he said, a 'red line' that he crossed at risk of arrest and imprisonment (Hansen 2012). In the new circumstances, Malek and his colleagues were eager to exploit opportunities denied to them for decades: their model was that of Turkey and the policies of the AK Party. In March 2012, Malek and Khairat al-Shatir established the Egyptian Business Development Association (Ebda – the acronym meaning 'Start' or 'Start it' in Arabic), which was launched with a gala event attended by business executives from Saudi Arabia, Turkey and the USA, and described as 'the coming-out party for the businessmen of the Brotherhood' (Hansen 2012). Their inspiration was the Independent Industrialists' and Businessmen's Association (MUSIAD) established by

Islamists in 1990 in Turkey as a forum to compete with the Association of Turkish Industrialists and Businessmen, long under the control of the Turkey's republican bourgeoisie.

MUSIAD had played a key role in advancing the interests of Islamist businessmen attached to the AK Party following the party's election in 2002 on a manifesto that declared for efficient government, intolerance of corruption and a fresh start in politics. The AK Party embraced neo-liberal policies, implementing IMF requirements for loans and imposing forceful austerity measures while advancing 'Islamic values'. In Egypt, the Brotherhood's leaders also embraced the free market, while repudiating what they saw as the cronyism of the Mubarak years and asserting commitments to Islamic principles of justice (*'adl*) and fairness (*insaf*) in economic policy. Sebnem Gumuscu (2008) identifies the aspirant, middling capitalists of Turkey's MUSIAD as a 'devout bourgeoisie' that successfully pursued its shared interests through the AK Party. The recent history of capitalism in Egypt, she suggests, differed from that in Turkey – in particular the embrace by Sadat and Mubarak of the policies of neo-liberalism meant that many 'devout' Egyptian businessmen remained close to the state and wary of political engagement that could bring punitive action of the sort experienced by Malek, Shatir and many others. The Brotherhood satirised the lifestyle of these pious but cautious bourgeois as an 'air-conditioned' Islam practised at a safe distance from activist currents. Gumuscu observed: 'The divided and apolitical nature of the devout bourgeoisie reduce[d] the political effectiveness and weight of the business class [in Egypt] within the political Islamic movements' (2008: 23). The Brotherhood failed to attract business interests that would have provided opportunities like those exploited by the AK Party. When Mubarak fell and leading Islamists such as Shatir emerged from prison, they were eager to make up for lost time and opportunities denied. Shatir travelled widely, preparing the ground for new initiatives including Ebda and soon after the presidential election of 2012, Mohamed Mursi led a large business delegation organised by the association to China; visits to Italy, Turkey and Qatar followed. Turkey promptly provided Egypt with a $2 billion loan: one Turkish official commented that the Mursi government viewed Turkey 'not as a model but an inspiration [...] and Turkey reciprocates this' (Awad 2012).

The 'bread file'

Ebda, suggests Hansen, sought to mobilise 'the Brothers of the 1 Percent' (2012). She observed prophetically:

> [They] believe they can empower a new class of businessmen – those Egyptians who didn't have clout during the Mubarak era – while also improving the lives of poor Egyptians and attracting investment from abroad. Their model resembles that of Turkey, where a religious middle class, encouraged by the country's Islamic government, has driven a spectacular economic boom. But talking the language of growth is one thing; making it real in a country whose economy is as ravaged as Egypt's is another.
>
> (Hansen 2012)

The Egyptian uprising gave testimony to the insecurity experienced by the mass of people and intensified during the latter period of Mubarak's rule by aggressive neo-liberalism. Now Mursi prepared to renew these policies. His prime minister, Hisham Qandil, declared: 'We want Egypt to be a mecca for investors [...] Allow me to confirm that the Egyptian government is committed to economic reform and free market economics' (Hyde 2012). Within weeks of his election, Mursi met IMF chief Christine Lagarde to begin talks over a $4.8 billion loan. The implications were clear: his government was ready to implement the Fund's demands for 'adjustment' measures including further cuts to subsidies of basic foods and fuel. The Islamist-dominated parliament dissolved by SCAF had earlier rejected terms for a proposed $3.2 billion loan: Mursi pressed ahead, knowing that the IMF would be uncompromising. According to the *Wall Street Journal*, the Fund viewed Egypt as a test case: 'Negotiations with Egypt will offer a laboratory for the world's emergency lender as it tries to aid the new democracies created by the so-called Arab Spring uprisings' (Reddy and Bradley 2012). Mursi's government faced a $30 billion annual spending deficit at a time when domestic banks were charging 16 per cent on loans to the state: the IMF's projected 1.1 per cent interest rate appeared to offer a lifeline. When agreed, said IMF officials, the loan would also release further resources from the World Bank, the African Development Bank and various

Middle East states; in addition, the USA would offer $1 billion in debt relief. In return, however, Mursi must phase out 'wasteful subsidies' and prepare for devaluation of the Egyptian pound (Wroughton 2012).

When ministers appointed by SCAF had earlier attempted to negotiate with the IMF, Egyptian activists established a Popular Campaign to Drop Egypt's Debt, committed to oppose the deal. The government should refuse to repay loans raised by the state both inside and outside Egypt, it argued: loans had been misused by the former regime and there should be no further indebtedness. The campaign asserted that negotiations with the IMF sent an unacceptable message to the people: 'We will borrow in your names so that your children and grandchildren continue paying off our debts' (Elmeshad 2012). Egypt's debts were 'illegitimate', it argued, and should be abandoned in the interests of 'people's welfare'.[1] Many members and supporters of the Brotherhood meanwhile declared that payment of interest to the IMF was *haram* – proscribed by Islamic principles in relation to usury. The vast majority of MPs had already expressed their opposition (before the dissolution of parliament in 2011): Islamist members of the people's Assembly had then declared, 'This loan will lead us all to hell' (Alabass 2012).

Caught between 'piety and expediency' (Alabass 2012), Mursi continued negotiations with the IMF, finding ample justification in Islamic traditions. Saad al-Husseini, a leading figure in the organisation, announced: 'Our decision not to reject borrowing is based on Egypt's supreme economic interest', quoting Shari'a (the Islamic legal code) to the effect that 'necessities allow the forbidden' (Alabass 2012). In October 2012, Mursi told a public rally that repayments to the IMF would not constitute *riba* – usury. 'I would never accept that Egyptians live off Riba [...] We would rather starve than eat off Riba', he said (AFP 2012). His anxieties were driven by the looming prospect of food shortages and specifically by a crisis in supplies of bread. During the Mubarak era, Egypt had become the world's largest importer of wheat, making the government particularly sensitive to changes in price, the availability of hard currencies and the value of the Egyptian pound. In January 2011, foreign currency reserves had amounted to $36 billion; by September 2012, they stood at $15.04 billion: barely enough to cover three months of imports (*Reuters* 2012a). Meanwhile the Egyptian pound had fallen continuously against the US dollar, reaching a new low in December 2012 when the Central Bank said that foreign currency reserves were at a 'critical' level (*Reuters* 2012a). Mursi announced that he had created a 'bread file' and was monitoring supplies regularly: when he spoke at a public rally in October 2012 he claimed that 80 per cent of targets set by the government for ending shortages had been met (Hussein 2012a). There was high scepticism among the public: revolutionary activists established an online Mursimeter to measure the president's success in fulfilling his promises, casting doubt on official claims.[2] Mursi faced similar challenges in relation to fuel, where the IMF also demanded cuts in subsidies. Cylinders of butane gas, used for cooking, had become unobtainable for many Egyptians, selling on the black market at 30 or 40 times the official price. Furious crowds demonstrated at gas distribution centres; there were similar scenes at service stations, where drivers waited for hours for deliveries of petrol and diesel.

When Christine Lagarde visited Cairo in August 2012 she was greeted by a protest that asserted: 'No to crony capitalism,' 'Down with capitalism,' and 'Reject the loans' (Mourad and Feteha 2012). In November 2012, a further demonstration opposed the IMF, organisers maintaining that any deal would amount to an abuse of power on the part of President Mursi. In a letter addressed jointly to Mursi and Lagarde, a large group of political parties, trade unions and NGOs argued that negotiations had been conducted in the absence of a parliament, without transparency, and with public consultations that were 'exclusionary and inaccessible' (EIPR 2012). The letter continued:

> We worry that this potential loan agreement and the policies connected to it will represent a continuation of the old regime's economic policies, particularly as they relate to the incursion of debt. The austerity measures associated with this potential loan agreement, including cutting subsidies as well as other deficit reduction policies, may aggravate the economic deprivation of a large section of the population, threatening their basic economic and social rights.
>
> (EIPR 2012)

'Egypt's new pharoah'

A mood of suspicion and mistrust towards Mursi and the Brotherhood was spreading nationwide, intensified by the president's determination to dictate the terms of a new constitution. Members of the Constituent

Assembly, dominated by the Brotherhood, were under continuous pressure to agree to contentious principles of which the most important was the organisation's insistence that Shari'a should be the main source of legislation. In November 2012, Mursi met leaders of both Islamist and non-Islamist parties in efforts to win their agreement. The initiative backfired, highlighting criticisms that the president had no authority in the Assembly and should stop interfering in its proceedings. As argument intensified, Mursi found himself at the centre of a new wave of mass protests. On 22 November, demonstrators assembled in central Cairo to mark the deaths of activists during the Mohamed Mahmoud protests of the previous year. Police attacked the commemorative event, killing Gaber Salah ('Jica') a journalist and prominent member of the 6 April Youth Movement. Liberal, radical and nationalist parties strongly criticised the police and the president, pointing out that his undertakings to reform the police and security agencies had not been fulfilled, nor had he sent for trial officials of the Mubarak regime said to have been responsible for hundreds of killings during 2011. The 6 April Movement said: 'Revolutionaries went to the streets to commemorate their martyrs but they became martyrs themselves' (*Ahram Online* 2012c). The Muslim Brotherhood blamed protestors: Mohamed El-Beltagy, Secretary-General of the FJP, said the clashes were 'planned organised chaos', prompting furious reactions from activists who recalled the Brotherhood's earlier denunciation of those involved in the Mohamed Mahmoud events (*Ahram Online* 2012c).

Mursi's response was contained in a startling statement – a Constitutional Declaration that began by committing to further investigation of the deaths of protestors in 2011 but went on to claim unprecedented new powers for the presidency. Article II asserted:

Previous constitutional declarations, laws, and decrees made by the president since he took office on 30 June 2012, until the constitution is approved and a new People's Assembly [lower house of parliament] is elected, are final and binding and cannot be appealed by any way or to any entity. Nor shall they be suspended or canceled and all lawsuits related to them and brought before any judicial body against these decisions are annulled.[3]

The edict empowered Mursi to appoint Egypt's prosecutor-general for a four-year period, installing in this position – that of the most senior legal official – Judge Talaat Ibrahim Mohamed Abdullah, a sympathiser of the Brotherhood. It also extended the life of the Constituent Assembly and provided the president with unrestricted general powers (Article VI) to take 'necessary actions and measures to protect the country and the goals of the revolution' (*Ahram Online* 2012d). The popular response was one of incredulity. Leading figures of liberal and nationalist parties and of Islamist rivals to the Brotherhood expressed outrage. For Abdel-Moneim Aboul-Futouh of the Strong Egypt Party the declaration was 'a package of dictatorial decisions which is a setback to the path of the revolution' (Ezzat 2012). Mohamed ElBaradei, leader of the Destour Party, said: 'Mursi today usurped all state powers and appointed himself Egypt's new pharaoh. [It is] a major blow to the revolution that could have dire consequences' (BBC 2012b). According to Hossam Issa, a leading Nasserist, 'With this declaration, the president has put an end to the law and the judiciary system. This is absolute fascism' (Ibrahim, E. 2012). The main opposition parties formed a National Salvation Front (NSF) – a coalition that aimed to force Mursi to rescind his decree and to form a more representative constituent assembly. This included the most assertively capitalist parties, the Free Egyptians, the Conference Party and the New Wafd; the main organisation of the established left, the Tagammu'; liberals and nationalists including the Egyptian Popular Current, the Destour Party, the Democratic Front, the Egyptian Social Democratic Party, and the Nasserist Democratic Party; and the Socialist Popular Alliance of the new left.

The Declaration brought to a head months of growing tension between the Brotherhood and revolutionary activists. While demonstrations of protest continued in Tahrir Square, now focused upon the president, at the presidential palace Mursi rallied his supporters, telling them there were 'weevils [sic] eating away at the nation of Egypt', adding, 'I don't like, want or need to resort to exceptional measures, but I will if I see that my people, nation and the revolution of Egypt are in danger' (*Al Jazeera* 2012). In several cities, large crowds attacked the offices of the Brotherhood: in Tahrir Square, opposition leaders called for a march on the presidential palace (Qasr al-Ittihadiyya, the 'Federation Palace' in Heliopolis) and activists soon established an encampment nearby. In an important development that suggested intensified hostility on the part of the security forces towards the president, police failed to protect the palace and the Brotherhood responded by mobilising against what it called an attempted 'coup' (Ibrahim 2015).[4] The FJP Deputy Secretary, Essam al-Erian, spoke live on television, calling on the party's supporters to hurry to the palace:

I call upon them to go in hundreds of thousands and to surround the thugs [critics of Mursi], because this is the opportunity to arrest them and reveal the third party that is behind the shooting of live ammunition, and the killing of protesters in the battle of the camel [February 2011], Mohamed Mahmoud, Maspero and the Cabinet [protests]. This is our opportunity now. [...] Everyone must go now to Ettihadiya and surround the thugs and separate the real revolutionaries out [...] for one or two nights and then we can arrest them all.[5]

Members of the Brotherhood seized protestors at the palace, among whom scores were brutally beaten. Human Rights Watch condemned Mursi for his role in the events: 'Instead of condemning illegal detentions and abuse right outside the presidential palace', it observed, 'President Morsy spoke out against the victims' (HRW 2012). Huge demonstrations converged on the palace, dwarfing the Brothers' rallies, to show solidarity with those attacked and to protest against Mursi and the Declaration. Protests were dominated by the slogan associated with the 18 Days of Tahrir Square – 'Irhal' ('Go'/'Leave'). Munir, a radical journalist, described the events:

I thought that Tahrir [in January–February 2011] was the summit of our movement but events at the Ittihadiyya exceeded everything. The scale of the protests was immense and mood was confident and defiant. When the Brotherhood tried to intervene their members were driven away ferociously. The army was helpless. It was another demonstration of the raw determination of the movement.[6]

Sara, a member of the revolutionary left, observed a change in the composition of the protests:

The demonstrations were huge and they were different. For the first time since Tahrir [the 18 Days] there were very big numbers of middle-class people, including the professionals and even, I think, the rich. The Brotherhood had scared them into doing something. The Brothers crossed a line and they gave an opportunity to many people who were still undecided about the revolution to oppose them. We didn't realise it at the time but the Ittihadiyya was a change in the climate of the revolution.[7]

As huge protests continued Mursi retreated, withdrawing the Constitutional Declaration but at the same time announcing a new decree that retained judicial immunity for the president. He insisted on proceeding with a referendum on the constitution and provided the army with powers of arrest and detention of civilians until the result of the referendum was announced. Heaping pressure on the mass of people, he also declared tax rises on more than 50 goods, including fuel, electricity, steel, cement, cigarettes and alcohol – an attempt to meet a deadline imposed by the IMF to meet the terms of the $4.8bn loan. Mursi and the Brotherhood were now reeling from one crisis to another. Within the space of 24 hours, Mursi had cancelled the tax rises, suspended his negotiations with the IMF and withdrawn the army's special powers. Meanwhile the Judges Association, mandated to supervise the referendum on the constitution, declined to participate. In an ominous sign for the president, his defence minister, Abdel-Fattah al-Sisi, took the initiative, calling for an emergency meeting – a 'national dialogue' to seek consensus between the Muslim Brotherhood and opposition groups. Using an official Armed Forces Facebook page, al-Sisi proposed to involve members of the Cabinet, the political elite, revolutionary youth, Al-Azhar (the centre of Islamic scholarship), the church, the Judges Association and the Supreme Constitutional Court. He also called on lawyers, journalists, artists, athletes, workers and peasants to attend 'out of love for Egypt' and in order to preserve national cohesion (Reuters 2012b).

When the referendum was eventually held in two stages (due to the shortage of judicial supervisors), the draft constitution was confirmed by a majority of two to one. The turnout had been low, however – less than 33 per cent – and unlike the parliamentary elections of the previous year, there were many allegations of fraud. The outcome did not assist Mursi. The demonstrations continued at the Ittihadiyya, where a new Museum of the Revolution, an annexe of the exhibition in Tahrir Square, commemorated martyrs of the movement. Across the country protestors meanwhile demanded electricity and fuel. Power cuts had become a daily occurrence: in late December 2012, the Egyptian Electricity Transmission Company said that 15 power stations were out of action: *Al-Ahram* reported that if the fuel crisis was not resolved, 'half of Egypt's governorates will plunge into darkness' (*Ahram Online* 2012f). Marwa, a doctor at one of Cairo's leading hospitals, recalled:

> It was the end of last year [2012] when things really got bad. We didn't know from one hour to the next if we'd have a power supply – for lighting, x-rays, to undertake operations. In the city we'd lose power for hours. Even government ministries and offices went dark without warning – Mohamed Mursi couldn't keep the lights on in his own capital city. What message did that send to Egyptians?[8]

Protests among workers had meanwhile been under way against both the Constitutional Declaration and a further edict in which Mursi announced changes to leading bodies of the ETUF, the official trade union federation. Decree Number 97 stipulated that senior officials of the federation, who were over the age 60, would be replaced by newly appointed members. This had the effect of removing Mubarak-era officials, many of whom had been members of the NDP. Worker activists expressed strong opposition to the decree, which they saw less as an expression of *taṭhir* than an attempt by the president to replace Mubarak's men with officials hand-picked by the Brotherhood. Fatma Ramadan of the independent union federation EFITU accused Mursi of 'Brotherhoodising' the official unions:

> Morsy is clearly preparing a systematic crackdown against Egypt's union movement, against the right to strike, against the right to organize and against union plurality. [He] is attempting to put on a mask of democracy as he points out that the ETUF leadership was appointed by the Mubarak regime. Yet he is not seeking democracy in the ETUF, he is only looking to fill the federation's seats with members of his own regime [...] This is a blatant and unwarranted intervention in union affairs from the state.[9]

Hisham, an activist in the independent health workers' union, condemned Mursi's intervention:

Why hasn't he organised elections so that workers can make their own decisions about who represents them? This revolution is about accountability and democracy. Mursi wants to put his own people in control in the unions – that's against everything this revolution has fought for.[10]

The EFITU issued a strong condemnation of the Constitutional Declaration.[11] There was soon strike action at Mehalla al-Kubra, where thousands of textile workers joined a protest in the city, clashing with supporters of the Brotherhood. A year earlier, the Brotherhood had led its campaign for the parliamentary election with promises to pursue social justice and equality, to eliminate poverty and unemployment, to ensure adequate education and welfare, and to improve the living conditions of workers and peasants. Under Mursi workers had experienced greater insecurity, a threat to supplies of basic foods and fuel, more aggressive intervention by international financial agencies, and unwanted Islamist influence in already flawed trade union bodies. Supporters who had been won to the Brotherhood by its years in opposition, its 'welfare reformism' and its rhetoric of democratisation were disillusioned; millions joined new protests.

Brotherhood and change

The leaders of the Brotherhood resisted the message coming from the streets and workplaces, maintaining that with Mursi's election they had acquired a popular mandate for change. The Brotherhood spokesman, Mahmoud Ghozlan, described the Constitutional Declaration of November 2012 as a 'revolutionary decision'.[12] Ali Abdel-Fattah, another key figure in the organisation, argued that Mursi was empowered to issue edicts on behalf of the people: 'As long as he is democratically elected, he has all the rights to issue such a declaration', he said; in a revealing comment Abdel-Fattah added that there were historic precedents for such action, quoting initiatives taken by President Nasser (*Ahram Online* 2012e). Some Islamists, however, were dismayed by the Brotherhood's approach. For Abdel-Moneim Aboul-Futouh, who had for decades been a leading figure within the organisation's reformist currents, the Declaration was an assault on the revolution (Kirkpatrick and Sheikh 2012). Ahmed Fahmi, leader of the Shura Council (the upper house in parliament) and a leading member of the FJP, argued that the president had 'severely divided the nation into Islamists and civilians [sic]' (Essam al-Din 2012).

These disagreements reflected debate and dissent within the Brotherhood and its constituencies of support. Many assessments of Islamism view organisations such as the Brotherhood as monolithic, with members adhering to unchanging theological and political principles. As we have seen, however, in Chapter 5, Islamist movements undergo continuous processes of change, modifying their agendas in response to new circumstances and experiencing inner tension and conflict. Bayat (2005) points out the dangers of identifying Islamist organisations as a whole with the beliefs and policies of their leaders on the assumption that the latters' views have been internalised unproblematically by members and supporters. This approach often converges with that of the leaders themselves, who present an account of the movements as unitary and even homogenous. In the case of Egypt, the leaders of the Brotherhood wished to present the organisation as coherent, loyal and disciplined. The upheaval of 2011 had in fact accelerated changes already under way within the organisation, which under a more conservative leadership had been in the process of withdrawing from activist political practice. Abstention from the early protests of January 2011 caused serious internal problems as the Brotherhood lost ground to new youth networks. Its standing among workers and the urban poor was also affected. Mass strikes and the emergence of independent unions drew workers towards collective forms of struggle, while the Brotherhood's complicity with SCAF and its endorsement of police actions repelled many erstwhile supporters. Young activists and key leaders of the reform wing left to join new parties or to form their own organisations. The weight of 'popular classes' and of liberal Islamists in the Brotherhood decreased; that of the traditional middle-class core increased, together with that of 'devout bourgeois', who aspired to obtain their share of the spoils of Egyptian capitalism.

As the Brotherhood's influence contracted in some areas it expanded in others, notably in the electoral field where for almost a year the organisation enjoyed unparalleled influence through the FJP. Wickham (2013: 268) suggests that by mid-2012 the Brotherhood could no longer be described as a single entity. Its move into new areas of public affairs, she suggests, had engendered the rise of separate entities with different institutional interests. These included the Society of the Muslim Brothers (the Muslim Brotherhood as founding entity), the FJP and the Mursi presidency. She adds: 'Treating the Brotherhood as a single entity is [...] problematic [...] What is clear is that the Brotherhood, like the state establishment, is not a monolith but a complex institutional network with different moving parts.' (Wickham 2013: 268).

As the revolution progressed, these different elements experienced varying fortunes. On the one hand, the Brotherhood (as the Society) lost the support of many members and supporters, especially those attracted by the welfare reformism of the Mubarak era. On the other hand, the FJP advanced into parliament, eventually obtaining the presidency and the means to establish a government responsive to its own agendas. For the Brotherhood leadership – conservatives grouped around the *murshid* – these were votes of confidence in the Society *tout court*, including its traditions and its project for change. In possession of the Egyptian presidency, they ignored the agendas of the popular movement and determined to advance towards specific goals: a programme of legal, social and cultural reforms shaped by their own interpretation of Islamic tradition; an advance to positions of authority within national politics of their trusted cadre of activists; and greater access to economic opportunity for members and supporters of their business lobby. These goals were to be achieved by working alongside SCAF and implementing key policies of the Mubarak regime.

'Pious vanguard'

Mursi and his colleagues had repeatedly misjudged the popular movement: now they made a huge miscalculation in relation to those holding power in the apparatus of state.

On 25 January 2013, large crowds gathered to mark the second anniversary of the revolution. Members of youth networks and parties of the left were prominent in marches in Cairo: to Maspero, to commemorate the killings of 2011; to the Shura Council (which had assumed legislative authority after dissolution of the lower house); and to Tahrir Square. For the first time a large group of anarchists, identifying as a 'Black Bloc', also appeared in Tahrir Square, having earlier participated in demonstrations in Alexandria. In Mohamed Mahmoud police fired teargas and birdshot at protestors who tried to dismantle a wall erected the previous year by military police; their slogans included: 'The people demand the fall of the regime' and 'Down with the rule of the *murshid*' (Trew *et al.* 2013). In several cities, there were attacks on offices of the Muslim Brotherhood, whose members were conspicuously absent from most events. There were also targeted attacks on female protestors. Assaults on women by the CSF and military police had taken place on many occasions – now groups of *baltagiyya* attacked women in an apparently co-ordinated programme of harassment aimed at creating fear and confusion. Anti-harassment groups, notably Operation Anti-Harrassment (*Quwwa did al-taharosh*, also known as OpantiSH) formed earlier by activists to identify and pursue assailants at public events, confronted large gangs who surrounded female demonstrators.[13] Habib, a member of the Marxist left with years of experience of protests in Tahrir Square, observed: 'The police and gangs were getting bolder. The second anniversary events were more confused than the anniversary events of the previous year. The people's movement was more fragmented, less sure about its targets, although the protests were still huge.'[14]

The Brotherhood was in a mode of denial. Its spokesman in Alexandria, Anas El-Qady, said that the day's demonstrations were not 'big enough to fill a street or a square', adding: 'What some political forces are doing now in spreading chaos and violence is only an attempt to make a coup against legitimacy' (Trew *et al.* 2013). Its leaders apparently approved mobilisations by the army, which placed large groups of soldiers at strategic points around major cities. Senior officers stated that they would not confront civilians and that the presence of detachments around Greater Cairo was part of a plan to intensify security measures on the road network. According to their spokesman, 'This is a precautionary routine procedure to secure the country through critical timing. We took the same procedure last November.'[15] As president, Mohamed Mursi had avoided challenging the authority and privileges of the armed forces. His reshuffle of senior posts in August 2012 had included praise for the outgoing head of SCAF Hussein Tantawi and his chief of staff Sami 'Anan, both of whom Mursi decorated with Egypt's top military medals and appointed as presidential advisers; other retiring officers were given lucrative civilian posts. New commissions, including that of al-Sisi as defence minister, were made from among a core group of senior commanders – all Mubarak appointees, who before January 2011 had been viewed as regime loyalists. Mursi insisted publicly on the autonomy of the armed forces and during the constitutional crisis of November 2012 attempted to expand their powers in relation to the civilian population. He adopted a similar approach to police and security agencies, declaring soon after his installation as president that the Interior Ministry had been rehabilitated – in effect he embraced the *mukharabat* and the CSF, viewed by millions of Egyptians as the chief organs of state repression. In November 2012, police protected the presidential palace while Mursi's supporters – summoned by senior officials of the Brotherhood – attacked protestors and declared that, 'the people and the police are one hand' (McCrummen 2012).

The leaders of the Brotherhood sought to align their organisation with the key coercive organs of the state. Although frustrated by the initial reluctance of SCAF to fulfil commitments to electoral change, success at the ballot box had confirmed the Brothers' determination to work alongside the military command and security agencies. At the first session of parliament in January 2012 the new speaker, Brotherhood member Saad al-Katatni, had proposed a thank you message to SCAF: 'The People's Assembly commends your historic stances in the great Egyptian Revolution. You have taken the side of the people and their peaceful revolution [...] and as brave fighters you shouldered the burden of making this choice' (Egypt Independent 2012). Following Mursi's election to the presidency, the Brothers expected to be treated as trusted equals in public affairs. In one of the few informed assessments of their rationales and expectations at this stage of the revolution, Hazem Kandil asks, 'Why did the Brotherhood adopt this position?' They had no stomach for taking on the 'formidable custodians of violence', he suggests (2015: 139); at the same time they believed that their theology of struggle and status as a 'pious vanguard' could win over generals, police chiefs and heads of the *mukhabarat* (Kandil, H. 2015: 139). For decades these bosses of the state machine had pursued the Brothers with zeal: their victims now sought to win them to the project of an Islamist future in which the organisation would share ownership of the state and the spoils of Egyptian capitalism.

State and capital

What was the character of the state in which the Brotherhood now sought its own stake? During the Nasser era the state had been reconstructed to serve a capitalism dominated by the armed forces command. An officer elite formed the core of a new ruling class that included senior managers, technocrats and security chiefs, and which directed an economy largely under public ownership. This state capitalism brought key economic activities under central control: at the same time, it accommodated private capital. Some private businesses flourished: public and private capital cohabited, the latter establishing a bridgehead from which it later advanced rapidly as the neo-liberal projects of Sadat and Mubarak transferred public assets to private hands. Coercive institutions of the state remained key instruments in the hands of successive regimes; at the same time, they were deeply affected by change, especially by the progressive engagement of the armed forces in the neo-liberal agenda.

Most assessments of the post-colonial period depict a process in which private capital was obliterated by zealous radicals. The reality was different: although from the mid-1950s Nasser's 'socialist' reforms took much of industry and commerce into public ownership, the state readily accommodated private capital (see Chapter 6). Large areas of land remained in private hands and the commercial bourgeoisie continued to play a key role internally and in external trade. Writing in 1962, at the height of his nationalisation programme, Nasser maintained: 'The private sector has its effective role in the development plan and must be protected to fulfil that part' (Abdel-Nasser 1972: 115). Huge sums were channelled into military spending: over 15 years from 1952 the armed forces' allocation of national resources was increased by some 300 per cent.[16] The military budget funded arms, equipment and vastly expanded programmes of conscription; it also supported new networks of privilege that extended beyond the armed forces. Officers received special bonuses and had access to exclusive social clubs, shops and holiday villages; on retirement, many senior officers moved into key positions in the state bureaucracy in which they interacted with private capitalists (Marfleet 2012). Raymond Baker quotes a contemporary observation by Soviet analysts (the Soviet Union then being the key supplier of arms and training for the Egyptian forces) on Egypt's 'officer businessmen'. These generals and former officers, they said, were 'more interested in business than in the military preparation of soldiers and sergeants' (Baker 1978: 60).

The expansion of the armed services and the public sector was accompanied by massive profiteering in construction and provision of services, facilitated by links between senior army officers, managers of public enterprises and private businessmen. The process was accelerated by the nationalisation of foreign capital and the departure from Egypt of communities of European origin that had been integral to finance, commerce and industry. Anouar Abdel-Malek observed that 'Egyptiani-sation' brought private enterprise back into the hands of local capitalists: 'people waiting to grow rich had finally found the means to do so under the banner of nationalism and revolution' (Abdel-Malek 1968: 155). The 'state bourgeoisie' of military men and technocrats was increasingly difficult to distinguish from private interests. Zaalouk observes:

> There were significant overlaps and alliances between both: i.e. some members of the state bourgeoisie were engaged in private enterprise, while alliances, interlinkages and interdependencies existed between the two groups – some by virtue of mutual business interests, others by virtue of kinship, or the social background of the top managerial elite.
>
> (Zaalouk 1989: 35–36)

Anwar Sadat, who succeeded Nasser in 1970, had close links with members of the old bourgeoisie and with senior technocrats at the interface of the state and private capital. He moved quickly to formalise networks of patronage within and outside the bureaucracy, facilitating links between senior military men, the old landowning aristocracy, entrepreneurs who had survived the Nasser era and merchants, traders and commercial intermediaries. In 1974, his *infitah* opened Egypt to imports and to foreign investment. The old bourgeoisie was back on centre stage, together with a new generation of aggressive import–export merchants, commission agents and speculators. The military elite was part of this process: its members had influence or even control over state budgets, which they now used freely to obtain commission from contractors and suppliers. The ministry of defence formalised these arrangements by establishing a new division of the armed forces, the National Service Products Organisation (NSPO), which participated in public infrastructure projects and produced a range of consumer goods. Sadat legitimised and encouraged public-private enterprise: building on networks established during the Nasser era, senior ranks of the armed forces were key players in the rush to profit.

Husni Mubarak, who became president in 1981, steered consistently towards private capital and the world market. He willingly accommodated the demands of the IMF and the World Bank, encouraging the entry to Egypt of large US and European companies and the integration of the local economy into a neo-liberal project that embraced the wider Middle East region (Hanieh 2013). His senior military commanders were important players in this process, although their role was obscured by the secrecy surrounding the state in general and the military establishment in particular: the army's economic activities were classified as state secrets and investigation could lead to imprisonment and worse. Robert Springborg (1988: 107) was among the first to identify its role in privatisation, describing a 'horizontal expansion' of the armed forces into strategically important areas of the economy. Later assessments confirm the consolidation of this 'officer economy', Marshall and Stacher observing that, 'The army's tentacles [...] grasped large shares of the civilian public sector as part of the "privatisation" process of the 1990s' (2012). During the final decade of Mubarak's rule, the armed forces entered every key area of economic activity, becoming Egypt's 'Military Incorporated' (Marroushi 2011). New military companies were established to run factories and agricultural enterprises. Together with the NSPO, established in the Sadat era, a Ministry of Military Production and a new Arab Organisation of Industrialisation ran 20 factories producing goods largely directed to civilian markets (Abdul-Magd 2013: 2). Marshall and Stacher (2012) identify involvement in arms production, construction, shipbuilding, oil and gas, railway engineering, IT, docks and container services, finance and real estate; Abdul-Magd also lists investments in steel, cement, automobiles, home appliances and foodstuffs (2013: 2). In addition, the army owned a large number of gas stations, hotels, wedding halls, supermarkets, parking lots, domestic cleaning services, transportation and shipping companies (Abdul-Magd 2012, 2013). At the same time, they were engaged with investment networks across the Middle East region. Adam Hanieh (2013: 138) demonstrates that in the years before the uprising of 2011, Egypt received a third of all private equity investment originating in the Gulf and placed within the Middle East and North Africa. Gulf capital entered every key sector of the Egyptian economy, including areas of industrial production such as textiles that for decades had been under public ownership. Private investment, observes Hanieh, was 'a key institutional form through which Gulf capital has become tightly integrated to local Egyptian elites' (2013: 168). The armed forces were important actors, entering a host of joint ventures including projects funded with Gulf investors such as the Kharafi group of Kuwait, a leading player in the oil engineering business whose links to the Egyptian military were described as a 'model of cooperation' between the state and the private sector.[17] Egyptian capitalism had been embedded in the political economy of the region – in structures of state and class produced by almost three decades of change driven by the neo-liberal agenda. The armed forces protected not only the specific interests of Egypt's ruling class but also those of investors linked more closely to the world market than at any time since the colonial era.

States of conflict

The Egyptian state with which Muslim Brothers of the post-Mubarak era sought collaboration was a complex formation. The post-colonial state of the Nasser era expressed the contradictory character of a regime that had removed the monarchy and expelled the British but that also protected Egyptian capitalism – the Free Officers' state of the 1950s first contained and then suppressed the mass movement that had brought them to power. By the end of the Nasser era, it accommodated the interests of the military command and security directorates; of senior bureaucrats and managers; and of sections of the landed aristocracy and the commercial bourgeoisie. Under Sadat, the state became an instrument for the rehabilitation of private capital, drawing together the old bourgeoisie with a new generation of capitalists and with networks of privilege within the armed forces, the civil administration and the public sector. Under Mubarak, the process went much further: now the machinery of state became a means of transferring public resources to private ownership and of integrating Egypt into the global market. Bodies of the state associated with public affairs, most importantly the armed forces, were active participants: Abdul-Magd observes that senior officers and retired officers were located across Egyptian society in positions at which 'authority and capital merged' (2013: 2). By the mid-1990s, suggest Henry and Springborg, Egypt was in the grip of 'a nexus of cronies, officers, bureaucrats and public sector managers' (2001). The term 'crony', with its implications of illicit practice, was to recur repeatedly as a means of characterising those most closely associated with the president.[18] If the latter were 'cronies', however, the entire Egyptian ruling class was implicated, as the Mubarak state facilitated the break-up of the public sector, the privatisation of land and utilities, and an unprecedented concentration of wealth within the networks of privilege.

Wickham observes that the state was not a monolith but 'a complex institutional network with different moving parts' (2013: 268). The component elements of the Egyptian state had specific interests: they both collaborated and competed. Kandil (2012) maintains that the long-standing rivalry between the armed forces, the security agencies and the presidency was in fact the key factor in the fall of Mubarak in 2011. All, however, had a stake in Egyptian capitalism and in the survival of the state. It was this state, a guardian of national and international capitalist interests, that the Brotherhood's leaders petitioned for a share in power and economic influence. Their project failed – with catastrophic consequences for the Islamists. Within months the leadership had been imprisoned on capital charges and thousands of supporters had been killed, while those in command of key institutions of the state turned upon the mass movement.

9

Towards the Coup

Many assessments of the revolution concluded that the attempts by the mass movement to bring lasting change were fruitless. In July 2011, *Foreign Affairs* had published an analysis of the impact of insurgent movements in the Middle East and an admission that academic experts had 'missed the Arab Spring' (Gause 2011). A year later, Ashraf Khalil used the same publication to declare that Tahrir Square was 'fading' (Khalil 2012). The movement was 'exhausted', he argued, its activists were disillusioned and becoming increasingly passive (Khalil 2012). In November 2012, Hussein Agha and Robert Malley proposed that the 'darkness' had descended upon Egypt and other Arab states. Peaceful demonstrations and the 'lofty values' that inspired them were distant memories, they argued, concluding: 'This is not a revolution' (Agha and Malley 2012: 71). On this account, those who had launched the uprisings were no more than plucky losers who were now in retreat. In fact mass struggles in Egypt had continued throughout 2012 and into 2013 with a surge of mass strikes and confrontations between protestors and security forces.

In 2012, the Egyptian Centre for Economic and Social Rights (ECESR) recorded 3,817 'labour strikes and economically motivated social protests': during the first quarter of 2013, it counted over 2,400 such events (Aboulenein 2013).[1] According to ECESR, over 70 per cent of all actions during 2012 occurred after Mursi took office, reaching an average of over 450 strikes and protests each month between July and December; between January and March 2013 they surged again, with an average of 800 separate events each month (Aboulenein 2013). Most strikes raised wage demands; other issues included job security, misman-agement, bullying, corruption and factory closures. Ashraf, a member of the Marxist left who monitored labour struggles closely, observed that action in the workplace was being used more and more often to address everyday problems:

> There's a much greater readiness now to use the strike as a default strategy when owners and managers won't respond to workers' demands. For decades under Mubarak repression made collective action very difficult but the revolution has allowed fast learning and now people move much more rapidly to the strike. This itself is part of political generalisation within the revolutionary process.[2]

The strikes of 2013 were not only more numerous but also more prolonged; many were also more closely linked across cities, regions and specific sectors of the economy. This was evident in the transport sector, in which stoppages affected strategically important networks, generalising strikers' demands and prompting panic measures from the government. In February 2013, 1,200 dockworkers at Ain Sukhna port on the Red Sea coast maintained a 16-day strike to demand secure jobs. According to *Bloomberg Business* 'not a single shipping container moved into or out of Egypt's principal port for Asian trade' and the dispute 'showcased workers' growing activism' (Lynch and Marroushi 2013). In March 2013, drivers of microbuses, integral to the road transport system in Egypt but who had not hitherto organised collectively, mobilised over availability of diesel fuel. In Mehalla al-Kubra drivers parked buses in squares and on railway lines: traffic across the city came to a halt (Fady 2013). There were similar stoppages in Alexandria, while in Giza drivers blockaded the Cairo ringroad, paralysing traffic around the city (*Ahram Online* 2013a). In April 2013, rail workers undertook a strike said to be the largest stoppage in the sector for over 30 years, with 73,000 workers involved, demanding increased pay and holidays. Government officials warned, implausibly, that the army would take over the railway system. One striking driver told Jano Charbel: 'neither the army nor the police are capable of driving or operating these trains [...] We even operate the army trains for the Armed Forces' (Charbel 2013a). When officials approached Cairo Metro workers to break the strike by driving railway trains, Metro unions also threatened to strike and eventually officials announced that they would conscript the rail workers, placing them under military discipline (MENA 2013).[3] The threat evaporated when Metro workers again threatened to strike, bringing a climbdown from the government and promises to implement the rail workers' demands. The dispute was soon followed by stoppages in the Cairo railway maintenance workshops and at Cairo Airport.

Although many strikes had uncertain outcomes (see Chapter 10), the idea of collective action to secure both specific local demands and more general aims had been generalised across the Egyptian working class. By 2012 over a quarter of disputes involved privately owned industrial enterprises in which strikes had earlier been rare or unknown (Aboulenein 2013). The trend continued into 2013, affecting areas of the economy in which there had been heavy foreign investment. *Bloomberg Business* noted that under Mubarak 'the promise of a compliant state union and low wages was instrumental in attracting investors from the U.S., Europe and the Persian Gulf' (Lynch and Marroushi 2013). Now foreign investment had evaporated and the prospect of more protests and strikes was a deterrent for those considering involvement in Egypt: by May 2013 foreign investment had fallen by 56 per cent in two years (Kingsley 2013). *Bloomberg* concluded: 'Labor unrest is just one element of the country's broader disorder. From the capital to Suez Canal ports, Egypt in recent weeks has come close to unraveling' (Lynch and Marroushi 2013).[4] The Mursi government had retreated from efforts to strike a deal with the IMF, further inhibiting inward investment. According to Samir Radwan, finance minister in the SCAF government of 2011, an IMF loan was 'the key' to economic recovery: 'if you sign with the IMF', he said, 'it means you have a sound financial and monetary programme to get you out of the crisis' (Kingsley 2013). There was neither progress on the IMF loan nor an easing of industrial action, which had its own specific impact on institutions of the state, for the military elite was not only a command centre for the armed forces but also an investor in private enterprise. As defence minister and head of the armed forces, Abdel-Fattah al-Sisi was challenged to assert the authority of state institutions and the interests of private capital based in Egypt and abroad.

Police 'on strike'

Mursi had turned more and more often to the police and security agencies to suppress street protests. Following the Ittihadiyya events he provided increased budgets and pay rises for senior ranks, together with assurances about their continuing role, and in February 2013 he warned that security forces would act 'with utmost decisiveness' to protect state institutions (BBC 2013). In the same month, the CSF was ordered to confront demonstrators in Port Said protesting over a court decision in which judges handed down capital sentences on 21 football fans – scapegoats for police violence in the city's stadium a year earlier. They used live weapons, killing 27 demonstrators: in response, furious crowds attacked police stations and drove security forces from the city; three CSF troops were killed. When Mursi declared a curfew, thousands of people occupied the streets to show their defiance: large numbers of CSF troops refused to comply and challenged the interior minister as to the legitimacy of his orders, a call that soon spread to CSF camps across the country. Some 8,000 members of the force in the Suez Canal area rejected instructions to enter Port Said. The CSF chief Maged Nouh was seized and held by 'strikers' who accused the interior minister of complicity with the Muslim Brotherhood and denounced President Mursi for 'repeating the mistakes of the former regime' (*Al-Masry Al-Youm* 2013). They demanded the minister's removal and their own replacement in Port Said by regular troops (*Al-Masry Al-Youm* 2013). Some reports identified 30 CSF camps affected in cities including Cairo, Giza, Ismailia, Port Said, Minya, Sohag and Alexandria, as well as 'tens' of CSF divisions in Sinai and the Nile Delta: in one camp in the governorate of Minufiya, 10,000 officers and troops were said to be involved (Kirkpatrick 2013).

In 2011, there had been many reports of CSF forces deserting, in some cases to join street protests (El-Hamalawy 2012a). In May 2012, CSF troops at a base in Obour City, north-east of Cairo, rebelled in protest at the abuse by their officers, occupying the highway until an army detachment arrived and concessions were negotiated. Over the following months, there were further protests in cities including Cairo and Alexandria over the ill-treatment by officers, long working hours and bad food (El-Hamalawy 2012a). The police 'strikes' of 2013 were a more complex development, however.[5] On the one hand, rank-and-file members of the CSF, all conscripts, had grievances focused upon pay and conditions, and on the bullying culture imposed by their officers – issues that had surfaced during the 'Auxiliary Forces mutiny' of 1986. On the other hand, CSF officers and regular police, not conscripts but employees of the interior ministry, were concerned mainly by the threat to their status and job security. Most were hostile to the Muslim Brotherhood. For years, they had pursued its members and supporters as enemies of the state: now, they were expected to protect them and to defend a president they associated with disorder and social chaos. The armed forces had maintained their own influence within the security agencies: as Sayigh (2012: 15) observes, 'officer-bureaucrats' had long been embedded in the security apparatus and SCAF had invested time and resources in repairing some of the damage inflicted on the CSF, the police and the *mukhabarat* by the mass movement of 2011. When in January 2013 Abdel-Fattah al-Sisi warned publicly that further political crisis could lead to collapse of the state, he made an indicative statement to those with a stake in the old order, including the cadres of the CSF, the police and security agencies, that executive action was needed to safeguard their interests (BBC 2013). Their 'strikes' became a means of opposing the presidency and undermining the government (ICG 2013: 4). Police activists who established a 7 March Movement, organising at some 60 police stations across the country, demanded not only a new pay structure but also the dismissal of the interior minister, seen as close to the president and whom they accused of forcing police to play a 'political role' in conflicts with the public (Halawa 2013). In the context of unexplained passivity of the police at the Ittihadiyya protests, these may have been further early moves against the Brotherhood within institutions of the state that were to culminate in the military coup and the counter-revolutionary offensive led by al-Sisi.

Crisis of the opposition

Public engagement in politics both formal and informal remained intense throughout the Spring of 2013. Maha Abdelrahman, who had monitored opposition movements closely for many years, observed:

> Egypt today is still teeming with millions of Egyptians who are taking to the streets on a daily basis in an unabashed struggle against the ruling elite's policies which continue to impoverish and marginalise them. Groups of activists are relentlessly trying to carve spaces for action.
>
> (Abdelrahman 2013)

At the same time, the popular movement faced a crisis of politics that had been in the making since the fall of Mubarak. This was expressed in part in the paralysis of secular opposition parties – the organisations of the National Salvation Front.

In November 2012, opposition parties had established a coalition against Mursi's constitutional declaration and the referendum that followed. The NSF combined radical nationalists such as Hamdeen Sabbahi of the Popular Current Party, with liberal reformers such as Mohamed ElBaradei of the Destour Party and Amr Mousa of the conservative Conference Party, with its links to the Mubarak networks. The Front soon alienated many supporters of participant parties by disowning protests in which activists were attacked by police. At the same time, its leading figures withdrew from the public arena, focusing on mutual rivalries and becoming more and more distant from their constituencies of support. Assessing the Front's record during its first six months, Taylor and Saleh (2013) proposed that the greatest threat to continuing change in Egypt might not come from the Brotherhood but from the inability of a weak and fragmented secular opposition to offer a coherent alternative. The Front had failed to agree on any of the pressing issues with which it was confronted:

> Should the opposition engage and compromise with Mursi for the sake of national unity, or boycott and try to weaken him to make it harder for the Brotherhood to control the country? Should they participate in parliamentary elections that many believe will be skewed towards the Brotherhood, as they say all post-revolution votes have been, or stay away at the risk of being marginalised and looking like bad losers? And should they back a proposed loan from the International Monetary Fund as essential to pull the economy out of crisis despite the tough terms that would be attached, or oppose it on grounds of national sovereignty and social justice – or just sit on the fence?
>
> (Taylor and Saleh 2013)

Most non-Islamist parties had emerged after the fall of Mubarak. They were beneficiaries of the mass movement, organising in the political space created by protestors of the streets, workplaces and neighbourhoods. Unable to prepare for the hurried parliamentary election of 2011, they had engaged more effectively the following year, when in the presidential election two candidates with wide public support – Hamdeen Sabbahi and Abdel-Moneim Aboul-Futouh – together captured a majority of the votes. Sabbahi's popularity was especially striking. He had aligned his campaign with the mass movement, with demands for social justice and the project of extending the revolution. His slogan, 'One of Us', resonated with millions of people seeking an alternative to *feloul* and to the Islamists. His overwhelming vote in large cities, especially industrial centres, was evidence of an increasingly radical mood among workers and the urban poor. The party he established following the election, however, proved a disappointment to many supporters. At a founding rally of the Popular Current in Cairo, Sabbahi had declared:

> We are the soldiers of the January 25 Revolution, who believe in the unity of our modern history, the sons of the July 23 Revolution [of 1952], the grandchildren of the 1919 great revolution [against British rule] [...] We Egyptians, who believe in the goals of the January 25 Revolution [of 2011] – freedom, social justice and human dignity – will not compromise a single one of its goals.
>
> (El-Sharnoubi 2012)

The Popular Current initially recruited young activists attracted by Sabbahi's commitment to secure basic needs, protect the historic interests of workers and peasants in the welfare state, and pursue the aim of social justice. Invoking the traditions of President Nasser – Sabbahi was a lifelong Nasserist – he also won much support for backing the Palestinian cause. Enthusiasm gave way to anger among young supporters, however, when the organisation joined the National Salvation Front (NSF). One of the party's leading activists, Khalid El-Sayed, argued: 'Most of the members of the Popular Current rejected the idea of forming a coalition with organisations led by *feloul*. It was against what the revolution stood for' (Rashwan 2013). Sabbahi steadily retreated from his stance in the presidential campaign, his radicalism fading as the Popular Current became entangled with the assertively capitalist parties of the NSF and as rival leaders jostled for a position in the coalition; many young members of the organisation resigned, disillusioned by their first experience of formal party politics. For many years, Sabbahi had drawn upon radical elements within Nasserism, especially upon memories of anti-colonial struggle, the triumph of Suez, land reform and the universal provision of education and health care. Buoyed by the mass movement, he had articulated demands for further change. Following the election of Mursi, however, and the prospect that the movement might challenge the state itself, he retreated towards the armed forces as a guardian of national interests. Other aspects of Nasserism came to the fore: a prescriptive, elitist politics focused upon the state and accompanied by mistrust of mass actions that could not be directed from above. Like Nasser, Sabbahi had been prepared to maintain working relations with the Brotherhood; like Nasser, he also turned upon the organisation as a threat to the state, simultaneously abandoning commitments undertaken in the presidential election only months earlier. Following a path set out decades earlier by the communist movement, he was prepared to ally with former enemies against the prospect of radical change.

Members of other organisations ostensibly committed to the popular movement also encountered leaders who had moved close to al-Sisi and to the prospect of participation in a new military backed government. Increasingly the NSF was paralysed by personal bids for influence among party leaders. One official of the coalition admitted that it was hobbled by a 'battle of the egos' (Taylor and Saleh 2013). In January 2013, the youth of the Destour Party, which had also grown rapidly since its foundation in September 2012, occupied the organisation's headquarters in Cairo to protest against undemocratic procedures and the unacceptable policies of the leadership. In March 2013, a number of leading activists resigned, declaring that the party was dominated by power-seekers. One defector said: 'There is a group of people controlling the party that believes they will win the majority in parliament and will become ministers' (El Gundy 2013). These developments also affected the most radical elements within the NSF, grouped in the Socialist Popular Alliance, or Tahaluf. The Alliance had been formed in 2011 by former members of the Egyptian Communist Party (ECP), who had for years operated within Tagammu', together with radical social democrats. Interviewed in April 2013, Nawal – a former member of the Alliance – observed,

> Neither the Salvation Front nor any of its leaders, including those in Tahaluf, offers a social strategy for the revolution. They do not address the questions faced by the people – prices of food and fuel, employment, a fair minimum wage, housing, rents, increasing poverty. They don't take care of the people – they take care of their own ambitions.[6]

For activists of the revolutionary movement, the conduct of the NSF was infuriating. Its leaders had vacated the democratic space created by the movement – erstwhile champions of social justice, notably Hamdeen Sabbahi, retreating from their commitments to radical change. In January 2013, NSF leaders refused Mursi's invitation to enter into dialogue; at the same time, they opened negotiations with key figures in the armed forces. According to Wael Kandil of *Al Shorouk*, as early as November 2012 there had been talks involving Sabbahi, ElBaradei and Mousa: 'mines are being laid', he suggested, 'the ground is being laid for a big explosion'.[7] Their willingness to engage with al-Sisi opened new options for the military command. Challenged in the streets and workplaces, and by the Brotherhood's aspiration to emplace itself within the structures of authority and networks of privilege, the military elite explored means to evict the president and to crush both his organisation and the popular movement. As liberal and reformist parties of the NSF retreated, al-Sisi and his advisers undertook to subvert the movement: their strategy was to undermine it from within.

Tamarud

Mursi had attempted to reassure the security agencies, providing them with new resources and summoning them to defence of the Brotherhood. They had other loyalties however. Since the time of Nasser, police and intelligence services had been integral to the apparatus of coercion: now, they had the interests of the state to protect and their own scores to settle with the revolutionary movement. In April 2013, a group of young activists who had established Tamarud ('Rebellion'), calling for an early presidential election, soon attracted the attention of the *mukhabarat*. Founding members of the group were well known within the youth movement: they drew around them others who wished to hold Mursi to account, initiating a petition that called on the president to step down before the anniversary of his election on 30 June. The campaign quickly developed momentum as the petition circulated widely in the streets, workplaces, campuses and neighbourhoods. Within weeks, Tamarud claimed 8 million signatures; by 30 June organisers claimed that 22 million had signed (Saleh 2014). Tamarud was a phenomenon, says Magda, a human rights activist with long experience of campaigning both before and after the fall of Mubarak:

I'd never seen anything like it. Petitions were everywhere. You could see people stopping cars Downtown [in central Cairo] and getting drivers and passengers to sign. People took them onto buses and into shops. Of course there was very strong feeling about Mursi, the economic crisis, the power cuts – but there was also something strange about it. Tamarud was getting huge coverage on television and in the newspapers – we'd never seen that before. We found later that the *mukhabarat* had been part of it from the beginning.[8]

Former members of Tamarud later explained that there had been close ties between the group's founders and state security agents who had 'influenced and guided' them (Saleh 2014). Ahmed Hassan, who abandoned Tamarud in 2014, said: 'At the beginning we had no doubts about them, but later after checking their background and gathering more information we realized they were state security recruits who had received special training' (Saleh 2014). Agencies of the state that for decades suppressed movements of protest had projected Tamarud to a national audience, co-ordinating support from business and media. Billionaire Naguib Sawiris, one of the wealthiest men in the Middle East and founder of the liberal capitalist Free Egyptians Party, boasted to the Reuters news agency of his own role:

> The Free Egyptians party, the party that I founded, used all its branches across Egypt to (gather) signatures for Tamarud [...] Also the TV station that I own and the newspaper, *Al-Masry Al-Youm*, were supporting the Tamarud movement with their media [...] It is fair to say that I encouraged all the affiliations I have to support the movement. But there was no financing, because there was no need [sic].
>
> (Blair *et al.* 2013)

Sawiris commissioned production of a popular music video to promote the campaign. 'Tamarud did not even know it was me!' he said: 'I am not ashamed of it' (Hubbard and Kirkpatrick 2013).

Tamarud's instant success reflected the distress of millions of people as prices continued to rise, jobs became increasingly insecure and power cuts struck across the country. It also demonstrated anger at the conduct of Mursi and the FJP, seen to have violated their promises, imposed changes to the constitution and relentlessly promoted 'Brotherhoodisation'. Tamarud's elevation to the role of leadership in a movement against the president, however, was the work of security agencies and of the military command, business interests and leaders of the secular opposition. It took place as state officials encouraged protests against the president in the CSF and the police, and – as later became clear – arranged power cuts and fuel shortages. The aim was to generalise a sense of disorder and insecurity, and of hostility vis-à-vis the president, opening the possibility of an intervention by the armed forces as a guardian of national interests. Throughout the Spring of 2013, a coup was in the making – carefully prepared in the form of an initiative apparently demanding change 'from below' in a movement that was administered from above.

A 30 June mobilising committee that included youth networks and the NSF called for protests against Mursi on the anniversary of the 2012 presidential election.[9] It was joined by businessmen such as Sawiris and by leading figures of the Muslim and Christian establishments, who had earlier disdained street activism. Intensive media coverage encouraged participation and huge crowds appeared in cities nationwide, including activists of the popular movement; veterans of the street battles of 2011 and of successive waves of strikes; large numbers of middle-class Egyptians; and, for the first time as participants in public protest, contingents of uniformed police (Haddon *et al.* 2013a). In several cities, military helicopters flew overhead to demonstrate support of the armed forces command. The June 30 Committee issued a statement welcoming the use of all 'democratic means' to oppose the Brotherhood, advocating demonstrations, strikes and sit-ins, and asking Egyptians to 'besiege' state institutions to demand the trial of all those responsible for 'torture, killing and announcing edicts inciting against the people and calls for terrorism which was called for [sic] by the Muslim Brotherhood' (Haddon *et al.* 2013b). The NSF also issued a statement:

> In the name of the Egyptian people with all their factions, the National Salvation Front announces public endorsement of the ouster of the regime of Mohamed Morsi and the Muslim Brotherhood [...] The Salvation Front also trusts that the Egyptian people will protect its revolution until peaceful transition of power is fulfilled [...] we also call on all political forces and all citizens to remain peaceful [...] and refrain from dealing with the failed Brotherhood government until the fall of this tyrannical organisation.
>
> (Haddon *et al.* 2013b)

Mursi declared Taramud and its demands to be 'absurd and uncon-stitutional' (ICG 2013: 3). The Brotherhood called rallies to support its president – most much smaller than those opposing him. Many activists hostile to Mursi said they were making 'a second revolution', taking up the slogan of Tamarud – 'Irhal' ('Go') – the same demand that had been placed upon Mubarak in January 2011. Following the 30 June protests, al-Sisi gave the president 48 hours to accept the 'people's demands' – early presidential elections – or, he said, the armed forces would impose their own 'roadmap'. Mursi refused and on 3 July officials informed him that he was no longer the president. He was taken from the presidential palace and held incommunicado at a secret location: three weeks later, he was charged with espionage. Al-Sisi meanwhile broadcast on television, asserting that although the armed forces had no intention of entering political life, they would 'never turn a blind eye to the aspirations of the Egyptian people' (*Ahram Online* 2013b). He suspended the constitution, directed the head of the High Constitutional Court (HCC) to run the country until a new president was elected, and appointed a new government. The broadcast was followed by statements from the shaikh of Al-Azhar, the Coptic Pope and Mohamed ElBaradei, who had been authorised by the NSF to speak on its behalf. 'I hope that this plan [of al-Sisi] will be a starting point for a new beginning for the January 25 revolution', said ElBaradei (*Ahram Online* 2013b). Meanwhile Tamarud called for further demonstrations to support the army and Hamdeen Sabbahi appealed to all Egyptians to rally in the streets as an expression of the 'success of the revolution' (Haddon *et al.* 2013c).

Mohamed El-Beltagy, deputy head of the FJP, declared: 'This is nothing short of a coup. [It is] a coup against legitimacy, against the will of the people, against the ballot box and the democratically approved constitution' (Haddon *et al.* 2013c). Al-Sisi urged 'honourable, faithful Egyptians' to demonstrate again with the aim of providing him with a 'mandate to confront violence and potential terrorism' and on 26 July there were further huge rallies dominated by the slogan 'the army, the police and the people are one hand'. The NSF mobilised enthusiastically: a handful of organisations refused to participate, including the Wasat Party, the 6 April movement and the Revolutionary Socialists. The latter, dissenting from mainstream opinions on the left, argued:

Not in our name! The Brotherhood was overthrown to deepen the revolution, not to support the regime. Whatever crimes the Brotherhood has committed against the people and against the Copts in defense of its power in the name of religion, we do not give Al-Sisi our authority. We will not go into the streets on Friday offering a blank cheque to commit massacre [...] [the army] wants a popular mobilisation behind it in order to increase the cohesion of the state and the ruling class behind its leadership. It wants to wipe out one of the most important features of the revolution so far, which is the masses' consciousness of the repressive role of the state apparatus and its intense hostility towards them. It wants to make true the lie that 'the army, the police and the people are one hand' [...] They want to finish off the revolution, and they will use [the excuse of] the Brotherhood to do it [...] The crimes that Morsi committed, he committed with the military, the police and Mubarak's state. They should all be tried together.

(Revolutionary Socialists 2013)

Arguing that he now had popular legitimacy to act in the national interest, al-Sisi ordered the arrest of key figures of the Brotherhood such as Deputy Guide Khairat al-Shatir, former Guide Mohamed Akef and FJP President Saad el-Katatni, and pro-Islamist broadcasting channels were shut down. When Brotherhood supporters refused to disperse from protests at Rab'a al-Adawiya Square and Nahda Square in Cairo, they were attacked over several days with unprecedented violence: at least 1,000 people died in the biggest state-sponsored killings in modern Egyptian history. After collecting testimony from protesters, doctors, journalists and local residents, Human Rights Watch concluded that the security forces had opened fire on protesters at Rab'a using live ammunition, with snipers firing from armoured personnel carriers and helicopters (HRW 2014: 1). The government (appointed by al-Sisi) had anticipated and planned for the deaths of thousands of protesters, said Human Rights Watch: it had supervised killings that 'likely amounted to crimes against humanity' (HRW 2014: 1). In the weeks that followed, said Amnesty International, security forces enjoyed 'a mandate for repression', attacking Islamists in the streets and on campus, and seizing and incarcerating thousands of people among whom many 'disappeared' into interrogation centres and prisons made notorious during the Mubarak era (Amnesty International 2014: 27). Sectarian conflict flared as Islamists and unidentified gangs targeted churches and properties owned by Christians, whom some Brotherhood supporters associated with the military offensive. Amnesty International noted that 'security forces stood idly by' (2014: 7).

Not just 'a coup'

In mid-August, the armed forces command imposed a State of Emergency in order to confront 'danger due to deliberate sabotage, and attacks on public and private buildings and the loss of life by extremist groups' (*Al Jazeera* 2013). The 'groups' in question were members and supporters of the Brotherhood, almost without exception unarmed and largely helpless in the face of military repression. At the same time, curfews were imposed in Cairo and most large population centres – measures familiar from military coups launched in many states worldwide. The developments in Egypt in 2013 differed, however, in being part of a project in which coercive institutions of the state were part of a coalition of political actors among which key players were bent upon erasure of an insurgent movement.

Al-Sisi's deposition of Mursi and his offensive on the Brotherhood were only part of a complex project in which the armed forces sought to restore the structures, practices and ideological resources of the Mubarak order. In an early analysis Adam Shatz (2013) identified key developments: 'The triumph of the counter-revolution has been obvious for a while,' he suggested, but most of Egypt's revolutionaries had preferred to deny it and some had actively colluded in the process, 'telling themselves that they were allying themselves with the army only in order to defend the revolution'. The involvement of organisations and political figures who had emerged from the revolutionary process was decisive in facilitating active support for the military. This was reflected in the composition of al-Sisi's new government. Mohamed ElBaradei, founder of the Destour Party, became deputy president; Hossam Eissa, a Nasserist and also a founding member of Destour, became minister of higher education; Hazem al-Beblawi, of the reformist Egyptian Social Democratic Party (EDSP), became prime minister; Ziad Bahaa El-Din, also of the EDSP, became deputy prime minister. Most strikingly, Kemal Abu-Eita, a member of the Popular Current Party – a Nasserist and key figure in the independent trade union movement – became minister of manpower. For a decade, Abu-Eita had been a key figure in advancing opposition to the Mubarak regime. He had participated in the Palestinian solidarity movement, in protests against the war in Iraq, in Kifaya, and most importantly in workers' struggles, as founder and effective leader of the Real Estate Tax Authority Union, Egypt's first independent union for 60 years. As a Nasserist and a prominent member of the Karama (Dignity) Party, he was a close associate of Hamdeen Sabbahi, one of the few independent MPs of the Mubarak era and a thorn in the side of the old regime.

Abu-Eita's journey from the picket line to the ministerial office – a move overnight from poacher to gamekeeper – was unthinkable without Sabbahi's support for the armed forces. As the most prominent radical in national politics, Sabbahi now gave unqualified backing to al-Sisi. Confirming in the summer of 2013 that he had been in extended talks with the military command, he insisted that the main obstacle to change in Egypt came from the 'terrorism' of the Muslim Brotherhood and that all political currents should unify with the armed forces against this existential threat (*Ahram Online* 2013b). His comrade-in-arms Abu-Eita accordingly joined al-Sisi's cabinet, resigning from his position as president of the EFITU. In his first public statement in office, the minister insisted that workers should abandon strikes in favour of a 'period of national reconstruction'. Karam Saber, Director of the Land Center for Human Rights spoke for many revolutionary activists and industrial militants astonished by the move: Abu-Eita had become part of a government, he said, 'which clearly sides with the interests of businessmen, investors and security forces' (Charbel 2013b).

The new ministers were soon associated with mass killings. Assaults on Brotherhood supporters in Cairo in August 2013 greatly exceeded in ferocity the most severe attacks on protestors during episodes such as those at Maspero and Mohamed Mahmoud. Most members of the Cabinet remained silent: only ElBaradei dissented, resigning his post and declaring, 'I cannot bear the responsibility for one drop of blood' (Fleishman 2013). Sabbahi continued to insist: 'the army and police are patriotic state institutions' (*Ahram Online* 2013b). His lieutenant Abu-Eita remained in his post as troops attacked protestors, imposed night-time curfews (shooting on sight after midnight), seized 'suspects' arbitrarily, and consigned thousands of people to prison.

Conspiracies

In December 2013, the government designated the Brotherhood a terrorist organisation and froze the assets of over a thousand affiliated charities. Mursi was charged with inciting violence and sent for trial on charges that carried a capital sentence. At the same time, Egypt's Court of Cassation overturned the conviction of Husni Mubarak for his role in multiple killings during the uprising of 2011; guilty verdicts on other senior officials were also reversed and army generals who had played a key role in assaults on the Brotherhood were quietly retired from public life. Activists who questioned al-Sisi's agenda were seized, independent media closed and most public gatherings and demonstrations prohibited. Police were licensed to attack protesters and the judiciary directed to punish them with long sentences. Among those jailed for allegedly breaking a new law on public assembly were Ahmed Maher, one of the founders of the 6 April Youth Movement; Ala' Abdel-Fattah, a prominent blogger and activist; and Mahinour El-Masry, a lawyer and member of the No to Military Trials Group and of the Revolutionary Socialists. According to Mohamed, a journalist who had reported on events throughout the revolution, 'Everything seemed to be turned upside down. We had managed to get Mubarak and the others to trial – now those who wanted justice and accountability like Ahmed [Maher] and Ala' [Abdel-Fattah] were being sent to the courts.'[10]

Economic pressures on the al-Sisi government had meanwhile diminished. The *New York Times* noted an 'apparently miraculous end' to crippling energy shortages; it speculated that power cuts and queues for gasoline, diesel and cooking gas had earlier been engineered by officials in order to generalise a sense of crisis and to focus hostility on Mursi and the Brotherhood (Hubbard and Fitzpatrick 2013). Within days of the July coup, the government's foreign exchange worries also lessened after it received $12 billion in aid from states of the Gulf: $5 billion from Saudi Arabia, $3 billion from the United Arab Emirates and $4 billion from Kuwait (MacDonald and El Baltaji 2013). The Brotherhood saw confirmation in these developments of international conspiracies against Egypt and Islam, organised variously by the United States, Israel, the Arab Gulf states and Iran (Abu Amer 2013). There was soon evidence that US strategists had indeed worked for months to support opposition figures prepared to remove Mursi. Citing material collected by academics in the United States, *Al Jazeera* proposed that American funding in the form of 'democracy assistance' had been directed to 'a coterie of [Egyptian] opposition politicians' who had worked to topple Mursi (Mekay 2013). Federal documents showed that groups supported by the US State Department sent funds to organisations in Egypt run by senior members of anti-Mursi political parties 'who double[d] as NGO activists' (Mekay 2013). Among organisations implicated by *Al Jazeera* were the Destour Party, the Reform and Development Party, and the Haya ('Life') Party (Mekay 2013).

The United States had long-standing links to core institutions of the Egyptian state. Since 1977, it had invested over $60 billion in the armed forces and security agencies, most in the form of equipment and training (Sharp 2007: 27–29). US officials enjoyed close relations with key figures of the armed forces, including senior officers among whom most had been trained in US military academies (in the case of al-Sisi at the United States Army War College). They worked closely with Egypt's General Intelligence Service, headed under Mubarak by Omar Suleiman, facilitator in Egypt for US programmes of extraordinary rendition – the kidnap and extra-legal transfer of 'suspects' for torture and interrogation (Hejjar 2011). The Central Intelligence Agency (CIA) maintained a key regional centre in Cairo, where Suleiman – appointed vice-president by Husni Mubarak shortly before the latter's fall in February 2011 – was often identified as the agency's 'main man' (Hejjar 2011). The United States had specific economic and political interests in Egypt and good reason to support the military intervention in July 2013. The coup and the events that followed were, however, home-made.

Co-optation

The counter-revolution launched in 2013 was a sophisticated initiative that had both institutional and ideological dimensions. Since the 1950s, the armed forces had enjoyed a disproportionate share of national economic resources, justified continuously by the need to prepare for war. After the 1973 conflict with Israel they did not, however, engage in state-on-state warfare; major mobilisations took place in relation to domestic crises, with offensives on protestors and strikers in 1977 and 1984, and against the CSF mutiny of 1986. Relations between the armed forces and the security apparatus were complex and changed as factions within the coercive institutions both collaborated and competed (Kandil 2012). In 2011, both the security agencies and the Muslim Brotherhood failed to contain the revolutionary movement. For the first time since the early years of the Nasser era, the armed forces were exposed to a sustained mass movement with radical aspirations.

The military command sought new allies by means of co-optation. This approach had been pioneered in Egypt by the British under a system of 'liberal constitutionalism' first employed in the 1920s. Following practices developed across the British Empire, military authorities encouraged consolidation of a local elite that mediated relations with the wider society (Maghraoui 2006). Nasser implemented a similar approach: during the 1950s he experimented with 'mobilisations' designed to draw workers' leaders and key figures of the left and of the Islamist movement behind the regime. According to Nasser's Free Officer colleague Ali Sabri, the Liberation Rally – the first such initiative – had 'the primary and basic goal [of] destruction of the political organisations opposing the revolution [i.e. the military regime]' (Baker 1978: 94). It was followed by the National Union and eventually by the Arab Socialist Union (ASU), which successfully incorporated trade unions and the communist movement into the apparatus of state (see Chapter 6). Under both Nasser and Sadat, the ASU operated as a 'collaboration movement' in which the leaders of participant groups (unions, professional syndicates, peasant associations) subordinated their particular claims to national interests that the regime claimed to represent (Hinnebusch 1985: 20). In the 1960s, leaders of the Egyptian Communist Party joined the ASU on the basis of the latter's radical nationalist agenda. Communist orthodoxy of the Stalinist era dictated a search for progressive national allies and accordingly, when Sadat reformed the Union in the 1970s, the left argued that it should take the form of a 'National Front'. The left-wing coalition or 'rally' that emerged in the form of Tagammu' attracted former communists, Nasserists and Arab nationalists: it saw its key task as the 'completion of the national-democratic revolution' (Hinnebusch 1985: 190). In 2013, al-Sisi's appeal for national unity also drew liberal reformers, social democrats and radical nationalists behind the military command.

Dunne points to striking parallels in the efforts of Nasser and al-Sisi to mobilise support, most importantly in appeals to 'a certain brand of pro-military, populist, anti-foreign nationalist sentiment' (2015: 5). In each case, she suggests, the military insisted that it must take extreme measures, seizing power from unpopular civilian rulers, to save the nation from the threat of chaos (Dunne 2015: 5). Both leaders also insisted that regime change constituted a 'revolution' that enacted the will of the people. Although, as we shall see in Chapter 10, al-Sisi differed sharply from Nasser in other respects, he successfully mobilised the latter's strategy and his legacy as a means of co-opting the left. In 2013 the military command, the security and intelligence agencies, business interests and the NSF worked to build a movement with the potential to evict Mursi and marginalise the Brotherhood. The parties of the NSF played a key role, providing 'progressive' credentials for the campaign and supplying some of their most prominent members to a government soon engaged in assaulting the mass movement.

Sectarianism and patriarchy

Leading religious figures also endorsed the coup. Of special significance was the support of the Coptic Orthodox Church. Pope Shenouda III had cultivated relations with the Mubarak regime, despite the latter's proven involvement in sectarian attacks on churches and Christian properties. In January 2011, he attempted to prevent Christians joining early protests against the president. Young Copts nonetheless participated in large numbers in rallies and marches: one feature of public mobilisations during 2011 was the prominence of symbols of Muslim–Christian unity, which soon appeared in street art and graffiti, and when Coptic youth were killed by security forces, they were celebrated equally as martyrs to the revolutionary cause.[11] Jason Brownlee comments that: 'The model of Tahrir showed once more how national solidarity trumped cynical attempts to stir discord along religious lines' (2013).

The participation of young Christians contributed to the democratic and secular character of the uprising, inhibiting efforts to divide the movement on sectarian lines. In 2012, however, election of Mohamed Mursi as president alarmed many Christians, especially those of the older generation who had less engagement with the popular movement. Sectarian attacks increased, with many allegations of involvement by members of the Muslim Brotherhood, security agencies and the baltagiyya.[12] Influential Christians, notably Naguib Sawiris, played a key role in backing Tamarud and in July 2013 Pope Tawadros II (who had succeeded Shenouda in 2012) appeared alongside al-Sisi to endorse military takeover. Al-Sisi pledged himself to the defence of religious freedoms, declaring for Muslim–Christian unity and identifying the Brotherhood as the chief enemy of national unity. When attacks on churches and Christian properties continued, however, police and officials stood aside. In a detailed assessment of the violence and discrimination against Christians before and after the coup, Brownlee (2013) concludes that al-Sisi's pledges to interfaith unity amounted to 'cosmetic gestures' – instrumental efforts to win Christian backing for an assault on the Islamists. As the Mubarak era demonstrated, he observes, state repression of Islamists does not necessarily protect Copts: on the contrary, officials are just as likely to pit the country's faith communities against one another, operating through 'a religious corporatism that treats Copts as members of the Church but not the nation' (Brownlee 2013).

The counter-revolutionary alliance organised by al-Sisi purposefully stimulated fears of Coptic oppression with the aim of mobilising Christians against the Brotherhood *and* against the popular movement. The same approach was pursued in relation to women. For years before the events of 2011 women had been prominent in movements of protest and in rising workers' struggles, often setting the pace in relation to their male counterparts. The uprising against Mubarak engaged millions of women in public protest – many testimonies of female activists record unprecedentedly high levels of involvement, including in mass rallies and marches, battles with police and the *baltagiyya*, local committees and community actions, and media and cultural initiatives.[13] Strikes undertaken throughout 2011–13 included very large numbers of women workers who in some cases constituted a majority of participants. The combined effect was to challenge deeply embedded gender relations, even if it did not rupture them.[14] These developments were particularly threatening to the machinery of state and its culture of patriarchal authority. Schenker describes how a process of state construction along familial lines had allocated women the status of 'juvenile dependency':

> Within Mubarak Country's model of the loving, stable family, men had to be honourable protectors and providers; women were always a wife, a mother, or a wife and a mother-to-be. Those operating outside this familial context, and who refused to couch their demands in

the manner of a child beseeching a parent, were often presented as an eccentric menace; in this arena, women are fallen and little more than prostitutes.

(Schenker 2016: 129)

During 2012 women engaging in public protest were more and more likely to face systematic sexual violence at the hands of the *baltagiyya* and uniformed police – as during the 'blue bra' assaults (see Chapter 4). Female demonstrators were seized and tortured by both male and female assailants, some subjected to intrusive 'virginity tests', a procedure defended at the time by an increasingly important senior officer, General Abdel-Fattah al-Sisi.[15]

The coup of July 2013 was followed by focused efforts to present al-Sisi in the role of father of the nation and protector of female integrity. He declared that the armed forces would defend women against the Muslim Brotherhood, said to be determined to enforce veiling and segregation. His speeches, notes Rabie, addressed women as 'housewives, mothers and sisters [...] he generally refuses to acknowledge that they are political players in society, as part of the work force, for example' (2014). Invoking models of the nation as a family under paternal direction, and women as virtuous, obedient and supplicant, al-Sisi used gender relations as part of a sustained campaign to return Egypt to the values and practices of the Mubarak era. The counter-revolutionary mobilisation as a whole, observes Sameh Naguib, was based on 'fear, conservatism, patriarchy, national chauvinism, and sectarian politics' (2016).

10

Counter-Revolution and Beyond

Abdel-Fattah al-Sisi had risen 'without trace'. An apparently bland career soldier, he was little known to most Egyptians until appointed by Mohamed Mursi in 2012 as head of the armed forces and minister of defence. Following the coup of July 2013, public and private media joined in a sustained campaign to present him as a national hero who had rescued the country from terrorism, chaos and foreign plots. His photograph appeared in government offices; in cafés and stores across the country where images of Nasser, Sadat and Mubarak had once been prominent; and on T-shirts, banners, Ramadan lanterns, and even chocolates and cakes. Newspapers carried laudatory accounts of his deeds and his vision for Egypt. Yasser Rizq, editor of *Al-Masry Al-Youm* (owned by billionaire Naguib Sawiris) set the tone in July 2013, writing that he was 'enthralled by the personality of this young leader [...] calm, cultured, religious, level-headed, articulate and full of pride for Egyptian nationalism and the deep-rooted military establishment' (Rizq 2013).

Amid a torrent of praise, Lubna Abdel-Aziz (also the name of a celebrated Egyptian actress of the 1950s) addressed efforts to promote a man whose face suddenly was everywhere and whose name was said to 'light up the darkness':

He stands straight and tall, impeccably attired and starched from head to toe. His freshly washed countenance and youthful zeal shield a Herculean strength and nerves of steel. He wears the feathers of a dove but has the piercing eyes of a hawk. During our thousand days of darkness, dozens of potential leaders pranced and boasted, to no avail. The leader of the people should combine a love of country, a deep faith in God and the desire to serve the nation's will [...]

He was called upon at a supreme moment in history; a kind of mysterious rendez-vous with destiny. He was a hero like no other!

He aroused attention without exhausting it. Nothing that touched the common run of mortals made any impression on him. All in all, he is but a common man, with an almost aristocratic aura of a nobleman [...] Composed and cool, Al-Sisi is everyman's man, with a sort of serene majesty on his brow [...] He will lead us to victory and never renounce the struggle, and we will be right there at his side.

(Abdel-Aziz 2013)

For some activists of the revolutionary movement the images of al-Sisi were both absurd and threatening. Maha, an academic who had been deeply involved in campus campaigns since 2011, said:

Here's another hero in uniform, with gold braid and medals. It's just a couple of years since we got rid of the last one! Now we can be sure that this man wants to bring back everything that the martyrs of the revolution opposed in struggles to change our society.[1]

Many Egyptians initially rallied to al-Sisi however. His promises of order and stability, and willingness to punish the Muslim Brotherhood for all manner of crimes, real and imagined, were greeted with relief by those associated with the armed forces and other agencies of the state, by the *feloul* networks, by business, by much of the middle class and by activists incensed by Mursi's arrogance and partisan policies. In December 2013, hundreds of thousands of Egyptians voted for al-Sisi as *Time* magazine's Person of the Year.[2]

Under al-Sisi's direction, police and CSF units returned to the streets, re-imposing the restrictions of the Mubarak era. City squares were again in possession of the state; streets that had become informal markets were cleared and restored to traffic; revolutionary graffiti and artworks were whitewashed to remove evidence of political upheaval. The media was placed on warning. Tamer, a journalist at an online newspaper that had gained an international reputation for accurate reporting and informed analysis, described the impact of the new regime:

Most of the space that had opened up to journalists – not just after the 25 January revolution but in the years preceding it – was closed. Some editors who'd pioneered a new sort of journalism, especially by encouraging 'citizen journalists', were thrown out of their jobs. We came to work not knowing if we'd be arrested that day. It wasn't just back to the Mubarak days – it was much worse.[3]

Industrial action declined – over six months from July 2013 the number of disputes decreased by some 60 per cent (El-Fiqi 2013). In part this was an outcome of new State of Emergency powers involving curfews and threats of arbitrary arrest; at the same time, it reflected the disorientation in the workplaces and unions produced by a crisis of the entire opposition, including the participation in government of the former president of the EFITU Kemal Abu-Eita, now calling for industrial peace and national unity. Six months after the coup labour journalist Mona El-Fiqi speculated that: 'the labour movements themselves now seem to have been tamed by the interim government' (El-Fiqi 2013).

A 'new Nasser'

Al-Sisi's discourse was that of conservative nationalism: an emphasis on national unity, on collective sacrifice for the national interest, and on vigilance against internal and external threat: he continuously pronounced that '*Misr lan tasqut*' ('Egypt will not fall'). He identified diverse enemies including terrorists, the Muslim Brotherhood, Israel, Iran, the United States, Hamas and Hezbollah; their malign intentions, he said, required a strong state and assertive measures. In January 2014, he obtained overwhelming approval in a referendum for a new constitution that confirmed the independence and power of the armed forces as guardian of national interests. Tens of thousands of Egyptians alleged to threaten the state were already in prison. The judiciary, which for decades had contained pockets of independence, was purged of independent minds and soon produced court rulings that exceeded the most punitive sentences of the Mubarak era. Reviewing the performance of the courts a year after the coup, Cabeza and Siegalbaum saw an 'increasingly fantastic' scenario:

> Scores of activists have been arrested for mathematically impossible crimes. Egyptian citizens with no political affiliation have been imprisoned for rioting and political protests they did not attend. Random civilians have been arrested as Muslim Brotherhood conspirators.
>
> (Cabeza and Siegalbaum 2014)

Hundreds of leading members of the Brotherhood, including Mohamed Mursi and Mohamed Badie, were sentenced to death. In a trial in the southern city of Minya the presiding judge, Sa'ed Yusef Sabri (widely known as *al-jazzar*, 'the Butcher'), passed 683 death sentences on local men alleged to be violent activists – over 500 sentences in the same case were issued *in absentia*. In a trial that served to highlight the regime's fixation with foreign enemies, three staff members of the *Al Jazeera* English bureau based in Cairo were sentenced to between seven and ten years' imprisonment on charges that included aiding the Muslim Brotherhood and reporting 'false' news.[4] Courts issued banning orders on the 6 April Youth Movement and the FJP, and the Ministry of Social Solidarity gave NGOs a 45-day deadline to register under a repressive Law on Associations, passed in the Mubarak era, warning ominously that it would hold accountable all those that failed to conform. Thousands of people were seized indiscriminately by the security services. In January 2014, the Interior Minister Mohamed Ibrahim declared:

> Every Friday, no less than 500 to 600 [pro-Mursi protesters] get arrested [...] Before we used to wait until [their assembly] is no longer peaceful, now we confront [their protests] as soon as they gather [...] some run, those we can catch, we catch.
>
> (HRW 2014)

Some detainees underwent 'enforced disappearance' and were held in secret detention, including at Al Azouly Prison, a unit within the Al Galaa military camp in Ismailia: public prosecutors told families of the disappeared that they had no jurisdiction over military prisons (Amnesty International 2015: 139). Meanwhile none of those responsible for the mass killings at Rab'a al-Adawiya and al-Nahda Squares in August 2013 were brought to trial and charges against Husni Mubarak, his interior minister and senior security officers for their role in the killings in 2011 were finally dismissed.

It was in these circumstances that al-Sisi was canvassed for the presidency as a candidate worthy of the mantle of Gamal Abdel-Nasser. Hoda Abdel-Nasser, daughter of the former president, wrote an open letter to the general (soon promoted to field-marshal) that was given wide press coverage:

We [Egyptians] toppled an unjust regime under which people had suffered from need, corruption, and oppression. We then waited for a leader who embodied the revolution so that the people could support him [...] Do you know that you achieved in less than two months what politicians cannot achieve in decades? [...] What I am asking is that you get involved in politics and stand for the presidential elections. Rest assured that the 30 million Egyptians who were happy and surprised on 26 July will cast their ballots for you. It is principles that make leaders. [...] You have overwhelming support. Look at the opposition. It's disassembled [sic]. Its leaders are not on your level in this great moment Egypt is currently witnessing [...] I personally call on you to step forward and take responsibility for the destiny that is yours [...] may God empower you for the sake of our beloved Egypt.

(Abdel-Nasser 2013)

Posters with juxtaposed images of Nasser and al-Sisi had appeared on the 30 June 2013 demonstration called by Tamarud and at subsequent rallies organised by al-Sisi to support his offensive against the Brotherhood; a host of articles in the national press had since identified al-Sisi closely with the former president. In May 2014, al-Sisi appeared in his first television interview to declare: 'I wish I was like Nasser. Nasser was not for Egyptians just a portrait on walls but a photo [image] and voice carved in their hearts' (*Ahram Online* 2014a). He also revealed that that he had decided to run for president when he detected an effort to 'destroy the state' that forced him to heed the calls of the people (*Ahram Online* 2014b). In a presidential election held in May 2014, al-Sisi received 96.9 per cent of the vote (on a modest turnout) – the remainder going to his sole challenger, Hamdeen Sabbahi, who had reappeared as a cautious critic of the new regime. Al-Sisi had been supported by almost the entire non-Islamist opposition, including liberal capitalists, the Wafd Party, the 'official' left (Tagammu'), the Nasserists and Tamarud. All but the most intransigent political currents organised in the Path of the Revolution Front ('the Revolutionaries', established in September 2013)[5] had fallen into line behind al-Sisi and the military command. The NSF was in disarray. Al-Sisi ignored its leaders, refusing to meet them and dismissing their proposals for electoral reform. When he eventually approved changes to the electoral law, parties of the NSF were sidelined by a system of independent lists that reinstated clandestine alliances of the Mubarak era.

NSF leaders who had taken positions in al-Sisi's post-coup government soon left office. First to go in February 2014 was Deputy Prime Minister Baha El-Din, hinting that he had finally had enough of the repression. In March the whole Cabinet, including Prime Minister Hazem el-Beblawi, was forced to stand down. Ministers had been exposed by 'mounting criticism from media and the public', said Farid Zahran of the ESDP, which had supplied members for key Cabinet posts (Al-Tawy 2014). Al-Sisi promptly appointed a new administration under Ibrahim Mehleb (formerly a member of Mubarak's NDP) that included businessmen and technocrats likely to be less squeamish about his policies. At the same time Tamarud, now greatly reduced in influence, split amid acrimonious exchanges among leading members. Mohamed Fawzi, leader of the breakaway faction Tamarud 2 Get Liberated, said that as members of the movement observed the outcomes of the July 2013 coup, many changed their attitude to al-Sisi: 'We wanted the army to help us oust Mursi, not take over power itself,' he said. 'The army's role is to protect and guard the state, not to rule [...] We are seeing a return of the police state, but with new faces' (Saleh 2014). The liberals, reformists and nationalists (including young activists of Tamarud) who had served as allies of the military command during the July coup were expendable: according to Farid Zahran of the ESDP, the '30 June alliance' was all but over (Al-Tawy 2014).

Nationalisms old and new

On taking up his ministerial position in July 2013, the EFITU leader Kemal Abu-Eita had admitted: 'This may spell political suicide for me' (Charbel 2013b). Within six months he had been ejected from office: at the same time, his former members were engaged in new industrial actions. The strike wave of early 2014 renewed labour struggles across the country, involving doctors, pharmacists, public transport employees, post office employees, workers in the textile industry and several other state-owned enterprises; it also once again engaged low-ranking police officers. Prime Minister Mehleb urged, unsuccessfully: 'Stop all kinds of sit-ins, protests and strikes. Let us start building the nation' (Hendaway 2014). The scale and persistence of these disputes surprised even experienced activists of the revolutionary left. 'Things were at a low ebb', says Reem, an activist in Cairo:

> After the July coup al-Sisi attacked the movement on many fronts. But he was not confident enough to assault the workplaces and it's there that people have been able to defend their interests and show how to maintain the momentum of the movement.[6]

Police had not been used in frontal assaults on striking workers since events in Mehalla in 2008 played a key role in fusing workers' struggles with wider calls for change. Al-Sisi attempted to exert pressure through the official trade union federation, the ETUF, which despite the emergence of independent unions remained intact in many large workplaces. In 2014, he issued a presidential decree extending the tenure of state-appointed officials of the federation, making the ETUF an instrument of the ministry of manpower. In April 2015, the Supreme Administrative Court ruled that strikes were illegal and that striking workers in the public sector could be dismissed and forced into retirement. A few days later, the ETUF presented al-Sisi with a 'Labour Honour Code' to mark Labour Day, 1 May. It asserted: 'Egypt's workers reject striking and confirm their commitment to social dialogue with the government and business owners as a mechanism to achieve social justice and stability' (Galal 2015).

Strikes continued: in August 2015 hundreds of government employees demonstrated in Cairo – the first major workers' protest in the city since the coup of 2013. Days later, a bitter dispute involving the lower ranks of the police resulted in strikes in several cities of the Delta and in October 2015 a dispute of symbolic importance engaged some 20,000 workers at textile mills in Mehalla al-Kubra and Kafr al-Dawwar who maintained a lengthy strike to demand unpaid bonuses. Unlike activists attempting to protest in the streets, they did not meet overwhelming force on the part of the CSF.[7]

Continuing industrial struggles reflected the serious problems of the regime's central project – the attempt to stabilise Egyptian capitalism in its neo-liberal mode. Al-Sisi had been promoted as a Nasser for the twenty-first century – a strong leader around whom the nation could unite to bring security, stability and prosperity. Media campaigns drew continuously on imagery of the Nasser period and on popular memory of the armed forces as champions of anti-colonialism who contested Egypt's enemies abroad and initiated economic and social reform at home. After a hesitant start, Nasser had pursued a coherent policy of anti-imperialism and an economic strategy consistent with agendas for change in many states of the post-colonial era. He had initiated land reform, vast infrastructural projects and welfare programmes that provided universal health care and free education, obtaining resources by means of nationalising foreign holdings and significant areas of Egyptian private capital. Nasser had been a developmentalist, using the machinery of state to pursue policies of redistribution: limited and flawed, these nonetheless benefited millions of Egyptians. Al-Sisi inherited a different agenda, to which he was wholly committed. Sadat and Mubarak had dismantled the developmental state, restored private capital, directed public resources into private hands, and integrated Egypt into a regional economic system focused upon the neo-liberal agenda. The uprising of 2011 gave testimony to the impact of their policies upon the mass of people – policies that al-Sisi proposed to pursue in an era of world crisis, austerity and insecurity.

These problems were intensified by the discourse of national redemption encouraged by the president and his supporters. Nasser had asserted a commitment to national development as a public good; he had also drawn on traditions of anti-colonial struggle, on identification with the Palestinian cause, on pan-Arabism and on solidarities across the 'Third' world. Notwithstanding his authoritarianism and eventual decline, Nasser's radical nationalism retained a powerful appeal and had been embedded in official Egyptian history and in popular memory. Al-Sisi attempted to draw on these traditions but his own conservative nationalism presented a sharp contrast in terms both of meaning and outcomes. Amr Aly (2014) addresses the contradictions: conservative nationalism, he observes, has its own limitations,

> Whereas it may prove to be a valuable tool for the newly-established [al-Sisi] regime in the short-term, it is not likely to furnish a strong ideological platform adequate enough for the longer-term process of re-establishing political authority and regaining legitimacy [...] conservative Egyptian nationalism cannot feed for too long on solely anti-Islamist overtones or anti-Arab and anti-Palestinian undertones. It will prove more and more difficult to claim its descent from earlier,

more established and more legitimate historical versions of Egyptian nationalism [...] the current version of conservative nationalism is at its heart pro-capitalist and in harmony with neo-liberalism.
(Aly 2014)

The key problem for al-Sisi, Aly suggests, is that of cultivating a broad social alliance with capacities to overcome the crisis of legitimacy that has led to recent political upheavals. Conservative nationalism, he concludes, 'does not seem to serve that end' (Aly 2014).

By 2015, parties with narrow nationalist agendas monopolised the electoral arena. They were clustered in a number of multi-party lists dominated by military and business interests and strongly supportive of al-Sisi. The voting system gave overwhelming influence to 'independent' candidates, reinstating the practices of the Mubarak era when candidates bought votes or used their influence as landowners, employers or local officials to secure support. More than 2,000 members of Mubarak's disbanded NDP were candidates and included NDP members earlier imprisoned for corruption, such as the former party chairman Ahmed 'Izz, or for supplying *baltagiyya* to attack protestors during the uprising of 2011 (Saleh 2015). When the delayed parliamentary elections were eventually held in October and November 2015, the turnout of 10 per cent was lower than on any occasion since the fall of Mubarak; even the pro-business daily *Al-Mal* headlined, 'An election without voters' (Noueihed 2015). The new parliament was dominated by al-Sisi loyalists and *feloul* who had repositioned themselves within the new party lists, notably the two largest groupings Love of Egypt and Call of Egypt. These were stridently nationalist – like al-Sisi they saw threats at home and abroad, dangers presented by 'foreign hands' and the need for strong centralised leadership. The Islamist opposition was absent, the Brotherhood having been banned and only the pro-Sisi Salafis of the Nour Party permitted to nominate candidates. A number of liberal and reformist parties had boycotted the election: those who participated gathered a mere handful of seats.

The movement and the state

George Ishak, a founder of Kifaya who had later backed the military coup, observed that under al-Sisi Egypt had become 'politics free'

(Dunne 2015: 1). The streets, the media and the electoral process were once again under regime control. Democratic space had been reoccupied by the state and the process of 'transition' anticipated by governments in Europe and North America, by think-tanks and by many academics, had failed to materialise. Liberal capitalist parties had been unsuccessful in their efforts to establish popular constituencies, advancing only when al-Sisi imposed an electoral system rigged in their favour in which liberal-reformists and social democrats had been driven to the margins. Politics in the wider sense of collective engagement in both formal and informal settings had not been stifled, however, as millions of people debated the revolution, their experiences and the implications.

Bayat observes that revolutions 'follow their own intriguing logic': they are subject to a complex mix of 'structural, international, coincidental and psychological factors' (2013: 2). We often analyse revolutions in retrospect, he adds, rarely engaging in processes that are expected or desired, 'for revolutions are never predictable' (Bayat 2013: 2). The Egyptian movement was tumultuous, full of creative energy expressed in political and social initiatives and in a surge of cultural activity. Participants were involved in a continuing process of discovery that could be illuminating and also frustrating and distressing. What were the strengths and weaknesses of the popular movement? How had it been suppressed? What might have been achieved? Would mass struggles resume? What was to be done?

Discussions were pursued intensively in Egypt; at the same time, the global impact of revolution and counter-revolution carried key debates into wider activist networks and into academic exchanges. A number of closely connected issues were of special importance: the nature of the state; the experiences of 'the streets' and of the workers' movement; the question of Islamism; and the legacies of the left.

The Egyptian state survived the upheaval that began in January 2011 – but with difficulty. Counter-revolution supervised by the military command gave testimony to the impacts of the popular movement. Months in preparation, mobilised with sophistication and ultimately with extreme violence, al-Sisi's project was evidence of the energy and resources required to re-establish the old order. The institutions of coercion consolidated over decades had been seriously affected by 'the forcible entry of the masses' into Egyptian politics (see Chapter 1): those intent on restoring the state were prepared to use all means to exclude them. The counter-revolution raised challenging questions, especially for those anticipating that the state could be reformed or modified to serve the interests of the majority. For many activists public protest had been the means to bring a fundamental change in social relations. Sharing a vision increasingly common among radical activists worldwide during the twenty-first century, they aimed to bring change without taking power – to effect a popular insurgency that would compel the retreat of those in command of the state. Analysing social movements worldwide, Colin Barker observes how such expectations 'can [...] leave a space for a movement's opponents to reorganise their forces and restructure their domination' (Barker 2014: 21).

Over three decades global opposition to neo-liberalism has taken a 'grass-roots turn', demonstrating the impatience felt by vast numbers of people with agendas for change proposed by social democrats and partisans of Stalinist Communism, who long dominated the politics of the left. Independent currents, including autonomists, libertarians and anarchists, have proposed that the practice of mass action – the work of 'the movement' mobilised through 'the crowd' and 'the multitude'– can attain a transformation in social relations. Much debate in Egypt since the coup of 2013 has focused on the fate of the movement in the face of the state understood as integral to the capitalist order – as what Karl Marx called 'a committee for managing the common affairs of the whole bourgeoisie' (Marx and Engels 1985 [1848]: 82). How did the movement address the state and its institutions of coercion?

The movement of January–February 2011 was massive and sustained. It engaged participants in continuous collective actions and debates about their demands and aspirations. For many of those involved, the experience was profound. Reflecting on the events in Tahrir, Sawsun recalled her desire to remain there 'for ever':

> The 18 Days were the best days of my life, when unimaginable things happened: people talked together, fought together, men and women, Muslims and Christians, young and old. And we made Mubarak fall [...] I thought if we could force him to go – 'irhal!' – we could do anything. But to do it we had to be there, showing ourselves and our power.[8]

In claiming Egypt's most important public space for the revolution, activists made Tahrir symbolic not only of their aspirations but also of the lived experience of a historic struggle. Gribbon and Hawas, participant observers during the events, describe the Square as a stronghold for the movement, a home for protestors and a space in which they could create continuous displays of civil resistance:

> The sense of collective energy in the *midan* was incredible. There was no hierarchy among the protestors, and lateral connections between people required a significant degree of organization [...] services were set up and run cooperatively in a remarkable display of burgeoning participatory democracy.
>
> (Gribbon and Hawas 2012: 104)

Here the authoritarian state was challenged by a movement that appeared to have no leaders: Jean-Pierre Filiu (2011: 57) describes a 'Copernican reversal of the tides' in which the mass of people pursued change by novel means manifested in their own practice.

For some activists the events of January and February realized long-held hopes for new social relations. The experiential dimension of the events offered not only confirmation that there could be further change but also that this could deliver in a more enduring form both the values and forms of organisation encountered in the Square.

Ahmed Shokr (2011) comments that those who seized the Square in January 2011 'did not come with the intention of creating a radical utopia'; as the revolution unfolded, however, 'Tahrir was elevated from a rally site to a model for an alternative society' (Shokr 2011). For many activists the collective organisation of the streets, apparently 'spontaneous' and leaderless, was prefigurative – not merely an aspect of the moment but an experience that could be projected as means of organisation for the future. Tahrir was 'a microcosm of civil utopia' – a template for radical change and, simultaneously, a means of pursuing such change (Alexander, J.C. 2011: 344).

The model of the Egyptian streets was soon generalised globally. For Alain Badiou (2012: 33) the protests were 'riots' – a form of uninhibited mass action of such significance that they would shape a new era of upheavals worldwide. The key feature of the Egyptian movement, much celebrated by libertarian, anarchist and autonomist currents, was its 'horizontalism'. John Chalcraft identifies key characteristics:

[The] decentralized or networked form of organizing; the leaderless protest movements; the eschewal of top-down command; the deliberative, rather than representative, democracy; the emphasis on participation, creativity and consensus; the opposition to dogma and sectarianism, often associated with older generations; and new links, respectful of diversity and often youth-inspired, between formerly sharply opposed political currents.

(Chalcraft 2012)

These and many similar assessments simplified and sometimes idealised the protests of January and February 2011. They also focused on 'youth' as an undifferentiated category in which the participants were without political allegiances and preferences. As Dina Shehata (2012: 130) notes, diverse parties and movements played a key role at an early stage in the uprising. Youth coalitions that unified in demands for the fall of Mubarak soon disintegrated, however, their members focusing on political currents old and new. Youth networks were challenged by problems of mobilisation: social media and direct action had initially played a key role in bypassing constraints imposed by the state but after the deposition of Mubarak they proved inadequate, prompting activists to seek alternative means and strategies (Shehata 2012: 122–23). This exposed an acute difficulty – as Maha Abdelrahman spells out – the absence of a central organised structure for the movement 'quickly became a liability' (Abdelrahman 2014: 74).

The mass strike

A focus on youth, social media and 'the streets' led some participants and many observers abroad to assume that class and class politics were of limited or no importance in the revolutionary process. Rabab El-Mahdi (2102: 143) comments on the frequency with which this argument was heard at conferences in Europe and North America. After two weeks of mass protest in January and February 2011, the movement faced deadlock as Mubarak refused to step down; mass strikes, which within 48 hours spread nationwide, compelled his resignation, El-Mahdi insists. It was in this context, she argues, that demands for social justice became general, reflecting the wish of millions of Egyptians for 'systemic change that met their class interests in resisting exploitation' (El-Mahdi 2012: 144).

Barker and colleagues point to a reluctance among activists and academic analysts to address the role of collective workers' action in contemporary social movements, especially the place of strikes in popular revolutions (Barker *et al.* 2014: 6–7). Barker emphasises the importance of workers' initiatives in the context of an encompassing approach to the issues of class struggle (Barker 2014). Of special importance, he argues, is the relationship between specific contestations with local capital or with forces of the state and the wider social movement. Mass strikes changed the dynamic of the Egyptian uprising: they not only compelled executive action by the military command but also expanded the horizons of the movement, focusing demands for radical change. This was not a sudden development. Egypt's workers had been present as part of social movements that challenged the Mubarak order for over a decade. Writing in 2008, Joel Beinin observed that mass strikes brought a qualitative change to the culture of protest:

> [T]he workers' movement along with the demonstrations of the intel-ligentsia organized by Kifaya and other extra-parliamentary protest groups established in response to the second Palestinian intifada and the 2003 US invasion of Iraq, have inculcated a culture of protest in Egypt. This has contributed to the formation of a consciousness of citizenship and rights in a far more profound manner than anything that has happened in the arenas of party politics or non-governmental organization work.
>
> (Beinin 2009: 454)

Decisive in the initial confrontations of 2011, mass strikes generalised ideas about workplace rights, minimum incomes, security of employment, and freedom of association and of expression – all central to the democratic aspirations of the revolution. They also carried forward campaigns of *taṭhir* in which the workplace collective challenged not only corrupt bosses and bullying managers but also police and military officials, government officers and bureaucrats of the state-run unions. As Alexander and Bassiouny argue, the most significant struggles for *taṭhir* 'breached the bounds of the existing form of the state to demand changes that represent a profound challenge to the existing regime' (2014: 298–99).

The popular movement advanced most rapidly and effectively in the context of such struggles. Industrial actions, often on a mass scale, continued from February 2011 until the coup of July 2013 and beyond. Millions of workers joined new unions, obtaining rights which they had been denied for generations. Independent union federations organised across industry, including in the private sector, from which the official federation had been largely excluded. Workers were present in countless demonstrations and rallies: in major industrial cities, the events in 'the streets' were largely working-class mobilisations. During periods of intensive industrial action, strikes fused with wider public protests: the Egyptian experience reinforced arguments advanced over a century earlier by Rosa Luxemburg that mass strikes break down the separation between economic and political issues, bringing forward questions about the state and society, and advancing the prospect of fundamental change in social relations (Luxemburg 1964 [1906]).

Unions old and new

The workers' movement faced pressing problems however. Many disputes concluded with undertakings from employers to meet strikers' demands. These often went unfulfilled, so that new strikes were undertaken and new promises made without resolution, increasing the unevenness of the movement. Local campaigns for *taṭhir* similarly brought undertakings to remove corrupt or bullying managers who continued in place, producing further strikes and increasing frustration in the workforce. At the same time, some aspects of labour organisation inhibited the movement. In key areas of the public sector, the official union federation, the ETUF, retained its authority. The federation had been officially dissolved in 2011 but SCAF encouraged officials of the old order to continue as before. Tamer, a labour lawyer, identifies the problems:

> The official unions belonged to the regime; at the same time in well-organised factories or [textile] mills the workforce could elect as officials people who improved things. Also welfare funds were controlled by the union.[9] In some big workplaces such as Mehalla al Kubra [textile mill] and Helwan [steelworks] independent unions never broke through.[10]

Workers were restrained by strategies of the new unions. Independent unions were clustered in two networks: the Egyptian Federation of Independent Trade Unions (EFITU), formed in January 2011, and the Egyptian Democratic Labour Congress (EDLC), launched officially in April 2013.[11] Each federation claimed some 250 unions, some organised at the national level, many organised locally at a single enterprise. Each federation was effective in facilitating unionisation: each however favoured a model that, under the circumstances of the revolution, inhibited the most effective forms of organisation. The new federations' emphasis on internal administration and national leadership quickly became a bureaucratic obstacle. Radical activists point to what they call the 'infatuation' of union leaders with international trade union networks. The emergence of independent unions in Egypt had been tracked closely by organisations such as the International Trade Union Confederation (ITUC) and the European Trade Union Confederation (ETUC). In 2010, the national trade union federation in the USA, the AFL-CIO, presented its George Meany-Lane Kirkland Award for Human Rights jointly to Abu-Eita and Abbas. Never slow to co-opt new union leaderships, the ITUC and other international networks intensified efforts to court the Egyptian federations. Ahmed, a revolutionary activist in Cairo says: 'We can do without constant invitations to Egyptian trade unionists to attend conferences at which they will be "taught how to negotiate". We need to develop strong organisation of the rank-and-file, not to train more bureaucrats.'[12]

A related issue much discussed on the revolutionary left is the absence within the Egyptian workers' movement of independent workplace committees or councils of the type often associated with revolutionary upheavals. Democratic workplace bodies emerged as part of revolutionary movements worldwide throughout the twentieth century, notably in Russia, Spain, France, Chile, Portugal and Iran, sometimes linking workplaces with delegate committees that, in the case of Russian soviets, became bases for a co-ordinated challenge to the state. Despite the scale and continuity of workers' struggles, in Egypt such developments were sketchy. By 2013, committees had begun to emerge in some industrial centres and there were isolated attempts at local self-management.[13] Inhibited by the continuing presence of the ETUF in historic centres of struggle, and by the orientation of independent unions on different aims, these initiatives did not progress. The workers' movement remained the most intransigent and effective component of the mass movement but did not produce forms of organisation by means of which its most radical elements could pose a direct challenge to institutions of the state.

Legacies of the Left

For the first time since the 1970s, the left had a huge audience. All manner of organisations identified as 'revolutionary', aligning with the popular movement against Mubarak and with continuing efforts to bring change. Among those advancing specifically socialist agendas in the traditions of the left were new reformist parties including the Egyptian Socialist Democratic Party (ESDP) and the Socialist Popular Alliance (Tahaluf); Marxist organisations, notably the Revolutionary Socialists; and in a novel development, libertarian and anarchist groups (Galian 2015). All faced a dual problem: the impact of years of repression and of the legacy of Stalinist Communism.

The effect of Mubarak's police state, says Amir – a former member of Tagammu' – had been the 'eradication of politics', with activists of the left confined to small circles and clandestine activity. 'The dictatorship voided politics,' he observes, 'isolating those who might have made a difference. As a result, when the revolution came there was no critical mass on the left which could relate directly to the workers' movement'.[14] For decades the state had inhibited independent activity, although after 2000 more adventurous political currents had been able to operate semi-legally. The problems of the left were associated not only with repression but also with the legacy of 'official' communism. The tortured history of the communist movement in Egypt during the Nasser era had concluded with its integration into the apparatus of state. When communists resurfaced in the form of Tagammu', they again moved into alliance with the regime, so that the established left became no more than an adjunct of the Mubarak networks, joining the regime's offensive on the Islamist opposition – the front line in its assault on dissidence.

Islamism prospered in proportion to the decline and defeat of the left. Mariam, a member of Kifaya, explains the impact of these developments:

> I come from an old communist family. My grandfather was with Haditu [the DMNL] and was very active in the years before Nasser. But he would never tell us [grandchildren] about the events of that

time and what followed. When I became involved in student politics I was puzzled that I couldn't find the left – there were no communists at my university. I discovered very slowly that the communists had supported dictators – first Nasser, then Sadat and then Mubarak – and had become invisible. We never saw them on campus – we never saw them anywhere.[15]

Politics of the 'official' left continued to have influence however. Although Stalinist Communism had collapsed organisationally with the fall of the Soviet Union, as an ideological current it had a continuing impact, especially in circumstances of radicalisation and in relation to currents such as Nasserism with which the left had intermittently collaborated. In 2012, Egypt's communists and Nasserists joined the alliance constructed by al-Sisi to facilitate counter-revolution. Their shared orientation on the state and on the armed forces as guardians of national integrity led to an embrace of *feloul* and the project of restoration. They endorsed al-Sisi's assault on the Brotherhood and (unlike ElBaradei) backed the NSF's celebratory statement following massacres perpetrated by the police and the army. The Front praised 'the firm leadership of the armed forces':

> The NSF salutes the police and military forces, and bows its head in tribute and respect for the great people, imposing their will of complete victory [...] Glory to the people, to the great army and to the courageous police.[16]

Abdelrahman identifies how 'the rush of progressive forces to join liberal and right-wing groups to confront the Islamist forces has impeded the development of a revolutionary project' (2014: 116). The headlong rush towards al-Sisi was explained on the left by the need to confront the Muslim Brotherhood as a 'fascist' tendency. This term had been used and abused on the Egyptian left for decades but took on increased importance in the 1990s in the context of Western military interventions in the Middle East. Tariq Ali (2002: 284) notes how 'the Hitler label' was applied by the United States to its erstwhile ally Saddam Hussein to justify military offensives in Iraq (to which the Mubarak regime had contributed Egyptian forces). The practice of dressing Iraqis in the garb of European fascism was 'grotesque', Ali argues, serving efforts by architects of the 2003 invasion to 'project the enemy' (Ali 2002: 285). In 2006, US President George W. Bush described the Hezbollah opposition to Israeli forces in Lebanon as 'Islamic fascism' (Greene 2006) and, following a Brotherhood demonstration in support of Hezbollah in Cairo in that same year, the official Egyptian press declared that, 'Fascism and Nazism are compatible with the Muslim Brotherhood's aims of toppling the [Egyptian] regime' (Wickham 2013: 121). After the election of Mohamed Mursi as president in 2012, the Brotherhood was routinely described by leaders of the NSF as fascist or crypto-fascist;[17] following the army assault on Brotherhood protestors in August 2013, the government spokesman Mustafa Hegazi declared that 'religious fascism' had been defeated.[18] In December 2013, Hegazi reasserted the government's determination to tackle the 'evil' Brotherhood, which he placed in the category of 'fascists and the Nazis' (Al-Ghamrawi 2013). He added, without irony:

> The state is now the only organization in Egypt. It is the singular institution to which all belong. No banners belonging to other organizations exist in the state which looks after all of us. There is no place for a new supreme guide or organization – for these elements have acquired an almost 'sinful' status in the public eye and no one will allow them to take root ever again.
>
> (Al-Ghamrawi 2013)

Egyptian governments had both accommodated and repudiated the Brotherhood. Communist organisations too had courted and castigated Islamism, just as they had presented the military regime of the post-colonial era as both 'progressive' and 'fascist'. The Brothers were not fascists: they did not share the politics of redemptive nationalism advanced by movements of the extreme right that emerged in Europe in the mid-twentieth century. The Brotherhood had originated and grown as part of the anti-colonial movement, becoming a movement of conservative reform that, in the context of communist retreat, became a mass opposition to the Mubarak regime. It had passed through many phases, including periods when the authoritarianism, elitism and a tendency towards sectarianism of its leadership were particularly pronounced. It had not, however, developed the hyper-nationalism and racist exclusivism associated with fascist currents, nor the latters' para-military modes of organisation and systematic practices of assault on minorities, working-class organisations and the left. In Egypt, the left's characterisation of the Brotherhood as fascist served to displace onto Islamists the responsibility for its own failures and what Abdelrahman calls 'the pitiful performance' of the NSF (2014: 115).[19] A revitalised left would require both the political and organisational independence necessary to avoid such accommodations to the state.

Old left – new left

The revolutionary process provided powerful evidence of the energies and potentials of the mass of Egyptians. It asserted their presence as political subjects – people with expectations, aspirations and their own agendas for change (Marfleet 2016). It demonstrated the significance in contemporary politics of conflict between social classes and of the profound importance of the state and its relations with the mass of people. Since the colonial era, Egyptian society had been dominated by institutions of the state – by *al-nizam*, 'the order'. State capitalism, initiated during the Nasser era, embedded the military command and a new bureaucratic elite within the structures of privilege. Institutions of coercion assumed special importance as the post-colonial regime struggled to control movements that had facilitated its rise to power; when the Sadat and Mubarak dictatorships later embraced neo-liberalism those who directed these bodies readily accommodated private capital. Egypt's bourgeoisie soon combined 'statist' and private interests: increasingly the two became interdependent and mutually supportive.

The revolutionary process that emerged as a societal conflict in 2011 counterposed a mass movement with those in authority in the state. The military command became a focal point for those committed to the status quo: SCAF became, in effect, an executive of the state as the manager of 'the common affairs of the whole bourgeoisie'. It mobilised those with an historic stake in the old order, including the 'official' ideologues of the Mubarak autocracy: executives and editors of national media; key figures of religious establishments both Muslim and Christian; university managers and senior academics. It also rallied ideological affiliates of the state for whom the latter was a foundational component of the political order. These included radical nationalists, communists and reformists ('liberals' and social democrats). Drawn behind the military command, they provided both ideological resources and organisational support for counter-revolution.

The counter-revolutionary alliance did not include the Muslim Brotherhood. Its leaders had long wished to exert their own authority over the institutions of the state. They were hostile to the mass movement to the extent that it threatened this ambition; unable to control the movement, however, they became the focus of an initiative undertaken to assault the movement as a whole and to end the process of change. In an unequal contest with the state, the Brotherhood was soon under intense pressure. The two had never been symmetrical, as in Springborg's invocation of the elemental conflict between rivals of the natural world (see Chapter 5). The Brotherhood could not rally forces of coercion such as those at the disposal of al-Sisi: it was soon decapitated as the military command moved on to attack the popular movement, targeting the leaders of the streets, the youth networks, NGOs and independent media.

In the face of this assault, much of the left was paralysed. As Shatz observed, al-Sisi and his alliance won through 'not only because the army and the *feloul* (remnants of the old regime) had superior resources at their disposal, but because they had a unified sense of their aims' (Shatz 2013). The military command successfully mobilised parties of the left that had earlier expressed commitment to the mass movement and its wider aims. From January 2011, radical currents had grown rapidly as activists sought to advance democratic gains and to progress struggles for social justice. When conflict with the state intensified, however, reformist organisations moved with speed into an alliance with the armed forces. The trajectory of radical nationalism was of special importance. Its leading figures had exerted significant influence on the popular movement. Hamdeen Sabbahi had emerged as the movement's champion in the electoral arena; Kemal Abu-Eita had personified aspirations for social justice pursued by means of workers' struggle. Their move to the right highlighted the absence of an independent pole within the popular movement. This 'liability', observed Maha Abdelrahman, had become an impediment to its survival. Writing before the military coup, she noted the need for 'structures capable of articulating alternatives around which the revolutionary potential of a broad swathe of the Egyptian people can be mobilized [...] [this] remains the main challenge facing a genuine, radical economic and political transformation' (2014: 74). The movement required an organisational and ideological presence independent of the state, free of the influences of Islamism, nationalism and Stalinist Communism.

Decades of accommodation to the autocracy by the official left had brought a legacy of scepticism and mistrust among many activists: as Abdelrahman observed, the 'rigid hierarchy and centralisation of power, iron discipline and leadership by a professional elite' constituted a 'tired old brand' (2013). In the summer of 2013, the independent left had modest forces – its sole organisational components being the April 6 Movement and the Revolutionary Socialists. Their efforts to establish a new brand of radical politics – to make good a historic political deficit – met a counter-revolutionary onslaught in which mainstream parties of the left joined with the state to strike the popular movement. The potentials of the mass of people to reshape Egyptian society were not in question but the legacy of the 'official' left had proved immensely costly. How to make good the deficit? How to organise forces for change capable of resisting the state and its institutions of coercion? How to focus workplace struggles that had been critical in removing Mubarak and in pursuing the most radical demands of the movement? What was to be the form of an independent revolutionary party? How could Egyptian women and men combine democratic methods with organisational coherence? These issues became matters of intense debate in the wake of military intervention and consolidation of a new autocracy.[20]

Back to the future?

The al-Sisi regime prepared for the fifth anniversary of the revolution as if anticipating a further uprising. In December 2015, the Ministry of Waqf (Islamic endowments) directed preachers in all mosques to use Friday prayers to warn against participation in public protests. Issuing a model sermon, it described those calling for January 25 protests as 'ill-hearted, weak believers; those who don't believe in the country and carry extremist ideas, who work on disintegrating society and destabilizing it' (*Mada Masr* 2015). Such calls were 'malignant conspiracies' that aimed to destroy the state, spread chaos, breach the state of law, threaten national security and fuel extremism and terrorism, said the ministry, telling Muslims to obey the nation's 'guardians' as they would obey God (*Mada Masr* 2015).

The ministry had earlier directed that sermons should be preached against industrial action: during 2015 there were nonetheless some 1,200 labour protests recorded across the country, including initiatives undertaken by the ministry's own employees (*Mada Masr* 2016a). During December 2015 and January 2016, the pace of industrial action increased sharply, with major strikes affecting Nile docks, food processing, hotels, the Suez Canal, petroleum processing and distribution, and key plants in heavy industry. Common to several disputes was the issue of unpaid bonuses; demands for *taṭhir* in relation to corrupt and incompetent managers were also raised (Charbel 2016). Growing frustration among workers reflected pressures affecting the whole economy. Financial backing from the Gulf regimes following the 2013 coup had fallen away and, with the decline in oil revenues during 2015, seemed unlikely to resume at the earlier level; Egypt's own energy exports had also been seriously affected. The contraction of the Chinese economy had hit Suez Canal revenues, and the downing of a Russian jet over Sinai had resulted in abrupt collapse of Red Sea tourism. Amr Adly (2015) described a 'vicious circle' in which the shortage of hard currency impeded economic recovery: recession was looming, he suggested, while Stacher (2016) concluded that Egypt was 'running on empty'.

Public protest had resumed, albeit at a much reduced level. After a long period of inaction in the streets demonstrators reappeared in Ismailiyya and Luxor after the deaths of local men in police stations in the two cities, fuelling anger nationally about torture and abuse, and the apparent impunity enjoyed by police and security agencies. Deeply embedded in the regional economy and in the global market, Egypt was more exposed to crisis and instability; committed to unprecedented authoritarian methods, the regime risked incendiary confrontations in the streets and workplaces. The mood of discontent had its impact on the presidency: in December, al-Sisi addressed members of the new loyalist parliament asking: 'Why am I hearing calls for another revolution? Why do you [sic] want to ruin [Egypt]?' (*Al Jazeera* 2016). The anxiety at the highest levels of the state was reflected in an intensive security clampdown before 25 January 2016, the fifth anniversary of the revolution. SSI teams searched thousands of homes in downtown Cairo, seizing alleged activists in dawn raids, and on 25 January unprecedented numbers of regular troops with tanks and armoured vehicles were deployed in city centres. For the first time since the 2013 coup, media analyses addressed the possibility of a new nationwide upheaval. *Al Jazeera* asked: 'Is another revolution brewing in Egypt?' (2016). The key issue, it suggested, was 'simmering popular discontent over the widening gap between what Egyptians were promised and what has been delivered to them', as a result: 'the regime has reason to worry' (*Al Jazeera* 2016).

In 2013, supporters of the al-Sisi coup had been quick to issue hubristic declarations that the revolution had been crushed. According to one retired general, 'the game is over and [...] Egyptians are back in unison with their armed forces' (ICG 2013: 9). By 2016, 'unison' was wearing thin: the process of change had not been concluded.

Postscript – Cairo, April 2016

On 24 February 2016, President al-Sisi spoke to the nation. His speech was billed as an introduction to 'Egypt Vision 2030' – the government's development programme. In the event a rambling and often highly charged presentation included alternate pleas and threats. He entreated Egyptians to listen to him, 'Because I know what I'm talking about' (Khalil 2016). He continued: 'Don't listen to anybody's words but me. I am speaking in all seriousness, don't listen to anybody's words but me ... I am a man who does not lie, nor do I beat around the bush. I have no interests except those of my country' (*Mada Masr* 2016b). In an abrupt change of tone al-Sisi added menacingly: 'Don't abuse my kindness', warning that he would 'wipe off the face of the earth' those who challenged the stability of the state (Khalil 2016).

This anxious performance reflected problems faced by a regime increasingly unpopular in the context of intense economic pressures and the state's relentless repression. Much of the speech addressed criticism of the government, parliament, state institutions and police brutality. 'Don't focus on the bad things,' al-Sisi suggested. 'Look at the glass half full because we have to raise our morale' (Khalil 2016). For weeks the government and security forces had been challenged by strikes and public protests including furious demonstrations against the police. Following an assault by police on medical staff at a Cairo hospital doctors held nationwide protests, including a 12,000-strong demonstration at the Interior Ministry. Days later thousands of residents of Darb al-Ahmar, a historic inner-city area of Cairo, also marched to the Interior Ministry after a policeman shot and killed a local taxi driver. At the ministry they chanted, 'All cops are thugs' and 'Revenge!'[1] Both protests defied the infamous anti-protest law of 2013, with police and security agencies keeping out of sight. In an unprecedented statement Interior Minister Magdy Abdel-Ghaffar said: 'We apologise for the acts of some policemen, we kiss the head of every citizen subjected to abuse or insult or any unkind act by policemen' (AFP 2016).

Anger directed at police is associated with more general discontent and with anxiety about wages, prices, job security and welfare, so that demonstrations called by the Doctors' Syndicate also demanded free medical treatment at all public hospitals. An activist in the syndicate points out: 'Things are very tense right now and questions about police brutality, welfare and social justice are all closely connected.'[2]

'Ghost towns'

Unemployment has risen relentlessly, driven by the decline and subsequent collapse of tourism. In 2010, 14.7 million foreign tourists arrived in Egypt: then, tourism contributed 13 per cent of GDP, generating $12.5 billion and employing one in seven of the Egyptian workforce (Economist 2013).[3] In 2011 tourist arrivals plummeted to 9.5 million (Economist 2013); after recovering briefly the number of visitors again collapsed: by the early months of 2016 even the most popular resorts were described as 'ghost towns' (Feteha 2016). According to an official of the Egyptian Tourism Federation the impact has been 'devastating'.[4]

By April 2016 the fall in both tourist income and foreign investment had reduced Egypt's foreign currency reserves to $16.5 billion (Ahram Online 2016), less than half the level at which they stood in January 2011 and inadequate to meet import bills averaging $6 billion each month (STRATFOR 2016). Imports of wheat and soybeans, crucial to maintain access to bread and cooking oil for the mass of Egyptians, could not be guaranteed.[5] As financial support from the Gulf states declined al-Sisi turned to the World Bank and the IMF. In December 2015 the Bank agreed a $3 billion loan accompanied by demands for cuts in subsidies and in public sector wages, increased energy prices and new tax laws favouring the private sector. According to the Bank, 'Jumpstarting the economy can't happen without enabling the private sector to play a catalytic role in diversifying the economy, increasing competitiveness and creating jobs.'[6] Maha, a member of the Marxist left, comments that Egyptians have heard similar propositions on countless occasions: 'We had 30 years of neo-liberalism – and that brought more corruption, more poverty and inequality, and more resistance. Al-Sisi is going down the same path but more aggressively. People who accepted the coup in 2013 have lost patience and everywhere frustration and anger are growing.'[7]

Demonstrations by civil servants against a law designed to cut wages and millions of jobs in state agencies (part of al-Sisi's deal with the World Bank) have been under way since the summer of 2015. In March 2016 thousands of state workers joined further protests. One response of the regime to such resistance is a renewed attempt to use official, state-run unions against independent union organisations. On 1 March 2016 the state declared that the stamps of independent unions would no longer be valid on official documents. According to Abdel-Monem al-Gamal, deputy chairman of the official federation ETUF, 'some workers have exploited the chaos that followed the January revolution to create fake entities'; all employees should operate exclusively through the official federation, he said (Hassan 2016). ETUF has called for the dissolution of independent unions.

'Mamluk state'

Official apologies for the conduct of the police have not inhibited the regime's repression, which touches tens of millions of people. Islam, a leading human rights activist, says: 'We've never had anything like this. The scale of disappearances and killings, and of torture and abuse in police stations in every part of the country is unprecedented – and it's irrational. The police and State Security seem to be out of control.'[8]

A widespread assessment holds that competing police and security agencies wish to demonstrate their effectiveness by outdoing one another in acts of violence, as in the disappearance and brutal murder of Italian student Giulio Regeni.[9] Encouraged by the regime to stimulate fear and compliance in the population at large, police and security agencies operate thousands of checkpoints, conduct random searches of apartments and houses, and seize 'suspects' at will, operating according to their own institutional agendas. 'It's the Mamluk state,' says Ala'a, an academic and a member of the radical left. Drawing parallels with the fratricidal Mamluks of Egypt's medieval and early modern eras, he suggests that institutions of coercion attempt to achieve advantage vis-à-vis one another within the apparatus of state. 'Is Sisi really running the show?' Islam asks: 'is there a logic to this – or are the police and intelligence [agencies] out of control?'

Many political activists are surprised at the rapid change in public mood during 2016, especially at the speed with which hopes for positive change under al-Sisi have been replaced by scepticism and greater willingness to undertake public protest despite the risks involved. The regime faces a prospect of increased opposition and, with an enfeebled parliament lacking popular authority, may feel compelled to seek allies among political opponents including the Muslim Brotherhood. The Brothers, still the main target of state repression, have been engaged in fierce internal debate about reconciliation with al-Sisi. During 2015 disputes in the organisation became public, with competing leaderships established among a series of factions (Dawoud 2015). In April 2016 the Brothers' official secretary-general, Mahmoud Hussein, issued a statement to the effect that talk of reconciliation was false. There would be no deals with al-Sisi, he said: '[W]e will never negotiate with the criminals whose hands are stained with the blood of innocent Egyptians' (Hussein 2016). An understanding with the regime would, however, be consistent with a long history of accommodations by the Brotherhood with the state.

Many Egyptians supported military intervention in 2013 as a continuation of revolution or as a 'second revolution'. Sherif, a senior academic who joined the liberal Destour Party of Mohamed ElBaradei and who backed al-Sisi's coup, now regrets his naivety: 'We lost our critical faculties. We allowed our feelings for the army and its place in our history to override suspicion about the generals' intentions. Since 2013 we've been going backwards – we lost the democracy we'd just found and now we have to find a new way to bring change.'[10]

The reformist left, used and discarded by al-Sisi, has been deeply disoriented by events. In January 2016 Hamdeen Sabbahi, its most important figure, declared that: 'The way we are being ruled is exactly like Hosni Mubarak's era ... The regime is using the same old policies that led to two mass uprisings.'[11] In March 2016 he announced moves to establish a new alliance under the slogan 'Let's Build an Alternative'. Implicitly recognising his error in enthusiastically backing the coup he nonetheless proposed to unite 'all forces that believe in the January 25 Revolution, and who do not see June 30, 2013 as a military coup' (Dawoud 2015). A much-diminished figure, Sabbahi has drawn little support for his project. There is now a larger space for the radical left, especially among young people whose first experiences of public politics were in the streets and workplaces during the 18 Days of 2011. Anarchists and those who celebrated a 'spontaneous' movement and 'the crowd' have disappeared from view but independent socialists have secured a growing audience. One activist interviewed in April 2016 explains his hopes and fears:

I was 20 when Mubarak fell – it seems a long time ago. We were all shocked by the military coup and for over a year we struggled to understand what had happened. Now we see people resisting and returning to politics – they've also been changed and I'm certain that the regime will be challenged again and again.

But will we be ready? Can we defend advances that will be made by our movement? Can we defend our democracy? Can we help to build workers' committees that are independent – that won't compromise with the regime? This should be our aim. We must make sure we don't make the same mistakes again.[12]

Notes

Preface

1. A film of what seems to be this very parade, held on CIA records, can be viewed on YouTube. Husni Mubarak, later to be president, is also pictured, at: www.youtube.com/watch?v=yODM1gTAovA (accessed 11 February 2015).

1. Introduction

1. Here the term 'popular' (popular participation/popular movement/popular demands) is used as an adjective deriving from the Latin root and with the meaning 'people's'.
2. Transcripts of communication between CSF officers published in *Al-Masry al-Youm*, 15 March 2011 and quoted in El-Ghobashy 2011.
3. Author's interview with Ibrahim, labour activist and democracy campaigner, Cairo, April 2011.
4. See Shebab 2011.
5. Typical of many analyses was that of the *New York Times*: 'Facebook and YouTube ... offered a way for the discontented to organize and mobilize' (Preston 2011). According to *USA Today*, 'Tech-savvy youths led the way in Egypt protests' (Michaels 2011).
6. The Arabic *'ashwa'iyya* means 'hazard', often translated as 'random', or 'haphazard'; *'ashwa'iyyat* is a plural noun for informal places of settlement, often used in the context of 'slums'. See Chapter 2 for an assessment of how this term is used and misused in relation to urban planning and political discourses of the Egyptian city.
7. Author's interview with Hussein, democracy activist, Cairo, April 2011.
8. Author's interview with Marwa, journalist and blogger, Cairo, April 2011.
9. Singular *baltagi* – literally 'axe-wielders' – gangs of paid thugs long used in Egypt by governing authorities, landowners or employers to enforce their will against political opposition, dissident communities or employees.
10. Author interview with Sara, Kifaya activist, Cairo, April 2011.
11. The *mulid*, pl. *mawalid* (*mawlid* in standard Arabic, sometimes *mulud* or *milad* in colloquial variations) is usually associated with celebrations of the birth of the Prophet (*mawlid al-nabi*, or more formally *'eid al-mawlid al-nabawi*). In some regions of the Islamic world and notably in Egypt, the term is used for birthdays or feast days of key figures in the Sufi tradition. In Egypt, it has long been associated with mass street processions and

expressive festivities that resist the control of authorities such as the police. See Schielke 2006.

12. *'Eid* – Arabic 'festival' or 'feast', usually associated with the annual *'eid al-fitr* (Breaking of the Fast) which marks the end of Ramadan, and *'eid al-adham* (Festival of the Sacrifice).

2. The Streets

1. See the account by British police chief Sir Thomas Russell of events in Cairo in 1919: Seth 1996: Ch. ix.
2. The idea of a 'clash of civilisations' is said to have been proposed by Lewis at a conference in the United States in 1957: Bonney 2008, p. 54.
3. Commenting on the mass movements of 2011 in Egypt and elsewhere, Lewis suggested that political factors should be taken into account in explaining the crises; at the same time, aspects of Islamic culture were relevant, notably sexual 'frustration' and 'raging sexual desire' [sic]. He observed:

   One has to remember that in the Muslim world, casual sex, Western-style, doesn't exist. If a young man wants sex, there are only two possibilities – marriage and the brothel. You have these vast numbers of young men growing up without the money, either for the brothel or the brideprice, with raging sexual desire. On the one hand, it can lead to the suicide bomber, who is attracted by the virgins of paradise – the only ones available to him. On the other hand, sheer frustration.

   (Lewis 2011)

   Lewis's conviction that Arab-Muslim society harboured distress and 'rage' continued to be influential: in a book published in 2012, Noueihed and Warren introduced their assessment of the 'Arab Spring' with an account of 'The Roots of Rage' (Noueihed and Warren 2012: 9).
4. Quoted in Beinin 2001: 108.
5. As an English-language publication directed to an expatriate audience and a fraction of the Egyptian population, *Al-Ahram Weekly* was for several years able to provide extensive coverage of protest movements with minimal official censorship, compiling an important archival record. It later adopted a much less independent approach.
6. Typical were those in the *New York Times* of February 2011: 'Movement began with outrage and a Facebook page that gave it an outlet' (Preston 2011); and in the *Washington Post*: 'Egypt's Facebook revolution faces identity crisis' (Wan 2011).
7. Author's interview with Ibrahim, Cairo, April 2011.
8. Author's interview with radical activist, Cairo, April 2011.
9. Figures quoted in this section are from sources mobilised by Alexander and Bassiouny 2014: Ch. 6.

10. Many were also speculative ventures, constructing property for rent and squeezing large numbers of people into inadequate spaces and poorly constructed buildings: see Sims 2010.

3. The Workers and the Movement

1. Observation of an Egyptian labour lawyer, quoted in Bishara 2012: 94.
2. Muhammed Abd al-Wahab, Minister of Industry, in *Al-Ahram*, 11 February 1986, quoted in El Shafei 1995: 29.
3. President Husni Mubarak, in *Al Ahram*, 9 March 1986, quoted in El Shafei 1995: 29.
4. Khalid Muntasir, "Tahrir Contagion," *Al-Masry Al-Youm*, 4 March 2011, quoted in Sallam 2011.
5. Figures compiled by the NGO Awlad al-Ard: A. Alexander 2011.
6. On experiences in the health sector, see Alexander and Bassiouny 2014: 296ff.
7. Author's interview with a teacher at the Cabinet Office protest, Cairo, September 2011.
8. Author's verbatim record of contributions at the meeting on 21 June 2011 with speakers Wael Khalil, Hossam El-Hamalawy, Kholoud Saber and Asmaa Aly. See also *Ahram Online* 2011c.
9. In a fascinating assessment of Fikri al-Khuli's memoire of factory life in the 1920s and 1930s, Joel Beinin comments on the general lack of materials authored by workers or peasants in which their own experiences are the main subject matter. See Beinin 2001: Ch 4.
10. Beinin and Lockman (1987: 462–478) provide a comprehensive bibliography of published and unpublished works on labour in Arabic, English, French and Hebrew.
11. Mustafa Khamis and Muhammed al-Baqari, leading activists at Misr Fine Spinning and Weaving in Kafr al-Dawwar, were executed on the orders of a military tribunal in September 1952.
12. Government notice published in *Al-Ahram Al-Iqtisadi*, 1 December 1961, quoted in Posusney 1997: 73.
13. Beinin (1994: 251) lists major workers' actions from 1971 to 1976, including demonstrations, strikes and occupations at a series of large public sector enterprises.
14. Author's interview with Ibrahim, labour activist, Cairo, April 2000.
15. Badr, in office from 1986 to 1990, told workers at the EISC plant in Helwan that if 1 per cent of the workforce died during police assaults on the occupation, he would consider the operation successful (Badr quoted in El Shafei 1995: 34). He told a journalist who interviewed him in 1988: 'I don't believe in political solutions, only military ones' (author's interview with the Cairo correspondent of a leading British newspaper, Cairo, 1988).
16. Editorials in *Al-Akhbar al-Youm*, quoted in El Shafei 1995: 35.
17. Author's interviews with EOHR activists and with an official of Amnesty International (International Secretariat), February 1990, Cairo.

18. Several leading figures were former student activists and members of the short-lived Communist Workers Party: see Chapter 6.
19. Food rationing and the provision of basic necessities began as a temporary measure under British military authorities in 1942; the post-colonial Nasser regime established a formal subsidy system that included transport, housing, energy, water and some non-food consumer products such as soap and cigarettes. Under President Sadat the system was extended to cover beans, lentils, frozen fish, meat – and eventually 18 food categories (Ahmed *et al.* 2001: 6).
20. *'Aysh baladi* – 'country bread'/'folk bread' is the key component of the diet for the majority of Egyptians.
21. Author's interview with Hisham Mubarak in Cairo, April 1997. Hisham Mubarak established The Office of Legal Aid for Human Rights in 1994 – one of the first campaigning rights organisations in Egypt. He died tragically in January 1998; his collaborators established the Hisham Mubarak Legal Center in 1999. Several, including Ahmed Seif al-Islam and Khalid Ali, were prominent in the uprising of 2011.
22. *Al-Akhbar*, 15 November 1996, quoted in Weiss and Wurzel 1998: 126.
23. World Bank figures, quoted in El-Naggar 2009: 42.
24. 'Desequestration' – reversal of laws under which land nationalised under the Nasser regime, having been taken into public ownership ('sequestered' by the state) was restored to families of former owners.
25. Palm Hills Development, which specialised in building gated residential communities, bought state land near Cairo at prices so far below the market rate that the deal was said to have wasted over $2.6 billion of public money (El-Wardani 2010). In the case of the vast Toshka New Valley, agricultural project land equivalent in area to 1 per cent of Egypt's total territory was sold to the Saudi prince and business tycoon Al-Waleed Bin Talal at cost of LE5 million – about £500,000. In 2011, he was compelled to surrender 75 per cent of the land (*Ahram Online* 2011b).
26. Author interview with Ashraf, Giza resident, April 2001, Cairo.
27. Author interview with Leila, anti-war campaigner, April 2003, Cairo.
28. The following year, two judges – Hesham Bastawisi and Mahmoud Mekki – were stripped of judicial immunity and punished with a show trial. In solidarity, 50 judges held an unprecedented three-day sit-in at the Judges' Association in Cairo.
29. Author interview with Alaa', a leading journalist, Cairo, June 2013.
30. Author interview with Khalid, labour journalist, Cairo, May 2012.

4. Crises and Confrontations

1. Excluded were those not physically fit for military service, those who were the sole male child of their parents, and in practice those whose influence by virtue of *wasta* ('connections', usually exercised through the family) provided exemption or a reduced term of service.

2. They underestimate casualties during the events in Egypt but show nonetheless that the number of victims was significantly lower than in other states of the region during the upheavals of 2011. See Bauer and Scheitzwer 2012: 1–2.
3. Testimony of Adly, quoted in Kandil 2012: 237.
4. Author's interview with Ali, former SSI detainee, Cairo, April 2011.
5. A video tour of SSI headquarters filmed by activists is posted on YouTube at: www.youtube.com/watch?v=sVkiYPChgwY (accessed 2 May 2015).
6. Brigadier General Safwat El Zayat, interviewed by *Ahram Online*: Eleiba 2011.
7. *Al-Ahram*, quoted in Ashour 2011.
8. AFP report quoted by *Al Arabiya News* 2011.
9. Dalia Mustafa and Aisha Khalil, participants in the 1 April demonstration in Tahrir, explain the significance of this slogan:

> 'Batil!' (null, false, void and untrue) [...] was derived from the Egyptian movie *Shay'a min al-Khuf* ('Fear'), made by well-known director Hussein Kamal in 1969, in which the population of an entire village live in fear of a despotic bandit leader. When he kidnaps a young woman and forces her into a false marriage, the villagers march to his palace, torch it and save her. As they do this they chant: 'Batil!' (in this case a void marriage contract). Our chants in Tahrir were: 'Hosni Mubarak – batil!' and 'ND Party – batil!'
>
> (Mustafa and Khalil 2011)

10. The officers were sentenced to ten years in prison, later reduced to three years (Ibrahim, E. 2012).
11. Author's interview with Omar, a member of the Marxist left, Cairo, May 2011.
12. Given the scale of the mass movement, the size of the vote was interpreted by many activists as expressing a lack of confidence in SCAF and confusion over the implications of constitutional change.
13. Abbasiya is an area of inner Cairo, north of the city centre.
14. As observed by the author at the Cairo demonstration, September 2011. Over several hours of protest, Muslim Brotherhood officials among the teachers were dislodged from the platform erected at the Cabinet Office by young teacher activists leading calls for the minister's resignation.
15. Author's interview with Marwa, a member of the Tahrir Doctors group, Cairo, December 2011.
16. Eyewitness observations by the author, Cairo, December 2011.
17. A cloak, usually covering women from the neck to the ankles.
18. Khaled (Khaled Said, a Muslim) had been murdered by police in 2010; Mina (Mina Daniel, a Christian) was killed during the Maspero massacre of October 2011.
19. Wages in the private sector rose from an average of LE299 per month in 2010 to LE397 in 2011; in the public sector, they rose from LE542 in 2010

to LE657 in 2011. Rising living costs consumed most of the increases: Alexander and Bassiouny 2014: 215. In July 2011, the government set a minimum wage for employees in both public and private sectors of LE700 per month – far short of the LE1,200 demanded by independent unions.

5. Islamism and the State

1. Author's interview with Ahmed, a radical activist, Cairo, April 2011.
2. Author's interview with Ali, left-wing activist, Cairo, April 2011.
3. Member of the Brotherhood, quoted by Tamman and Haenni 2011.
4. Kedive Muhammed Tawfiq was Muhammed Ali's great-grandson. Khedive was a title conferred by the Ottoman Sultan on a local ruler, with implication of 'governor' or 'viceroy'.
5. Mitchell (1969: 8–9) discusses competing accounts of the founding of the Brotherhood; see also Wickham (2013: 20–26).
6. Khaled Mohi el-Din, one of the senior officers in the group, recalled that within days of the coup they met for dinner with the US ambassador in Cairo, Jefferson Caffery, making concessions to his demands over ministerial appointments: see Muhieddin (1996: 128). Gordon (1992: Ch. 9) examines evidence that the Free Officers had long had contact with US officials and that the CIA played a role in setting the agenda for their coup.
7. At the time of the coup, the Executive Committee had 14 members, with Nasser as 'president': Gordon (1992: 59).
8. *Akhir Sa'a*, quoted in Mitchell (1969: 66).
9. Mitchell notes that, 'one of his greatest dreams was to be welcomed into the royal presence' (1969: 40).
10. See Mitchell (1969: 42) on 'aid' to the Brotherhood in the form of contributions to its education, social and welfare activities.
11. This complex episode brought tensions in the RCC to a head, with resignations and counter-resignations within the ruling group. Nasser emerged more fully in control.
12. Qutb set out his strategy in detail in *Ma'alim fi al-Tariq* (*Milestones on the Road*, often referred to in English as *Milestones* or *Signposts*), written in prison and published in 1964 – later to become the key text of the *jihadi* movement. See Qutb 1988.
13. Mohamed Uthman Ismail, secretary of the regime's Arab Socialist Union, played a key role in facilitating activities of the radical Islamist groups: see Abdalla (1985: 226).
14. The Brotherhood put huge efforts into elections in the syndicates, running sustained campaigns and focusing its efforts on polling day with large teams of canvassers. Its presence on these occasions provided evidence of the scale of support within these constituencies.
15. Author's interview with Maya, a member of the doctor's syndicate, Cairo, April 1996.

16. Akef appeared on joint platforms with liberals, radical nationalists and members of various left-wing currents, participating for example in the Cairo Conference. This event, held annually at the Journalists Syndicate in Cairo from 2002 to 2008, brought together Islamists, liberals, nationalists and socialists from Egypt with secular radicals from Europe, North America and elsewhere. See discussion on the conference and its significance for the Egyptian opposition in Abdelrahman 2014.
17. Akef quoted in Brown (2012: 92).
18. Badie had been an associate of Sayyid Qutb and had been jailed under Nasser but later emerged as a cautious conservative.

6. Fate of the Left

1. In 1951 the DMNL explained that, 'the organisation [the DMNL] has always drawn a distinction between the Wafd and all other bourgeois political parties'. The Wafd, it argued, 'because of its makeup and history never rested in the least bit on reaction or imperialism'. Quoted in Gordon (1992: 31).
2. Author's interview with the late Armas 'Ed' Suvanto, Cairo, October 1989.
3. As at the Bayda Dyers Company: see Beinin and Lockman (1987: 421–22).
4. Mustafa Khamis and Mohamed al-Baqari were hanged on 7 September 1952.
5. Peasants owning five *feddan*s (just over five acres or about 2.5 hectares) or less made some gains from the reforms. In 1952 they represented 94 per cent of owners, controlling 35 per cent of the cultivated area. After the first reforms, they owned 52 per cent of cultivated land. Middle peasants, those with 11–50 *feddan*s, gained the most: after the reforms they accounted for 3 per cent of all landowners, owning 24 per cent of the cultivated area. See Bush 2009.
6. During the 1960s, half of ministerial positions and almost all provincial governorships were occupied by serving or former officers: Baker (1978: 48–49, 55).
7. In 1952 the DMNL seems to have had some 5,000 registered members; other groups including the Egyptian Communist Party (ECP) and Workers' Vanguard had about half this number combined: all had much larger numbers of sympathisers and significant influence among workers and students. For estimates of membership and support, see Agwani (1969: 48–49); Gordon (1992: 31); and Ismael and El-Sa'id (1990: 68–73).
8. According to Mohi el-Din: 'Nasser did not feel uneasy about dealing with communists. He and I believed that socialism, by necessity, was the closest to our movement' (1996: 38).
9. The DMNL even printed leaflets and other material for the Officers, using Nasser as a middleman (Botman 1988: 122).
10. Ismael Sabri Abdallah of the ECP recalled:

we believed that nothing good and durable could come from the army
[…] We were against coups. We were for revolutions […] In the first days
our position was ambiguous, saluting the overthrow of the king but asking
the military to fraternize with the population and form neighbourhood
committees and village committees of workers and soldiers. Then there
was a strike at Kafr al-Dawwar. The army intervened and two leaders of
the strike were hanged. Then we said this is a fascist regime.

(Quoted in Botman 1988: 123)

11. The Central Treaty Organisation (Cento – usually known as the Baghdad
    Pact) linked Iran, Iraq, Turkey, Pakistan and Britain, under American
    auspices. It was a key element in US efforts to construct a southern front
    against the advance of the Soviet Union in the Middle East and Central Asia
    – a Nato of the East.

12. Between 1955 and 1979, 6,250 Egyptian military personnel were trained in
    Eastern bloc states, the great majority in the Soviet Union. This was more
    than in any other country in the region, including Iraq and Syria, with
    which the Soviet Union enjoyed close relations after its links with Egypt
    were effectively broken in the early 1970s. See Moreton (1982: 66).

13. L.N. Vatolina, quoted in Agwani (1969: 51).

14. Krushchev, addressing the 20th Congress of the Communist Party of the
    Soviet Union, quoted in Behbehani (1986: 124).

15. A new leftist publication, *Al-Misa'*, was established under the editorship of
    the rehabilitated Khaled Muhieddin, together with a series of other titles
    run by key figures of the left who had spent years in Nasser's prison camps.
    See Abdel-Malek (1968: 121).

16. Telegram sent to Nasser, quoted from the original by Ismael and El-Sa'id
    (1990: 124).

17. See Mitchell's account of these contradictions and their implications:
    Mitchell 1969: 224–31).

18. See Beinin and Lockman (1987: 281–83), on 'Uthman's move from the
    Islamists to the left.

19. Author's interview with Ahmed, a veteran union activist in the Iron and
    Steel Company, Tibbin, April 1987.

20. NCWS statement of 1946, quoted in Beinin and Lockman (1987: 369–70).

21. Nasser made an unprecedented personal visit to Helwan, a key industrial
    centre south of Cairo, to address workers – a mark of the impact of the
    strikes after years of passivity in major workplaces.

22. This is the assessment of Ismael and El-Sa'id (1990: 129). Rifa'at El-Sa'id
    had been a member of DMNL and an enthusiastic supporter of the Popular
    Front approach. In the 1970s, he became a key figure in Tagammu', later
    steering the organisation into an effective alliance with the Mubarak
    regime. His recognition of the impacts on the communist movement of
    accommodation with Nasser and dissolution of the Egyptian Communist
    Party (ECP) is particularly interesting.

23. Officials of the ECP, quoted in El-Hamalawy (2009 [2000]: 8).
24. Author's interview with 'Amr, human rights activist, interviewed in Cairo, March 2004.
25. The Brotherhood had an inconsistent relationship with Kifaya. Individual members supported the movement, while the leadership kept a wary distance without expressing hostility. In 2005, the leading Brotherhood member 'Issam el-Erian said:

> Unfortunately the Kifaya movement has the wrong goal; they stress the amendment of the constitution. We support this but we don't make it the first priority. The priority is to end the situation of martial law and the false multi-party system.
>
> (ICG 2005: 19)

7. Egypt under Mursi

1. Author's interview with Fatma, Cairo, June 2013.
2. Ali El-Selmi, the SCAF-appointed deputy prime minister, proposed 'supra-constitutional' principles that would give armed forces command rights to appoint most members of the constitution drafting committee, would protect the military budget from parliamentary oversight, and would preserve the military's power to veto decisions relating to war and to laws dealing with the military. See Chapter 3.
3. Here 'secular' is applied to political parties without explicitly Islamist agendas. There are high levels of religiosity across Egyptian society, so that all parties draw on support from, variously, Muslims and Christians. The term 'Islamist' refers to parties and movements mobilising Islamic traditions and principles as part of a political project.
4. A complex arrangement of electoral lists favoured organisations with well-established structures and candidates with high public profiles. See the discussion in S. Tadros 2012.
5. Comment made as part of a debate on 'Twenty years of multipartyism in Egypt', in Hussein *et al.* (1999: 77).
6. As evoked in Max Weber's *The Protestant Ethic and the Spirit of Capitalism* and R.H. Tawney's *Religion and the Rise of Capitalism*. Beinin and Lockman (1987: 378) also see similarities with the aspiration for a 'moral economy' identified by E.P. Thompson as a characteristic of the 'English Crowd' in the eighteenth century.
7. The Brotherhood had not developed formal economic theory or even a focused economic policy: its strategists were said to be 'little more than glorified merchants'; they were 'skilled commodity movers' with 'a wholesale trade mentality'. See Kandil, W. 2015 (113–14).
8. Nine other candidates were also rejected on the basis of 'legal irregularities', including Mubarak's former Director of Intelligence, Omar Suleiman. The

decision was widely held, however, to have been directed against Shatir and the Brotherhood.

9. Author's interview with participants in the first anniversary demonstration, Cairo, January 2012.
10. Author's interview with Ibrahim, Cairo, April 2012.
11. Demonstration of Friday 1 June 2012, Tahrir Square, author's testimony.

8. Brotherhood, People, State

1. See www.dropegyptsdebt.org
2. The Mursimeter can be viewed at: http://morsimeter.com/en (English) and at: http://morsimeter.com/ar (Arabic).
3. See the full text of the Declaration at *Ahram Online* 2012d.
4. Events at the initial Ittihadiyya protests have never been successfully explained, with competing accounts suggesting that Brotherhood supporters attacked those protesting against Mursi; others have claimed that the *baltagiyya* attacked supporters of the Brotherhood while police stood by, with the implication that the security services encouraged the clashes. See Ibrahim 2015.
5. El-Erian speaking live on Masr25, a television channel sympathetic to the Muslim Brotherhood, on 5 December. Quoted by Human Rights Watch, see HRW 2012.
6. Author's interview with Munir, a leading journalist, Cairo, December 2012.
7. Author's interview with Sara, Cairo, April 2013.
8. Author's interview with Marwa, interviewed in Cairo, June 2013.
9. Fatma Ramadan, member of the Executive Bureau of EFITU, quoted in Charbel 2012b.
10. Author's interview with Hisham, worker in a Cairo hospital, December 2012.
11. See the statement by EFITU: MENA Solidarity 2012.
12. Ghozlan quoted in Al Ahram: *Ahram Online* 2012e.
13. OpantiSH organised groups of women and men, dressed in the group's distinctive T-shirts, to identify and mark as aggressors (with spray paint) those seen to attack women in public spaces. OpantiSH declared:

> We will not be silenced. We will not be broken. We will not shy away. There are mob sexual assaults in Tahrir Square. Come and stand against the rapists because we do not plan to hide in our homes. This is our square, this is our revolution, and we will fight this battle to the last breath.
> (From leaflets of OpantiSH distributed in Tahrir Square, January 2013.)

14. Habib, radical activist, interviewed in Cairo, April 2013.
15. Army spokesman Ahmed Mohamed Ali, quoted in Trew *et al.* 2013.
16. Spending increased from an estimated 3.9 per cent of GNP to 12.3 per cent of GNP. See Baker (1978: 56).

17. A former Egyptian minister, quoted in Marshall and Stacher 2012.
18. See Marfleet 2013a, for an assessment of the notion of 'crony capitalism' and its use as a means of distancing governments and international financial agencies from practices they have routinely endorsed in states such as Egypt.

9. Towards the Coup

1. In addition to collective withdrawals of labour and workplace occupations, ECESR recorded vigils, demonstrations, blockades and hunger strikes among which some were 'citizen actions' including protests over rising prices, lack of fuel and clean water, and power cuts. See Aboulenein 2013.
2. Author's interview with Ashraf, Cairo 2013.
3. Drivers were told that they had been assigned to work 'in a military capacity for the Armed Forces'; those who were slow reporting for duty would face a six-month jail term or a fine of 5000 Egyptian pounds [£500] or both (MENA 2013).
4. Bloomberg quoted an Egyptian manufacturer who lamented a 'breakdown of discipline' in Egyptian factories as endless political debates distracted workers from their assembly lines. 'Someone has to go and say: "enough is enough"', he said, 'The economy is bleeding.' See Lynch and Marroushi 2013.
5. For an interesting assessment of police strikes, see Abdelrahman 2015.
6. Author's interview with Nawal, Cairo, April 2013.
7. Kandil, editor of *Al Shorouk*, proposed in November 2012 that the architect of a plan to remove Mursi was Ahmed Shafiq, defeated candidate in the presidential election. The initiative was taken up and pursued to a conclusion by al-Sisi, he argues. See Kandil 2015.
8. Author's interview with Magda, London, September 2014.
9. The committee included the Revolutionary Youth Union, the Maspero Youth Union, the Socialist Youth Union, the Liberal Youth Front, the Justice and Freedom Youth, the April 6 Democratic Front, the Mina Daniel Movement, and the NSF member parties – the Democratic Front Party, the Constitution Party, the Wafd Party, the Free Egyptians Party, the Egyptian Communist Party, the Egyptian Socialist Party, the Socialist Popular Alliance Party, the Tagammu' Party, the Nasserist Party, the Egyptian Social Democratic Party, the Karama Party, the Egypt Freedom Party, the Egyptian Popular Current and the National Association for Change. See Haddon *et al.* 2013b.
10. Author's interview with Mohamed, January 2014.
11. See Cole 2011. Churches of several denominations in Cairo became support centres for activists engaged in street fighting with police and troops, notably Qasr al-Dubara near Tahrir Square, an evangelical institution soon known as 'The Church of the Revolution', in which for months wounded protestors were treated by emergency medical teams.
12. As in the case of an assault on the headquarters of the Coptic Orthodox Church, St Mark's Cathedral, in April 2013. The perpetrators – 'unknown

assailants' according to press reports – were not pursued by police or officials and were never charged. See Al-Tawy 2013.

13. Among many such testimonies, see those quoted by Naib 2011.

14. See the analysis by Jessica Winegar (2012) of both opportunities and limits to women's activism during the uprising.

15. According to al-Sisi, the procedure had been necessary 'to protect [sic] the girls from rape, and the soldiers and officers from accusations of rape' (BBC News 2014).

10. Counter-Revolution and Beyond

1. Author's interview with Maha, radical activist, London, January 2014.

2. In February 2011, the same publication had featured five young activists of Tahrir Square as its cover personalities. See *Time*, 6 December 2013 and 28 February 2011.

3. Author's interview with Tamer, online journalist, April 2014.

4. The court convicted Mohamed Fahmy, a Canadian-Egyptian dual national; Peter Greste, an Australian; and Baher Mohamed, an Egyptian. Amnesty International (2015: 138) described the trial as 'grossly unfair'.

5. The Front was established by members of the April 6 Youth Movement, the April 6 Democratic Front, the Strong Egypt Party and the Revolutionary Socialists; it included independent academics, lawyers and journalists, and a number of leading cultural figures.

6. Author's interview with Reem, April 2014.

7. Police had appeared at some workplaces in dispute and in April 2015 military police opened fire on workers at a factory in al-Arish, killing one and wounding several. These incidents were rare however: see Youssef 2015.

8. Author's interview with Sawsun, Cairo, December 2012.

9. ETUF officials not only worked closely with employers and the intelligence agencies but also controlled local welfare schemes – *al-sanadiq al-khasr* ('private boxes') – to which groups of workers contribute and which are of vital importance to working-class families.

10. Author's interview with Tamer, Cairo, May 2013.

11. The EDLC originated in a split in 2011, when the Centre for Trade Union and Workers Services (CTUWS) and unions under its influence broke from the EFITU. The EFITU was formed under the influence of Kemal Abu-Eita, the leader of the Egyptian Real Estate Tax Authority Union; EDLC was led by Kemal Abbas, who founded CTUWS in 1990.

12. Author interview with Ahmed, Cairo, June 2013.

13. Committees were established in some factories in Suez and in Sadat City; in 10 Ramadan City activists initiated moves to form a council of Suez workers. These initiatives were limited however: see Alexander and Bassiouny 2014; Marfleet 2013b.

14. Author's interview with Amir, Cairo, September 2012.

15. Author's interview with Mariam, member of Kifaya, Cairo, April 2005.
16. NSF statement of 14 August 2013: in Arabic and English at: https://nilerevolt. wordpress.com/2013/08/14/statement-by-the-national-salvation-front/? utm_content=buffer56fc9&utm_source=buffer&utm_medium=twitter &utm_campaign=Buffer (accessed 1 July 2015).
17. The Tagammu' leader Rifa'at el-Sa'id repeatedly accused the Brotherhood of 'fascism and aiding terrorism': see Salah and Abdel Aziz 2010. Mohamed ElBaradei made similar allegations: see Taylor and Saleh 2013.
18. Official notice of the State Information Service, see SIS 2013.
19. Debates in Egypt about the Brotherhood, the revolution and the counter-revolution intensified in 2015, focusing on the strategic relations between the left and the Islamists. Some key documents and standpoints are at: www. revso.me; English page at: http://global.revsoc.me/2015/07/on-the-counter-revolution-and-the-islamists-an-invitation-to-open-discussion/
20. The al-Sisi regime's assault on freedom of expression has restricted open debate on the left about issues of theory, strategy and tactics. The intensive discussion under way on social media is not reflected in public forums but surfaces periodically on the websites of independent online publications. See, for example, *Mada Masr* in both Arabic and English at: www.madamasr. com; also *Jadaliyya* at: www: egypt.jadaliyya.com. For perspectives from the Marxist left, see documents of the Revolutionary Socialists archived at www. revso.me, and (in European languages) at: www.global.revsoc.me

Postscript – Cairo, April 2016

1. Author's interview with an eyewitness to the demonstration, Cairo, April 2016.
2. Author's interview with Amal, a member of the Doctors' Syndicate, Cairo, April 2016.
3. This figure does not express the significance of tourist expenditure for millions of Egyptians. The 'tourist dollar' passes through complex networks and many hands, with small sums of money critical for the survival strategies of countless families, especially in the urban economy.
4. Amani El-Torgoman, member of the board of the Egyptian Tourism Federation, quoted in Feteha 2016.
5. Several shipments of wheat and soybean were turned away at Egyptian ports, ostensibly because of contamination of cargoes but in reality, suggested the business press, because the government was unable to pay (El Dahan 2016).
6. Mouayed Makhlouf, regional director for the Middle East and North Africa at the World Bank's International Finance Corporation, quoted in World Bank 2015.
7. Author's interview with Maha, Giza, April 2016.
8. Author's interview with Islam, official of a human rights organisation in Cairo, April 2016.

9. Regeni's body was found in February 2016 outside Cairo bearing multiple marks of torture usually associated with the security services. A PhD student researching the Egyptian trade union movement, he had disappeared on 25 January – the fifth anniversary of the uprising against Mubarak. For an account of the case as investigated up to 8 April 2016 see Egypt Solidarity: https://egyptsolidarityinitiative.org/2016/04/09/justice-for-giulio-italian-ambassador-recalled-but-uk-government-stays-silent/

10. Author's interview with Sherif, Cairo, April 2016.

11. In a television interview on Dream TV Sabbahi made a number of outspoken criticisms of the al-Sisi regime. He said: 'The [Egyptian] people sacrificed a lot but they still live in poverty, corruption, dependence, and tyranny', adding that al-Sisi was losing popularity for failing to provide solutions to the people (Al Fekki 2016).

12. Author's interview with 'Amr, Cairo, April 2016.

Bibliography

Abdalla, A. (1985) *The Student Movement and National Politics in Egypt, 1923–1973* (London: Saqi).

Abdel-Aziz, L. (2013) 'Catch the Al-Sisi mania', *Ahram Weekly*, 19 September, at: http://weekly.ahram.org.eg/News/4103/44/Catch-the-Al-Sisi-mania.aspx (accessed 26 June 2015).

Abdelhadi, M. (2012) 'Mohamed Morsi's choice of prime minister confirms Egyptian fears', *Guardian*, 26 July, at: www.theguardian.com/commentisfree/2012/jul/26/mohamed-morsi-prime-minister-egyptian (accessed 8 June 2015).

Abdel-Malek, A. (1968) *Egypt, Military, Society: The Army Regime, the Left, and Social Change under Nasser* (New York: Vintage Books).

Abdel-Nasser, G. (1955), *The Philosophy of the Revolution* (Washington, DC: Public Affairs Office).

Abdel-Nasser, G. (1972) 'The National Charter', in A.M. Said, *Arab Socialism*, (London: Blandford Press).

Abdel-Nasser, H. (2013) 'Open letter to Lieutenant General Abdel Fattah al-Sisi', *Egypt Independent*, 7 August, at: www.egyptindependent.com/opinion/open-letter-lieutenant-general-abdel-fattah-al-sisi (accessed 30 June 2015).

Abdelrahman, M. (2013) 'The Egyptian opposition: From protestors to revolutionaries?', *Open Democracy*, 22 April, at: www.opendemocracy.net/5050/maha-abdelrahman/egyptian-opposition-from-protestors-to-revolutionaries (accessed 23 June 2015).

Abdelrahman, M. (2014) *Egypt's Long Revolution: Protest Movements and Uprisings* (London: Routledge).

Abdelrahman, M. (2015) 'A force divided: Interpreting the police protests', *Mada Masr*, 1 August, at: www.madamasr.com/opinion/politics/force-divided-interpreting-police-protests (accessed 20 January 2016).

Abdul-Magd, Z. (2012) 'The Egyptian Republic of Retired Generals', *Foreign Policy*, 8 May.

Abdul-Magd, Z. (2013) 'The Egyptian military in politics and the economy: Recent history and current transition status', *CMI Insight*, October, No. 2 (Bergen: Chr Michelsen Institute).

Aboulenein, A. (2013) 'Labour strikes and protests double under Morsi', *Daily News*, 28 April, at: www.dailynewsegypt.com/2013/04/28/labour-strikes-and-protests-double-under-morsi/ (accessed 10 March 2016).

Abouzeid, R. (2011) 'Did prison breakout reveal a plan to sow chaos in Egypt?' *Time*, 16 March, at: http://content.time.com/time/world/article/0,8599,2059301,00.html (accessed 26 February 2015).

Abu Amer, A. (2013) 'Brotherhood document blames Israel, Iran, Gulf for Egypt Coup', *Al Monitor*, at: www.al-monitor.com/pulse/originals/2013/08/muslim-brotherhood-morsi-iran.html#ixzz3xjVDHCWW (accessed 27 June 2015).

Abu-Eita, K. *et al.* (2011) *'Matalib al-'ummal fi al-thawra'* ['Demands of the Workers in the Revolution'], 19 February, at: www.e-socialists.net/node/6509 (accessed May 2012).

Achcar, G. (2013) *The People Want: A Radical Exploration of the Arab Uprising* (London: Saqi Books).

Adam, M. and Carr, S. (2012) 'Brute force: Inside the Central Security Forces', *Egypt Independent*, 11 November, at: www.egyptindependent.com/news/brute-force-inside-central-security-forces (accessed 20 May 2015).

Adly, A. (2015) 'Analysis: Egypt economy "entered a vicious circle"', *Al Jazeera*, 10 December, at: www.aljazeera.com/news/2015/12/analysis-egypt-economy-entered-vicious-circle-151203112708562.html (accessed 20 January 2016).

AFP (2012) 'Morsi says IMF loan compatible with Islamic banking', *AFP*, 6 October, at: https://au.finance.yahoo.com/news/morsi-says-imf-loan-compatible-084805151.html (accessed 13 June 2015).

AFP (2016) 'Egypt minister apologises over police abuses', *France 24*, 22 February. Online at: http://www.france24.com/en/20160222-egypt-minister-apologises-over-police-abuses?ns_campaign=reseaux_sociaux&ns_source=twitter&ns_mchannel=social&ns_linkname=editorial&aef_campaign_ref=partage_aef&aef_campaign_date=2016-02-22&dlvrit=66745; accessed 10 April 2016.

Agha, H. and Malley, R. (2012) 'This is not a revolution', *New York Review of Books*, 8 November, at: www.nybooks.com/articles/2012/11/08/not-revolution/ (accessed 10 March 2016).

Agwani, M.S. (1969) *Communism in the Arab East* (Bombay: Asia Publishing House).

Ahmed, A., Bouis, H., Gutner, T. and Löfgren, H. (2001) *The Egyptian Food Subsidy System: Structure, Performance and Options for Reform*, IFPRI Research Report 119 (Washington, DC: International Food Policy Research Institute).

Ahram Online (2011a) '"Save the Revolution" day begins in Tahrir, Egypt', 1 April, at: http://english.ahram.org.eg/News/9046.aspx (accessed 2 May 2015).

Ahram Online (2011b) 'Egyptian government and Saudi prince reach agreement on Toshka', *Ahram Online*, 20 April, at: http://english.ahram.org.eg/NewsContent/3/12/10457/Business/Economy/Egyptian-government-and-Saudi-prince-reach-agreeme.aspx (accessed 23 March 2016).

Ahram Online (2011c) 'Tweeters' forum #tweetnadwa discusses roots of the Egyptian revolution', *Ahram Online*, 22 June, http://english.ahram.org.eg/NewsContentP/1/14804/Egypt/Tweeters-forum-tweetnadwa-discusses-roots-of-the-E.aspx (accessed 23 March 2016).

Ahram Online (2011d) '296 injured in Abbasiya clashes', 24 July, at: http://english.ahram.org.eg/NewsContent/1/64/17154/Egypt/Politics/-/-injured-in-Abbasiya-clashes.aspx (accessed 23 March 2016).

Ahram Online (2011e) 'Muslim Brotherhood threaten mass protests and new martyrs if elections are postponed', 14 September, at: http://english.ahram.org. eg/NewsContent/1/0/21186/Egypt/0/Muslim-Brotherhood-threaten-mass-protests-and-new-.aspx (accessed 3 June 2015).

Ahram Online (2012a) 'Chronicles of Day 1 of Egypt's historic post-Mubarak People's Assembly', 23 January, at: http://english.ahram.org.eg/ NewsContent/33/0/32412/Elections-/0/Chronicles-of-day--of-Egypts-historic-postMubarak-.aspx (accessed 5 May 2015).

Ahram Online (2012b) 'Relive vote count in 1st round of Egypt presidential race: How Morsi and Shafiq moved on', *Ahram Online*, 25 May, at: http://english. ahram.org.eg/News/42755.aspx (accessed 7 June 2015).

Ahram Online (2012c) 'Renewed clashes in Cairo leave scores injured', *Ahram Online*, 21 November, at: http://english.ahram.org.eg/NewsContent/1/64/58760/ Egypt/Politics-/Renewed-clashes-in-Cairo-leave-scores-injured.aspx (accessed 13 June 2015).

Ahram Online (2012d) 'English text of Morsi's Constitutional Declaration', *Ahram Online*, 22 November, at: http://english.ahram.org.eg/NewsContent/1/0/58947/ Egypt/0/English-text-of-Morsis-Constitutional-Declaration-.aspx (accessed 14 June 2015).

Ahram Online (2012e) 'Morsi declaration hailed by supporters, deemed "coup" by opposition', *Ahram Online*, 22 November, at: http://english.ahram.org. eg/NewsContent/1/64/58950/Egypt/Politics-/Morsi-declaration-hailed-by-supporters,-deemed-cou.aspx (accessed 13 June 2015).

Ahram Online (2012f) 'Egypt suffers power outage, could face "dark winter" due to fuel crisis', *Ahram Online*, 28 December, at: http://english.ahram.org.eg/ NewsContent/3/12/61427/Business/Economy/Egypt-suffers-power-outage,-could-face-dark-winter.aspx (accessed 26 June 2015).

Ahram Online (2013a) 'Microbus drivers strike strangles traffic in Cairo', *Ahram Online*, 10 March, at: http://english.ahram.org.eg/NewsContent/1/64/66512/ Egypt/Politics-/Microbus-drivers-strike-strangles-traffic-in-Cairo.aspx (accessed 22 June 2015).

Ahram Online (2013b) 'Not a coup, but popular revolution: Egypt's Sabbahi', *Ahram Online*, 24 August, at: http://english.ahram.org.eg/ NewsContentPrint/1/0/79809/Egypt/0/Not-a-coup,-but-popular-revolution-Egypt%E2%80%99s-Sabbahi.aspx (accessed 26 June 2015).

Ahram Online (2014a) 'I wish I was Gamal Abdel Nasser, El-Sisi says', *Ahram Online*, 5 May, at: http://english.ahram.org.eg/News/100583.aspx (accessed 23 March 2016).

Ahram Online (2014b) '"I ran for Egypt president to save the state" says El-Sisi', *Ahram Online*, 5 May, at: http://english.ahram.org.eg/NewsContent/ 1/0/100577/Egypt/0/I-ran-for-Egypt-president-to-save-the-state,-says-.aspx (accessed 27 June 2015).

Ahram Online (2016) 'Egypt's foreign currency reserves slightly up in March', *Ahram Online*, 4 April. Online at: http://english.ahram.org.eg/

NewsContent/3/12/198759/Business/Economy/Egypts-foreign-currency-reserves-slightly-up-in-Ma.aspx; accessed 10 April 2016.

Alabass, A. (2012) 'Piety versus expediency: Egypt Islamists change tack on IMF loan', *Ahram Online*, 28 August, at: http://english.ahram.org.eg/NewsContent/3/0/51412/Business/0/Piety-versus-expediency-Egypt-Islamists-change-tac.aspx (accessed 12 June 2015).

Al-Ahram Weekly (2005) 'A Chronicle of Dissent', *Al-Ahram Weekly*, 23–29 June 2005.

Al-Ahram Weekly (2009a) 'Seasons of protest', *Al-Ahram Weekly*, 1–6 January.

Al-Ahram Weekly (2009b) 'Brother trouble', *Al-Ahram Weekly*, 28 October.

Al Arabiya News (2011) 'Egyptians rally in Cairo's Tahrir to "save revolution"', 1 April, at: http://english.alarabiya.net/articles/2011/04/01/143823.html (accessed 2 May 2015).

Albrecht, H. (2012) 'Authoritarian transformation or transition from authoritarianism? Insights on regime change in Egypt', in B. Kotany and R. El-Mahdi (eds), *Arab Spring in Egypt: Revolution and Beyond* (Cairo: The American University in Cairo Press).

Alexander, A. (2011) 'The strike wave and the crisis of the Egyptian state', *Ahram Online*, 16 December.

Alexander, J.C. (2011) *Performative Revolution in Egypt: An Essay in Cultural Power* (London: Bloomsbury Academic).

Alexander, J.C. (2013) 'The arc of civil liberation: Obama–Tahrir–Occupy', in *Philosophy and Social Criticism* 39 (4–5): 341–47.

Alexander, A. and Bassiouny, M. (2014) *Bread, Freedom, Social Justice: Workers and the Egyptian Revolution* (London: Zed Press).

Al-Fekki, A. (2016) 'Former rival presidential candidate Sabahy slams Al-Sisi's regime', *Daily News*, January 7. Online at: http://www.dailynewsegypt.com/2016/01/07/former-rival-presidential-candidate-sabahy-slams-al-sisis-regime/; accessed 10 April 2016.

Al-Ghamrawi, A. (2013) 'Egyptian presidential advisor: Brotherhood ideology a crime against society', *Al-Sharq al-Awsat*, 30 December, at: http://english.aawsat.com/2013/12/article55326181/egyptian-presidential-advisor-brotherhood-ideology-a-crime-against-society (accessed 1 July 2015).

Ali, M. (2011) 'Egypt's Islamists and Secularists avoid confrontation and join hands for yet another Friday of protest', *Ahram Online*, 28 July, at: http://english.ahram.org.eg/NewsContent/1/64/17498/Egypt/Politics-/Search.aspx?Text=%20leftists (accessed 2 May 2015).

Ali, T. (2002) *The Clash of Fundamentalisms: Crusades, Jihads and Modernity* (London: Verso).

Al Jazeera (2011a) 'Protesters torch Egypt police post', *Al Jazeera*, 27 January, at: www.aljazeera.com/news/middleeast/2011/01/201112734210243448.html (accessed 2 May 2011).

Al Jazeera (2011b) 'Timeline: Egypt's revolution', *Al Jazeera*, 14 February, at: www.aljazeera.com/news/middleeast/2011/01/201112515334871490.html (accessed 5 May 2015).

Al Jazeera (2012) 'Egypt's top judges condemn Morsi's decree', *Al Jazeera*, 24 November, at: www.aljazeera.com/news/middleeast/2012/11/201211241217 56983310.html (accessed 14 June 2015).

Al Jazeera (2013) 'Egypt declares state of emergency', *Al Jazeera*, 14 July, at: www.aljazeera.com/news/middleeast/2013/08/201381413509551214.html (accessed 25 June 2015).

Al Jazeera (2016) 'Is another revolution brewing in Egypt?', *Al Jazeera*, 24 January, at: www.aljazeera.com/news/2016/01/160122114637805.html (accessed 25 January 2016).

Al-Masry Al-Youm (2013) 'CSF officers strike over planned Port Said deployment', *Egypt Independent*, 6 March, at: www.egyptindependent.com/news/csf-officers-strike-over-planned-port-said-deployment (accessed 23 June 2015).

Al-Tawy, A. (2013) 'Egyptian figures condemn cathedral violence but disagree on causes', *Ahram Online*, 8 April, at: http://english.ahram.org.eg/NewsContent/1/0/68762/Egypt/0/Egyptian-figures-condemn-cathedral-violence-but-di.aspx (accessed 20 January 2016).

Al-Tawy, A. (2014) 'Egypt cabinet reshuffle hints at "dissolution of 30 June alliance"', *Ahram Online*, 1 March, at: http://english.ahram.org.eg/NewsContent/1/64/95573/Egypt/Politics-/Egypt-cabinet-reshuffle-hints-at-dissolution-of--J.aspx (accessed 27 June 2015).

Aly, A. (2014) 'Egypt's conservative nationalism: Discourse and praxis of the new regime', *Jadaliyya*, 14 October, at: www.jadaliyya.com/pages/index/19628/egypt%E2%80%99s-conservative-nationalism_discourse-and-pra (accessed 1 July 2015).

Amnesty International (2002) *Egypt No protection – systematic torture continues.* (London: Amnesty International), at: www.amnesty.org/en/library/info/MDE12/031/2002 (accessed 10 June 2015).

Amnesty International (2012) *Egypt: Brutality Unpunished and Unchecked: Egypt's Military Kill and Torture Protestors with Impunity* (London: Amnesty International).

Amnesty International (2014) 'Egypt: Roadmap to repression: No end in sight to human rights violations', Amnesty International, London, 23 January, at: www.amnesty.org/en/documents/MDE12/005/2014/en/ (accessed 10 March 2016).

Amnesty International (2015) Amnesty International Report 2014/15 (London: Amnesty International).

Ansari, H. (1987) *Egypt, The Stalled Society* (Cairo: The American University in Cairo Press).

Aouragh, M. and Alexander, A. (2011) 'The Egyptian experience: Sense and nonsense of the Internet revolution', *International Journal of Communication* 5: 1344–58.

Arab Barometer Project (2011) *Public Opinion Report on the Most Important Political and Social Issues in Egypt*, at: www.arabbarometer.org/sites/default/files/Egypt%20ABII%20Country%20Report%20English.pdf (accessed 10 May 2015).

Arafat, A. (2009) *Hosni Mubarak and the Future of Democracy in Egypt* (Basingstoke: Palgrave).

Asad, T. (2012) 'Fear and the ruptured state: Reflections on Egypt after Mubarak', *Social Research* 79 (2).

Asad, T. (2015) 'Thinking about tradition, religion, and politics in Egypt today', *Critical Enquiry*, Special Feature, 14 April, at: http://criticalinquiry.uchicago.edu/thinking_about_tradition_religion_and_politics_in_egypt_today/ (accessed 28 April 2015).

Ashour, O. (2011) 'History's lessons: Dismantling Egypt's security agency', *BBC News*, 9 March, at: www.bbc.co.uk/news/world-middle-east-12679632 (accessed 2 May 2015).

Attalah, L. (2010) 'Workers, activists demand national minimum wage', *Egypt Independent*, 2 May.

Awad, M. (2012) 'Islamist businessmen challenge Egypt's old money', *Reuters*, 17 October, at: www.reuters.com/article/egypt-economy-brotherhood-idUSL6E8L9NQ420121017#TgeHEtTI7d2ctBOP.97 (accessed 11 June 2015).

Badiou, A. (2012) *The Rebirth of History: Times of Riots and Uprisings* (London: Verso).

Badr El-Din, K. (2014) 'Privatization: A key to solving Egypt's economic woes', *Voices and Views: Middle East and North Africa*, World Bank, 3 November, at: http://blogs.worldbank.org/arabvoices/privatization-key-solving-egypt-s-economic-woes (accessed 19 March 2015).

Baker, R.W. (1978) *Egypt's Uncertain Revolution under Nasser and Sadat* (Cambridge, MA: Harvard University Press).

Baker, R. W. (1990) *Sadat and After: Struggles for Egypt's Political Soul* (London: I.B. Tauris).

Barghouti, T. (2008) *The Umma and the Dawla: The Nation-State and the Arab Middle East* (London: Pluto).

Baring, E. (2000 [1908]) *Modern Egypt*, vol. 6 (London: Macmillan).

Barker, C. (2014) 'Class struggle and social movements', in C. Barker, L. Cox, J. Krinsky and A.G. Nilsen, *Marxism and Social Movements* (Chicago, IL: Haymarket).

Barker, C., Cox, L., Krinsky, J. and Nilsen, A.G. (2014) 'Marxism and social movements: An introduction', in C. Barker, L. Cox, J. Krinsky and A.G. Nilsen, *Marxism and Social Movements* (Chicago, IL: Haymarket).

Barsamian, D. (2003) *Culture and Resistance: Conversations with Edward W. Said* (London: Pluto Press).

Bauer, B. and Schweitzer, P. (2012) 'The Egyptian Revolution 2011: Mechanisms of violence and non-violence', *State of Peace Conference & Peace Report 2012 Democracy in Crisis: The Dynamics of Civic Protest and Civic Resistance*, at:

www.friedensburg.at/uploads/files/Bauer_Schweitzer_StoP2012_paper.pdf (accessed 2 May 2015).

Bayat, A. (1987) *Workers and Revolution in Iran* (London: Zed).

Bayat, A. (2003) 'The "street" and the politics of dissent in the Arab world', *Middle East Report* 226, at: www.merip.org/mer/mer226/street-politics-dissent-arab-world (accessed 20 March 2015).

Bayat, A. (2005) 'Islamism and social movement theory', *Third World Quarterly* 26 (6): 891–908.

Bayat, A. (2012) 'The Arab Street', in J. Sowers and C. Toensing, *The Journey to Tahrir: Revolution, Protest, and Social Change in Egypt* (London: Verso).

Bayat, A. (2013) *Life as Politics: How Ordinary People Change the Middle East* (Redwood City, CA: Stanford University Press).

Bayat, A. and Denis, E. (2000) 'Who is afraid of *ashwaiyyat*? Urban change and politics in Egypt', *Environment and Urbanization* 12 (2): 185–99.

BBC (2012a) 'Egyptian pound falls further despite currency intervention', *BBC News*, 31 December, at: www.bbc.co.uk/news/business-20875179 (accessed 13 June 2015).

BBC (2012b) 'Egypt fury over Mohammed Mursi "coup against legitimacy"', *BBC News*, 23 November, at: www.bbc.co.uk/news/world-middle-east- 20457058 (accessed 15 June 2015).

BBC (2013) 'Egypt protesters clash with police at presidential palace', *BBC News*, 1 February, at: www.bbc.co.uk/news/world-middle-east-21289729 (accessed 23 June 2015).

BBC News (2014) 'Egypt: Abdul Fattah al-Sisi profile', *BBC News*, 16 May, at: www.bbc.co.uk/news/world-middle-east-19256730 (accessed 20 January 2016).

Beaumont, P. and Sherwood, H. (2011) 'Egypt protesters defy tanks and teargas to make the streets their own', *Guardian*, 28 January.

Behbehani, H. (1986) *The Soviet Union and Arab Nationalism* (London: Kegan Paul).

Beinin, J. (1990) *Was the Red Flag Flying There?: Marxist Politics and the Arab–Israeli Conflict in Eqypt and Israel 1948–1965* (Berkeley, CA: University of California Press).

Beinin, J. (1994) 'Will the real Egyptian working class please stand up?', in Z. Lockman (ed.), *Workers and Working Classes in the Middle East* (Albany, NY: State University of New York Press).

Beinin, J. (2001) *Workers and Peasants in the Modern Middle East* (Cambridge: Cambridge University Press).

Beinin, J. (2007) 'The Egyptian Workers Movement in 2007', *Chroniques Egyptiennes 2007*.

Beinin, J. (2009) 'Workers' protest in Egypt: Neo-liberalism and class struggle in 21st century', *Social Movement Studies* 8 (4).

Beinin, J. (2011) 'Egyptian workers play crucial role in fight for democracy', *Clarion – PSC CUNY* (Professional Staff Congress, City University of New

York), August, at: www.psc-cuny.org/clarion/august-2011/egyptian-workers-play-crucial-role-fight-democracy (accessed 1 March 2015).

Beinin, J. (2012) *The Rise of Egypt's Workers* (Washington, DC: Carnegie Endowment for International Peace).

Beinin, J. and El-Hamalawy, H. (2007) 'Egyptian textile workers confront the new economic order', 25 March, *Middle East Report Online*, at: http://www.merip.org/mero/mero032507 (accessed 12 March 2016).

Beinin, J. and Lockman, Z. (1987) *Workers on the Nile: Nationalism, Communism, Islam and the Egyptian Working Class, 1882–1954* (Princeton, NJ: Princeton University Press).

Beissinger, M., Jamal, A. and Mazur K. (2013) 'Who participated in the Arab Spring?: A comparison of Egyptian and Tunisian Revolutions', Princeton University, at: www.princeton.edu/~mbeissin/beissinger.tunisiaegyptcoalitions.pdf (accessed 10 May 2015).

Bilal, M. (2011) 'Egypt's "Ultras" pitch in at Tahrir protest', *Al Jazeera*, 29 November, at: www.aljazeera.com/indepth/features/2011/11/2011112849129 60586.html; (accessed 2 May 2015).

Bishara, D. (2011) 'The power of workers in Egypt's 2011 Uprising', in B. Korany and R. El-Mahdi, *Arab Spring in Egypt: Revolution and Beyond* (Cairo: The American University in Cairo Press).

Blair, E., Taylor, P. and Perry, T. (2013) 'Special Report: How the Muslim Brotherhood lost Egypt', *Reuters*, 26 July, at: www.reuters.com/article/us-egypt-mistakes-specialreport-idUSBRE96O07H20130726 (accessed 24 June 2015).

Bonney, R. (2008) *The 'Clash of Civilizations' and the Global War on Terror* (Oxford: Peter Lang).

Botman, S. (1988) *The Rise of Egyptian Communism, 1939–1970* (Syracuse, NY: Syracuse University Press).

Brown, N. (2012) *When Victory Is Not an Option: Islamist Movements in Arab Politics* (Ithaca, NY: Cornell University Press).

Brownlee, J. (2013) 'Violence against Copts in Egypt' (Washington, DC: Carnegie Endowment for International Peace), at: http://carnegieendowment.org/files/violence_against_copts3.pdf (accessed 20 January 2016).

Bush, R. (ed.) (2002) *Counter-Revolution in Egypt's Countryside: Land and Farmers in the Era of Economic Reform* (London: Zed).

Bush, R. (2009) 'The land and the people', in R. El-Mahdi and P. Marfleet (eds), *Egypt: The Moment of Change* (London: Zed).

Büttner, F. (1979), 'Political stability without stable institutions: The retraditionalization of Egypt's polity', *Orient* 20 (1): 51–67.

Byman, D. (2011) 'After the hope of the Arab Spring, the chill of an Arab Winter', *Washington Post*, 1 December, at: www.washingtonpost.com/opinions/after-the-hope-of-the-arab-spring-the-chill-of-an-arab-winter/2011/11/28/gIQABGqHIO_story.html (accessed 1 November 2012).

Cabeza, S. and Siegalbaum, M. (2014) 'Egyptian courts in peril', *Middle East Eye*, 21 October, at: www.middleeasteye.net/in-depth/features/egyptian-courts-peril-663392890#sthash.Y41QPcog.dpuf (accessed 27 June 2015).

Campbell, D.G. (2011) *Egypt Unshackled: Using social media to @#:) the system* (Camarthenshire: Cambria).

Campagna, J. (1996) 'From accommodation to confrontation: the Muslim Brotherhood in the Mubarak years', *Journal of International Affairs* 50 (1): 278–304.

Carapico, S. (2012) 'Egypt's civic revolution turns "Democracy Promotion" on its head', in B. Korany and R. El-Mahdi (eds), *Arab Spring in Egypt: Revolution and Beyond* (Cairo: The American University in Cairo Press).

Carnegie (Carnegie Endowment for International Peace) (2011) *Egypt's Democratic Transition*. Washington, DC: Carnegie Endowment / Legatum.

Chalcraft, J. (2012) 'Horizontalism in the Egyptian revolutionary process', *Middle East Report* 42 (262), at: www.merip.org/mer/mer262/horizontalism-egyptian-revolutionary-process (accessed 12 March 2016).

Charbel, J. (2012a) 'SCAF takes strike-breaking into its own hands', *Egypt Independent*, 13 March, at: www.egyptindependent.com/news/scaf-takes-strike-breaking-its-own-hands (accessed 7 June 2015).

Charbel. J. (2012b) 'Labor activists: New decree eyes "Brotherhoodization" of unions', *Egypt Independent*, 26 November, at: www.egyptindependent.com/news/labor-activists-new-decree-eyes-brotherhoodization-unions (accessed 16 June 2015).

Charbel, J. (2013a) 'Egypt's railways see biggest strike in almost 30 years', *Egypt Independent*, 8 April, at: www.egyptindependent.com/news/egypt-s-railways-see-biggest-strike-almost-30-years (accessed 22 June 2015).

Charbel, J. (2013b) 'Labor activist wades into the deep state', *Mada Masr*, 30 September, at: www.madamasr.com/content/labor-activist-wades-deep-state (accessed 26 June 2015).

Charbel, J. (2016) 'Strikes and labor protests hit state-owned companies', *Mada Masr*, 5 January, at: www.madamasr.com/sections/economy/strikes-and-labor-protests-hit-state-owned-companies (accessed 20 January 2016).

Cole, J. (2011) 'Christians, Muslims "One Hand" in Egypt's Youth Revolution', *Informed Comment*, 7 February, at: www.juancole.com/2011/02/christians-muslims-one-hand-in-egypts-youth-revolution.html (accessed 20 January 2016).

Cook, S. (2012) *The Struggle for Egypt: From Nasser to Tahrir Square* (Cairo: The American University in Cairo Press).

Creswell, R. (2011) 'Egypt: The Cultural Revolution', *New York Times*, 10 February.

Cromer [Earl of] (1913) 'The government of subject races', *Political and Literary essays, 1908–1913* (London: Macmillan).

CTUWS (Centre for Trade Union and Workers' Services) (2013) 'Shubra Metro workers on strike and trains work without maintenance', at: www.ctuws.com/?item=1208 (accessed 26 June 2015).

Dale, T. (2012) 'Draft law threatens independent unions, but workers vow to fight', *Egypt Independent*, 14 March, at: www.egyptindependent.com//news/draft-law-threatens-independent-unions-workers-vow-fight (accessed 8 June 2015).

Dawoud, K. (2015) 'Splits within the Brotherhood', *Al-Ahram Weekly*, 31 December. Online at: http://weekly.ahram.org.eg/News/15107/17/Splits-within-the-Brotherhood.aspx; accessed 10 April 2016.

Dunne, M. (2015) *Egypt's Nationalists Dominate in a Politics-Free Zone*, Carnegie Endowment for International Peace, April. (Beirut: Carnegie Endowment).

Dunne, M. and Revkin, M. (2011) *Rethinking Internal Security in Egypt*, Carnegie Endowment for International Peace, 16 March, at: http://carnegieeurope.eu/publications/?fa=43081 (accessed 1 May 2015).

EAAT [Egyptian Association Against Torture] (2003), statement, at: www.aloufok.net/article.php3?id_article=484 (accessed 30 March 2008).

Economist (2013) 'Arab spring break', *Economist*, 4 May.

Egypt Independent (2012) 'Thank-you telegram to Tantawi stirs up People's Assembly spat', *Egypt Independent*, 24 January, at: www.egyptindependent.com//news/thank-you-telegram-tantawi-stirs-peoples-assembly-spat (accessed 3 June 2015).

EIPR [Egyptian Initiative for Personal Rights] (2012) 'Letter from parties, NGOs, syndicates and political movements to the IMF', 12 November, at: http://eipr.org/en/pressrelease/2012/11/12/1534 (accessed 13 June 2015).

El Dahan, M. (2016) 'UPDATE 1-Egypt rejects Canadian wheat shipment over ergot fungus', *Reuters*, 16 February. Online at: www.reuters.com/article/egypt-wheat-idUSL8N15V5A5; accessed 10 April 2016.

Eleiba (2011) 'The counter revolution, Shafiq and state security', *Ahram Online*, 7 March, at: http://english.ahram.org.eg/NewsContent/1/64/7155/Egypt/Politics-/The-counter-revolution,-Shafiq-and-State-Security-.aspx (accessed 2 May 2015).

El-Erian, E. (2011) 'Rise of the Brothers', *The Cairo Review of Global Affairs* 1 (1): 94–100.

El-Fiqi, M. (2013) 'Strikes under control', *Ahram Weekly*, 19 December, at: http://weekly.ahram.org.eg/News/4970/18/Strikes-under-control.aspx (accessed 27 June 2015).

El-Ghobashy, M. (2011) 'The Praxis of the Egyptian Revolution', *Middle East Report* 258, at: www.merip.org/mer/mer258/praxis-egyptian-revolution#_31_ (accessed 10 March 2015).

El-Ghobashy, M. (2012) 'Egyptian politics upended', *MERIP*, 20 August, at: www.merip.org/mero/mero082012 (accessed 6 May 2015).

El Gundy, Z. (2013) 'Generational conflicts shake ElBaradei's Constitution Party', *Ahram Online*, 28 March, at: http://english.ahram.org.eg/NewsContent/1/64/67797/Egypt/Politics-/Generational-conflicts-shake-ElBaradeis-Constituti.aspx (accessed 23 June 2015).

El-Hamalawy, H. (2009 [2000]) *1977: The Lost Revolution* (MA thesis, The American University in Cairo), at: www.scribd.com/doc/12893045/1977-Bread-Uprising#scribd (accessed 1 June 2015).

El-Hamalawy, H. (2011a) 'Egypt protests continue in the factories', *Guardian*, 14 February.

El-Hamalawy, H (2011b) #Jan25 'The workers, middle class, military junta and the permanent revolution', '*Arabawy* blog, 12 February, at: http://arabawy.org/24959/permanent-revolution (accessed 4 April 2015).

El-Hamalawy, H. (2011c) 'Egypt's revolution has been 10 years in the making', *Guardian*, 2 March.

El-Hamalawy, H. (2011d) 'Anti-SCAF (Army) march attacked in Egypt', *Jadaliyya*, 24 July, at: www.jadaliyya.com/pages/index/2222/anti-scaf-(army)-march-attacked-in-egypt

El-Hamalawy, H. (2012a) 'In Egypt, Mubarak's repression machine is still alive and well', *Guardian*, 16 May, at: www.guardian.co.uk/commentisfree/2012/may/16/egypt-mubaraks-repression-machine-alive-wel (accessed 23 June 2015).

El-Hamalawy, H. (2012b) 'Hossam El-Hamalawy on social media and protests in Egypt', *Jadaliyya*, 19 October, at: www.jadaliyya.com/pages/index/7942/hossam-el-hamalawy-on-social-media-and-protests-in (accessed 10 May 2015).

El-Mahdi, R. (2009) 'The democracy movement: Cycles of protest', in R. El-Mahdi and P. Marfleet (eds), *Egypt: The Moment of Change* (London: Zed).

El-Mahdi, R. (2012) 'Against marginalization: workers, youth and class in the 25 January revolution', in R. Bush and H. Ayeb (eds), *Marginality and Exclusion in Egypt* (Cairo: The American University in Cairo Press).

El-Meehy, A. (2012) 'Egypt's popular committees: From moments of madness to NGO dilemma', *Middle East Report* 42 (265), Winter, at: www.merip.org/mer/mer265/egypts-popular-committees (accessed 1 March 2015).

El-Menawy, A. (2012) *Tahrir: The Last 18 Days of Mubarak* (London: Gilgamesh Publishing).

Elmeshad, M. (2012) 'Advocacy group rejects government's IMF-pleasing reform plan', *Egypt Independent*, 22 March, at: www.egyptindependent.com/news/advocacy-group-rejects-government's-imf-pleasing-reform-plan (accessed 12 June 2015).

El-Naggar, A. (2009) 'Economic policy: From state control to decay and corruption', in R. El-Mahdi and P. Marfleet (eds), *Egypt – the Moment of Change* (London: Zed).

El-Nahas (2005) 'Judges into the fray', *Al-Ahram Weekly*, 21–27 April.

El-Nahhas, M. (2011) 'New faces, new hope', *Al-Ahram Weekly*, 24–30 November.

El Shafei, O. (1995) 'Workers, trade unions and the state in Egypt 1984–1989', *Cairo Papers in Social Science* 18 (2).

El-Sharnoubi, O. (2012) 'Unity movement launched at mass rally to counter Egypt's Islamists', *Ahram Online*, 22 September, at: http://english.ahram.org.

eg/NewsContent/1/64/53500/Egypt/Politics-/Unity-movement-launched-at-mass-rally-to-counter-E.aspx (accessed 24 June 2015).

El-Sharnoubi, O. (2013) 'Revolutionary history relived: The Mahalla strike of 6 April 2008', *Ahram Online*, 6 April.

El Wardani, S. (2010) 'Palm Hills: engine of growth or example of crony capitalism?', *Ahram Online*, 17 December, at: http://english.ahram.org.eg/NewsContent/3/0/1861/Business/0/Palm-Hills-engine-of-growth-or-example-of-crony-ca.aspx (accessed 23 March 2016).

Elyan, T. (2011) 'MB says to participate "symbolically" in Jan. 25 demos', *Daily News Egypt*, 23 January, at: www.dailynewsegypt.com/2011/01/23/mb-says-will-have-symbolic-participation-in-jan-25-demos/ (accessed 23 January 2011).

Engels, F. (1968 [1884]) 'Origins of the Family, Private Property and the State', in K. Marx and F. Engels, *Collected Works*. London: Lawrence & Wishart.

Engineer, A.A. (1980) *Origin and Development of Islam: An Essay on Its Socio-Economic Growth* (Hyderabad: Orient Longman).

Essam al-Din (2012) 'Brotherhood's Shura Council chairman criticises Morsi declaration', *Ahram Online*, 25 November, at: http://english.ahram.org.eg/NewsContent/1/64/59123/Egypt/Politics-/Brotherhoods-Shura-Council-chairman-criticises-Mor.aspx (accessed 15 June 2015).

Esterman, I. (2016) 'Exclusive: Mada Masr obtains Sisi's presidential decree for World Bank loan', *Mada Masr*, February 3. Online at: www.madamasr.com/sections/economy/exclusive-mada-masr-obtains-sisi's-presidential-decree-world-bank-loan-0; accessed 10 April 2016.

Ez-Eldin, M. (2011) 'Date with a revolution', *New York Times*, 30 January.

Ezzat, D. (2012) 'Morsi rocks the boat', *Al-Ahram Weekly*, 22 November, at: http://weekly.ahram.org.eg/News/354/17/Morsi-rocks-the-boat.aspx (accessed 14 June 2015).

Fadel, L. (2012) 'Egypt's Muslim Brotherhood faces sharp internal divisions over presidential race', *Washington Post*, 26 March, at: www.washingtonpost.com/world/middle_east/egypts-muslim-brotherhood-faces-sharp-internal-divisions-over-presidential-race/2012/03/26/gIQASa7qcS_story.html (accessed June 7 2015).

Fady, S. (2013) 'Mahalla drivers shut down city roads', *Daily News*, 17 March, at: www.dailynewsegypt.com/2013/03/17/mahalla-drivers-shut-down-city-roads/ (accessed 22 June 2015).

Fahmi, G. (2012) 'Egypt presidential election 2012: The survival of the July 1952 regime', *Arab Reform Brief*, no. 60 (Amman: Arab Reform Initiative).

Fahmy, H. (2011) 'Muslim Brotherhood reconsiders refusal to participate in Jan 25 demo', *Daily News Egypt*, 20 January, at: www.dailynewsegypt.com/2011/01/20/muslim-brotherhood-reconsiders-refusal-to-participate-in-jan-25-demo/ (accessed 20 January 2011).

Fahmy, K. (1997) *All the Pasha's Men: Mehmed Ali, his Army and the Making of Modern Egypt* (Cambridge: Cambridge University Press).

Fahmy, K. (2013) 'A Revolutionary People', *Ahram Online*, 8 June.

Fayed, S. (2011) 'Police shoot dead 17 attacking Egypt police stations', *Reuters*, 29 January, at: www.reuters.com/article/2011/01/29/us-egypt-benisuef-idUSTRE70S3T420110129 (accessed 2 May 2015).

Feteha, A. (2011) 'Egypt military attacks Occupy Cabinet protesters: Updates from the day', *Ahram Online*, 16 December, at: http://english.ahram.org.eg/NewsContent/1/64/29489/Egypt/Politics-/Egypt-military-attacks-Occupy-Cabinet-protesters-U.aspx (accessed 3 May 2015).

Feteha, A. (2016) 'Egypt's Tourism Collapse Stretches From the Pyramids to the Beach', *Bloomberg*, 1 February. Online at: www.bloomberg.com/news/articles/2016-02-01/egypt-resorts-become-ghost-towns-as-tourist-arrivals-plummet; accessed 10 April 2016.

Filiu, J-P (2011) *The Arab Revolution: Ten Lessons from the Democratic Uprising* (London: C. Hurst & Co.).

FJP [Freedom and Justice Party] (2011) *Election Program – the Freedom and Justice Party*, at: www.scribd.com/doc/73955131/FJP-Program-En (accessed 4 June 2015).

Fleishman, J. (2013) 'Egypt's VP Mohamed ElBaradei resigns in protest against crackdown', *Los Angeles Times*, 14 August, at: www.latimes.com/news/world/worldnow/la-fg-wn-egypt-mohamed-elbaradei-resigns-20130814,0,5082837.story#ixzz2vZgD5lNR (accessed 26 June 2015).

Friedman, G. (2011) 'Egypt: The distance between enthusiasm and reality', *Stratfor Global Intelligence*, 14 February, at: www.stratfor.com/weekly/20110213-egypt-distance-between-enthusiasm-and-reality (accessed 10 March 2015).

Galal, R. (2015) 'Egypt outlaws workers' right to strike', *Al Monitor*, 12 May, at: www.al-monitor.com/pulse/originals/2015/05/egypt-court-ruling-strike-right-sharia-law-sisi-badawi-labor.html# (accessed 28 June 2015).

Galian, L. (2015) 'New modes of collective actions: The reemergence of anarchism in Egypt', in F. Gerges (ed.), *Contentious Politics in the Middle East* (Basingstoke: Palgrave).

Gamal, W. (2013) 'Sons of Thatcher in the Brotherhood and Salvation Front', *Ahram Online*, 25 April.

Gause, F. (2011) 'Why Middle East Studies missed the Arab Spring: The myth of authoritarian stability', *Foreign Affairs*, July–August, pp. 81–90, at: www.foreignaffairs.com/articles/middle-east/2011-07-01/why-middle-east-studies-missed-arab-spring (accessed 21 March 2016).

Gerges, F. (ed.) (2014) *The New Middle East: Protest and Revolution in the Arab World* (Cambridge: Cambridge University Press).

Ghonim, W. (2012), *Revolution 2.0: The Power of the People is Greater Than the People in Power: A Memoir* (Boston, MA: Houghton Mifflin Harcourt).

Gordon, J. (1992) *Nasser's Blessed Movement: Egypt's Free Officers and the July Revolution* (Oxford: Oxford University Press).

Greene, R. (2006), 'Bush's language angers US Muslims', *BBC News*, 12 August, at: http://news.bbc.co.uk/1/hi/world/americas/4785065.stm (accessed 1 July 2015).

Gribbon, L. and Hawas, S. (2012) 'Signs and signifiers: Visual translations of revolt', in S. Mehrez (ed.), *Translating Egypt's Revolution: The Language of Tahrir* (Cairo: The American University in Cairo Press).

Gumuscu, S. (2008) *Economic Liberalization, Devout Bourgeoisie, and Change in Political Islam: Comparing Turkey and Egypt*, EUI Working Papers RSCAS 2008/19 (Florence: European University Institute).

Haddon, H., Rashwan, N., Ali, A., Tarek S., Shukrallah, S., Abo El-Abbas, B. and El-Sharnoubi, O. (2013a) 'Live updates: Millions join anti-Morsi protests in Egypt', *Ahram Online*, 30 June, at: http://english.ahram.org.eg/NewsContent/1/152/75297/Egypt/Morsi,-one-year-on/Live-Updates-Millions-join-antiMorsi-protests-in-E.aspx (accessed 24 June 2015).

Haddon, H., Rashwan, N., Ali, A., Tarek S., Shukrallah, S., Abo El-Abbas, B., and O. El-Sharnoubi (2013b) 'Live updates 2: Millions on streets for anti-Morsi protests; 4 dead in Upper Egypt', *Ahram Online*, 30 June, at: http://english.ahram.org.eg/News/75341.aspx (accessed 24 June 2015).

Haddon, H., Shukrallah, S., Adel, M., Al-Tawy, A., Rashwan, N. and Ali, R. (2013c) 'Live updates: Morsi ousted; head of constitutional court to take over Egypt presidency', *Ahram Online*, 3 July, at: http://english.ahram.org.eg/NewsContent/1/0/75594/Egypt/0/Live-updates-Morsi-ousted;-head-of-constitutional-.aspx (accessed 24 June 2015).

Halawa, O. (2013) 'Divisions among police result in intermittent "strike" action', *Egypt Independent*, 13 March, at: www.egyptindependent.com/news/divisions-among-police-result-intermittent-%E2%80%98strike-action (accessed 22 June 2015).

Hamid, S. (2011) 'The struggle for Middle East democracy', *The Cairo Review of Global Affairs* 1 (1): 18–29.

Hanieh, A. (2013) *Lineages of Revolt: Issues of Contemporary Capitalism in the Middle East* (Chicago, IL: Haymarket).

Hansen, S. (2012) 'The economic vision of Egypt's Muslim Brotherhood millionaires', *Business Week*, 19 April.

Harman, C. (1994) 'The prophet and the proletariat', *International Socialism Journal* 64 (Autumn).

Hassan, K. (2016) 'Egyptian state takes on independent trade unions', *Al Monitor*, 24 March. Online at: www.al-monitor.com/pulse/originals/2016/03/egypt-independent-trade-unions-battle-decision-law.html#; accessed 10 April 2016.

Hejjar, L. (2011) 'Omar Suleiman, the CIA's man in Cairo and Egypt's Torturer-in-Chief', *Jadaliyya*, 30 January, at: www.jadaliyya.com/pages/index/503/omar-suleiman-the-cias-man-in-cairo-and-egypts-tor (accessed 10 March 2016).

Hendaway, H. (2014), 'Egypt's new premier calls for protests to end', *ABC News* [Associated Press], 1 March, at: http://abcnews.go.com/International/

wireStory/egypt-cabinet-sworn-ahead-presidential-vote-22731595 (accessed 27 June 2015).

Henry, C. and Springborg, R. (2001) *Globalization and the Politics of Development in the Middle East* (Cambridge: Cambridge University Press).

Herrera, L. (2011) 'Egypt's Revolution 2.0: The Facebook factor', *Jadaliyya*, 12 February, at: www.jadaliyya.com/pages/index/612/egypts-revolution-2.0_the-facebook-factor (accessed 10 March 2015).

Hill, E. (2012a) 'Egypt's surprise candidate: Hamdeen Sabbahi', *Al Jazeera*, 25 May, at: http://www.aljazeera.com/blogs/middleeast/2012/05/2313.html (accessed 26 June 2015).

Hill, E. (2012b) 'Background: SCAF's last-minute power grab', *Al Jazeera*, 18 June, at: www.aljazeera.com/indepth/spotlight/egypt/2012/06/201261812449990250.html (accessed 9 June 2015).

Hinnebusch, R.A. (1985) *Egyptian Politics under Sadat: The Post-Populist Development of an Authoritarian-Modernizing State* (Cambridge: Cambridge University Press, 1985).

Hirst, D. and Beeson, I. (1981) *Sadat* (London: Faber & Faber).

Howeidy, A. (2002) 'In the heart of Cairo', *Al-Ahram Weekly*, 16–22 May.

Howeidy, A. (2012) 'Meet the Brotherhood's enforcer: Khairat El-Shater', *Ahram Online*, 29 March, at: http://english.ahram.org.eg/News/37993.aspx (accessed 7 June 2015).

HRW [Human Rights Watch] (2003) 'Egypt's emergency without end', (New York: Human Rights Watch).

HRW [Human Rights Watch] (2011) 'Egypt: End use of live fire at peaceful protests', 29 January, at: www.hrw.org/news/2011/01/29/egypt-end-use-live-fire-peaceful-protests (accessed 2 May 2015).

HRW [Human Rights Watch] (2012) 'Egypt: Investigate Brotherhood's abuse of protesters', Human Rights Watch, 12 December, at: www.hrw.org/news/2012/12/12/egypt-investigate-brotherhoods-abuse-protesters (accessed 15 June 2015).

HRW [Human Rights Watch] (2013) 'All according to plan: The Rab'a Massacre and mass killings of protesters in Egypt' (New York: Human Rights Watch).

HRW [Human Rights Watch] (2014) 'Egypt: Activists arrested for "No" campaign', 13 January (New York: Human Rights Watch).

Hubbard, B. and Kirkpatrick, D. (2013) 'Sudden improvements in Egypt suggest a campaign to undermine Morsi', *New York Times*, 10 July, at: www.nytimes.com/2013/07/11/world/middleeast/improvements-in-egypt-suggest-a-campaign-that-undermined-morsi.html (accessed June 24 2015).

Hussein, M. (2012a) 'Egypt's bread: Morsi kneads life into subsidised staple', *Ahram Online*, 8 October, at: http://english.ahram.org.eg/NewsContent/1/140/54982/Egypt/First--days/Egypts-bread-Morsi-kneads-life-into-subsidised-sta.aspx (accessed 13 June 2015).

Hussein, M. (2012b) 'Egypt textile workers in revolt: Seven companies join Mahalla strike', *Ahram Online*, 17 July, at: http://english.ahram.org.eg/

NewsContent/1/0/47965/Egypt/0/Egypt-textile-workers-in-revolt-Seven-companies-jo.aspx (accessed 10 June 2015).

Hussein, M. (2016) Muslim Brotherhood Press Statement: Coup Media Machine Launch Lie Campaign Against Group, *Ikhwanweb*, April 6. Online at: www.ikhwanweb.com/article.php?id=32502; accessed 10 April 2011.

Hussein, A., al-Said, R. and al-Sayyid, M. (1999) 'Twenty years of multipartyism in Egypt', in M. Kennedy (ed.), *Twenty Years of Development in Egypt*, Cairo Papers in Social Science, vol. 21, no. 3. (Cairo: The American University in Cairo Press).

Hyde, M. (2012) 'At Euromoney, officials try to calm investor fears', *Egypt Independent*, 9 October, at: www.egyptindependent.com//news/euromoney-officials-try-calm-investor-fears (accessed 12 June 2015).

Ibrahim, A. (2015) 'Ittihadiya clashes: Planned coup or deadly attack on sit-in?' *Middle East Eye*, 21 April, at: www.middleeasteye.net/news/ittihadiya-clashes-planned-coup-or-attack-sit-1693049448#sthash.dsy05fpI.dpuf (accessed 3 July 2015).

Ibrahim, E. (2012) 'New decree will allow Morsi to reinstate Egypt parliament: Legal expert', *Ahram Online*, 22 November, at: http://english.ahram.org.eg/NewsContent/1/64/58946/Egypt/Politics-/New-decree-will-allow-Morsi-to-reinstate-Egypt-par.aspx (accessed 15 June 2015).

Ibrahim, E., Shukrallah, S., Ali, M., Hanna, S., Samak, S., Fathi, Y. and Tarek, S. (2011) 'Live updates: A blow by blow account of Egypt's "Friday of popular will and united front"', *Ahram Online*, 29 July, at: http://english.ahram.org.eg/NewsContentP/1/17572/Egypt/Aboutus.aspx (accessed 30 April 2015).

Ibrahim, I. (2012) '9 April, 2011: When the SCAF, people went their separate ways', *Ahram Online*, 9 April, at: http://english.ahram.org.eg/WriterArticles/NewsContentP/1/38881/Egypt/Aboutus.aspx (accessed May 2 2015).

ICG [International Crisis Group] (2005) *Reforming Egypt: in Search of a Strategy* Middle East/North Africa Report, no. 46, 4 October (Brussels: ICG).

ICG [International Crisis Group] (2011) *Popular Protest in North Africa and the Middle East (I): Egypt Victorious?*, 24 February (Brussels: ICG).

ICG [International Crisis Group] (2012) *Lost in Transition: the World According to Egypt's SCAF*, 24 April (Brussels: ICG).

ICG [International Crisis Group] (2013) *Marching in Circles: Egypt's Dangerous Second Transition*, 7 August (Brussels: ICG).

Ikhwanweb (2010) 'Egypt's Muslim Brotherhood chooses new leader', *Ikhwanweb*, 22 January, at: www.ikhwanweb.com/article.php?id=22751 (accessed 10 May 2015).

Ismael, T.Y. and El-Sa'id, R. (1990) *The Communist Movement in Egypt, 1920–1988* (Syracuse, NY: Syracuse University Press).

Kandil, H. (2011) 'Revolt in Egypt', *New Left Review*, 68, March–April.

Kandil, H. (2012) *Soldiers, Spies and Statesmen: Egypt's Road to Revolt* (London: Verso).

Kandil, H. (2015) *Inside the Brotherhood* (Cambridge: Polity Press).

Kandil, W. (2015) 'Sisi stole another general's coup, and ultimately Egypt', *The New Arab*, 22 April, at: www.alaraby.co.uk/english/comment/2015/4/22/sisi-stole-another-generals-coup-and-ultimately-egypt (accessed 24 June 2015).

Kassem, M. (2004) *Egyptian Politics: The Dynamics of Authoritarian Rule* (Boulder, CO: Lynne Rienner).

Keraitim, S. and Mehrez, S. (2012) '*Mulid al-Tahrir*: Semiotics of a revolution', in Samia Mehrez (ed.), *Translating Egypt's Revolution: The Language of Tahrir* (Cairo: The American University in Cairo Press).

Khalil, A. (2012) 'The fading of Tahrir Square', *Foreign Affairs*, 3 July.

Khalil, N. (2016) 'The power of words', *Al-Ahram Weekly*, 3 March. Online at: http://weekly.ahram.org.eg/Print/15682.aspx; accessed 10 April 2016.

Kingsley, P. (2013) 'Egypt suffering "worst economic crisis since the 1930s"', *Guardian*, 16 May, at: www.theguardian.com/world/2013/may/16/egypt-worst-economic-crisis-1930s (accessed 23 June 2015).

Kholaif, D. (2013) 'The Egyptian army's economic juggernaut', *Al Jazeera*, 5 August, at: www.aljazeera.com/indepth/features/2013/08/20138435433181894.html (accessed 20 June 2015).

Kirkpatrick, D. (2011a) 'Wired and shrewd, young Egyptians guide revolt', *New York Times*, 9 February.

Kirkpatrick, D. (2011b) 'Military flexes its muscles as Islamists gain in Egypt', *New York Times*, 7 December, at: www.nytimes.com/2011/12/08/world/middleeast/egyptian-general-mukhtar-al-mulla-asserts-continuing-control-despite-elections.html (accessed 6 May 2015).

Kirkpatrick, D. (2011c) 'Leader denies use of violence as Cairo crackdown persists', *New York Times*, 17 December.

Kirkpatrick, D. (2011d) 'Mass march by Cairo women in protest over abuse by soldiers', *New York Times*, 20 December, at: www.nytimes.com/2011/12/21/world/middleeast/violence-enters-5th-day-as-egyptian-general-blames-protesters.html?_r=0 (accessed 5 May 2015).

Kirkpatrick, D. (2013) 'Angry at public and officials, security forces strike in Egypt', *New York Times*, 7 March, at: www.nytimes.com/2013/03/08/world/middleeast/angry-at-public-and-officials-police-strike-in-egypt.html?_r=0 (accessed 23 June 2015).

Kirkpatrick, D. and El Sheikh, M. (2012) 'Citing deadlock, Egypt's leader seizes new power and plans Mubarak retrial', *New York Times*, 22 November, at: www.nytimes.com/2012/11/23/world/middleeast/egypts-president-morsi-gives-himself-new-powers.html (accessed 16 June 2015).

Korany, B. and El-Mahdi, R. (eds) (2012) *Arab Spring in Egypt: Revolution and Beyond* (Cairo: The American University in Cairo Press).

Kurtz, S. (2011) 'Is there an Arab spring?', *National Review Online*, 21 March, at: www.nationalreview.com/corner/262618/there-arab-spring-stanley-kurtz (accessed 18 March 2015).

LCHR (Land Center for Human Rights [Markaz el-Ard]) (2002) 'Farmer Struggles against Law 96 of 1992', in R. Bush (ed.) *Counter Revolution in Egypt's Countryside* (London: Zed).

Lenin, V.I. (1964 [1916]) 'The discussion on self-emancipation summed up', *Lenin Collected Works* vol. 22 (London: Lawrence & Wishart).

Levinson, C. and Bradley, M. (2013) 'In Egypt, the "Deep State" rises again', *Wall Street Journal*, 19 July.

Lewis, B. (1990) 'The roots of Muslim rage', *The Atlantic* 266 (3).

Lewis, B. (2001) 'A mass expression of outrage against injustice', *Jerusalem Post*, 25 February, at: www.jpost.com/Opinion/Columnists/A-mass-expression-of-outrage-against-injustice (accessed 14 April 2015).

Lewis, B. (2006) 'Freedom and justice in Islam', *Imprimis* (September) 35 (9).

Lewis, B. (2011) 'A mass expression of outrage against injustice', *The Jerusalem Post*, 25 February, at: www.jpost.com/Opinion/Columnists/A-mass-expression-of-outrage-against-injustice (accessed 12 March 2016).

Lockman, Z. (1994) 'Introduction', in Z. Lockman (ed.) *Workers and Working Classes in the Middle East* (Albany, NY: State University of New York Press).

Lübben, I. (2015) 'The economic ideology of Hasan al-Banna and the Egyptian Muslim Brotherhood', in H. Elsenhans, R. Ouaissa, S. Schweke and M-A. Tétreault (eds), *The Transformation of Politicised Religion: From Zealots into Leaders* (Farnham: Ashgate).

Luxemburg, R. (1964 [1906]) *The Mass Strike, the Political Party and the Trade Unions* (London: Merlin Press).

Lynch, M. (2003) 'Beyond the Arab Street: Iraq and the Arab public sphere', *Politics & Society*, 31, no. 55.

Lynch, D. and Marroushi, N. (2013), 'Workers adding to Egyptian chaos as strike wave disrupts economy', *Bloomberg*, 27 February, at: www.bloomberg.com/news/2013-02-27/workers-adding-to-egyptian-chaos-as-strike-wave-disrupts-economy.html (accessed 21 June 2015).

MacDonald, F. and El Baltaji, D. (2013) 'Kuwait Egypt aid pushes Gulf pledges to $12 billion in 24 Hours', *Bloomberg Business*, 10 July, at: www.bloomberg.com/news/articles/2013-07-10/kuwait-egypt-aid-pushes-gulf-pledges-to-12-billion-in-24-hours (accessed 26 June 2015).

Mada Masr (2015) 'Ministry uses Friday sermon to warn against January 25 protests', *Mada Masr*, 8 December, at: www.madamasr.com/news/ministry-uses-friday-sermon-warn-against-january-25-protests (accessed 20 January 2016).

Mada Masr (2016a) '1,117 labor protests across Egypt in 2015: Democracy Meter report', *Mada Masr*, 11 January, at: www.madamasr.com/news/economy/1117-labor-protests-across-egypt-2015-democracy-meter-report (accessed 20 January 2016).

Mada Masr (2016b) 'Sisi: Don't listen to anyone but me', *Mada Masr*, 24 February. Online at: www.madamasr.com/news/sisi-dont-listen-anyone-me; accessed 10 April 2016.

Maghraoui, A.M. (2006) *Liberalism without Democracy: Nationhood and Citizenship in Egypt, 1922–1936* (Durham, NC: Duke University Press).

Mahdawy, H. (2016) 'On the eve of the revolution's anniversary, the state cajoles and intimidates', *Mada Masr*, 5 January, at: www.madamasr.com/sections/politics/eve-revolutions-anniversary-state-cajoles-and-intimidates (accessed 20 January 2016).

Makram-Ebeid, M. (2009) 'The power of Egypt's street', *Al-Ahram Weekly*, 29 January–4 February.

Mansfield, P. (1971) *The British in Egypt* (London: Weidenfeld and Nicolson).

Marfleet, P. (1998) 'Islamist politics', in A. Lent (ed.). *The New Politics* (London: Lawrence & Wishart), pp. 89–111.

Marfleet, P. (2012) 'Egypt – never "one hand"', in Gonzalez, M. and Barakat, H. (eds) *Arms and the People* (London: Pluto Press).

Marfleet, P. (2013a) 'Mubarak's Egypt: Nexus of criminality', *State Crime* 2 (2).

Marfleet, P. (2013b) 'Egypt – the workers advance', *International Socialism* 139.

Marfleet, P. (2016) 'The political subject in the "Arab Spring"', *Contemporary Levant* 1 (1).

Marroushi, N. (2011) 'US expert: leadership of "Military Inc." is running Egypt', *Egypt Independent*, 26 October.

Marshall, S. and Stacher, J. (2012) 'Egypt's generals and transnational capital', *Middle East Research and Information Project*, MERIP 262.

Martini, J. and Taylor, J. (2011) 'Commanding democracy in Egypt: The military's attempt to manage the future', *Foreign Affairs*, September–October, pp. 127–37.

Marx, K. and Engels, F. (1985 [1848]) *The Communist Manifesto* (London: Penguin Books).

Mayton, J. (2010) 'Muslim Brotherhood is young at heart', *Guardian*, 16 February, at: www.theguardian.com/commentisfree/2010/feb/16/muslim-brotherhood-young-egypt (accessed 10 May 2015).

McCrummen, S. (2012) 'In Egypt, Morsi's supporters see themselves as righteous protectors', *Washington Post*, 11 December, at: www.washingtonpost.com/world/middle_east/anti-morsi-protesters-challenge-barriers-around-presidential-palace/2012/12/11/9efb66bc-439d-11e2-8e70-e1993528222d_story.html (accessed 20 June 2015).

Mehrez, S. (ed.) (2012) *Translating Egypt's Revolution: The Language of Tahrir* (Cairo: The American University in Cairo Press).

Mekay, E. (2013) 'Exclusive: US bankrolled anti-Morsi activists', *Al Jazeera*, 10 July, at: www.aljazeera.com/indepth/features/2013/07/201371011 3522489801.html (accessed 26 June 2015).

MENA [MENA Solidarity Network] (2011) 'Egypt: Teachers tell generals "meet our demands ... or no school this year"', 13 September, at: http://menasolidaritynetwork.com/2011/09/13/egypt-teachers-tell-generals-meet-our-demands-or-no-school-this-year/ (accessed 2 May 2015).

MENA [MENA Solidarity Network] (2012) 'Egypt: Independent union federation rejects president's power grab', 27 November, at: http://menasolidarity

network.com/2012/11/27/egypt-independent-union-federation-rejects-presidents-power-grab/ <http://menasolidaritynetwork.com/2012/11/27/egypt-independent-union-federation-rejects-presidents-power-grab/> (accessed 24 March 2016).

MENA [MENA Solidarity Network] (2013), 'Egypt: Independent unions, revolutionary activists slam conscription of rail strikers', 10 April, at: http://menasolidaritynetwork.com/2013/04/10/egypt-independent-union-federation-condemns-conscriptio/ (accessed 22 June 2015).

Michael, M. and El Deeb, S. (2012) 'Egyptians gather in Cairo to mark anniversary of uprising, *The Independent*, 25 January, at: www.independent.co.uk/news/world/africa/egyptians-gather-in-cairo-to-mark-anniversary-of-uprising-6294228.html (accessed 5 May 2015).

Michaels, J. (2011) 'Tech-savvy youths led the way in Egypt protests', *USA Today*, 7 February.

Middle East Quarterly (2009), 'Gamal Mubarak: "We Need Audacious Leaders"', (interview) *Middle East Quarterly*, Winter, pp. 67–73, at: www.meforum.org/2063/gamal-mubarak-we-need-audacious-leaders (accessed 15 March 2015).

Milner, A. (2002 [1892]) *England in Egypt* (Piscataway, NJ: Gorgias Press).

Mitchell, R. (1969) *The Society of the Muslim Brothers* (Oxford: Oxford University Press).

Moazzam, A. (1983) *Jamal al-Din al-Afghani: A Muslim Intellectual* (New Delhi: Concept).

Mohi el-Din, K. (1996) *Memories of a Revolution: Egypt 1952* (Cairo: The American University in Cairo Press).

Montasser, F. (2012) '"Happy Birthday, Revolution" from the Muslim Brotherhood', *Ahram Online*, 26 January, at: http://english.ahram.org.eg/NewsContent/5/0/32819/Arts--Culture/0/Happy-Birthday,-Revolution-from-the-Muslim-Brother.aspx (accessed 6 June 2015).

Moreton, E. (1982) 'The Eastern Europeans and the Cubans in the Middle East', in A. Dawisha and K. Dawisha (eds), *The Soviet Union in the Middle East: Policies and Perspectives* (London: Heinemann).

Mourad, S. and Feteha, A. (2012) 'IMF's Lagarde concludes Egypt visit amid modest protests', *Ahram Online*, 22 August, at: http://english.ahram.org.eg/NewsContent/3/12/51011/Business/Economy/IMFs-Lagarde-concludes-Egypt-visit-amid-modest-pro.aspx (accessed 13 June 2015).

Mubarak, M.H. (2011) 'Hosni Mubarak's speech: full text', *Guardian*, 2 February.

Muhamadeen, H. (2015) 'Khaled Ali: Privatisation has stolen Egypt from its people', *Al Araby al-Jadeed*, 23 January, at: www.alaraby.co.uk/english/features/2015/1/27/khaled-ali-privatisation-has-stolen-egypt-from-its-people#sthash.SGYwAL98.dpuf (accessed 19 March 2015).

Muslim Brotherhood (2011) 'FJP 2011 Program on Social Justice', *Ikhwanweb*, 4 December, at: www.ikhwanweb.com/article.php?id=29300 (accessed 4 June 2015).

Mustafa, D. and Khalil, A. (2011) 'The culture of the revolution', *Socialist Review* 357, April.

Naguib, S. (2009) 'Islamism(s) old and new', in R. El-Mahdi and P. Marfleet (eds), *Egypt: The Moment of Change* (London: Zed).

Naguib, S. (2011a) *The Egyptian Revolution: A Political Analysis and Eyewitness Account* (London: Bookmarks).

Naguib, S. (2011b) 'Egypt's unfinished revolution: Egypt since the fall of Mubarak', *Internationalist Socialist Review*, 79.

Naguib, S. (2016) 'The Egyptian Counterrevolution', *Jacobin*, 11 March, at: www.jacobinmag.com/2016/03/egypt-revolution-sisi-mubarak-muslim-brotherhood/ (accessed 12 March 2016).

Naib, F. (2011) 'Women of the revolution', *Al Jazeera*, 16 February, at: www.aljazeera.com/indepth/features/2011/02/2011217134411934738.html (accessed 20 January 2016).

Netanyahu, B. (2011) 'PM addresses opening of Knesset winter session', Israel Ministry of Foreign Affairs, official statement, 31 October, at: http://mfa.gov.il/MFA/PressRoom/2011/Pages/PM_Netanyahu_opening_Knesset_winter_session_31-Oct-2011.aspx (accessed 20 March 2015).

Noueihad, L. (2015) 'Egypt in second day of "election without voters"', *Reuters*, 20 October.

Noueihed, L. and Warren, A. (2012) *The Battle for the Arab Spring* (New Haven, CT: Yale University Press).

Obama, B. (2011) 'Remarks by the President on Egypt', The White House, official statement, 11 February, at: www.whitehouse.gov/the-press-office/2011/02/11/remarks-president-egypt (accessed 20 March 2015).

Oweidat, N., Benard, C., Stahl, D., Kildani, W., O'Connell, E. and Grant. A. (2008) *The Kefaya Movement: A Case Study of a Grassroots Reform Initiative*. Santa Monica, CA: RAND National Defense Research Institute.

Owen, R. (2014) 'From the revolutionary overthrow of the dictatorships to the struggle to establish a new constitutional order', in F. Gerges, (ed.), *The New Middle East: Protest and Revolution in the Arab World* (Cambridge: Cambridge University Press).

Parties and Movements (2011) [Jadaliyya and Ahram Online] 'National Progressive Unionist (Tagammu) Party', *Jadaliyya*, 18 November.

PCSU [Privatization Coordination Support Unit] (2002) *The Results and Impacts of Egypt's Privatization Program* (for USAID), at: www1.aucegypt.edu/src/wsite1/Pdfs/Results%20and%20Impacts%20of%20Privatization%20in%20Egypt.pdf (accessed 19 March 2015).

Petersen, S. (2011) 'Egypt's revolution redefines what's possible in the Arab world', *Christian Science Monitor*, 11 February.

Posusney, M.P. (1997) *Labor and the State in Egypt: Workers, Unions, and Economic Restructuring* (New York: Columbia University Press).

PIP (Privatization Implementation Project) [USAID] (2004) 'Privatization in Egypt', *Quarterly Review*, January–March, at: http://pdf.usaid.gov/pdf_docs/PDACA341.pdf

Pipes, D. (2002) 'A new round of anger and humiliation: Islam after 9/11', in D. Pleszcynski (ed.), *Our Brave New World: Essays on the Impact of September 11* (Stanford, CA: Hoover Institution).

Preston, J. (2011) 'Movement began with outrage and a Facebook page that gave it an outlet', *New York Times*, 5 February.

Qutb, S. (1988) *Milestones* (Karachi: International Islamic Publishers).

Rabie, D. (2014) 'Sisi and his women', *Mada Masr*, 25 May, at: www.madamasr.com/sections/politics/sisi-and-his-women (accessed 20 January 2016).

Rady, F. (2008) 'Sayed Habib: portrait of an activist', *Al-Ahram Weekly*, 1–7 May.

Rady, F. (2011) 'Mahalla wins showdown', *Al-Ahram Weekly*, 24 February–2 March.

Rashwan, N. (2013) 'Egypt's National Salvation Front faces existential challenges', *Ahram Online*, 25 February, at: http://english.ahram.org.eg/NewsContentPrint/1/0/65497/Egypt/0/Egypts-National-Salvation-Front-faces-existential-.aspx (accessed 23 June 2015).

Ravid, B. (2011) 'Netanyahu: Arab Spring pushing Mideast backward, not forward', *Haaretz*, 24 November, at: www.haaretz.com/news/netanyahu-arab-spring-pushing-mideast-backward-not-forward-1.397353 (accessed 20 March 2015).

Reddy, S. and Bradley, M. (2012) 'IMF's Egypt loan is Mideast Test Case', *Wall Street Journal*, 15 October, at: www.wsj.com/articles/SB10000872396390443854204578058703824706178 (accessed 12 June 2015).

Rennick, S.A. (2013) 'Contested meanings in the Egyptian Revolution', *Socio* 2: 81–98.

Reuters (2012a) 'Egypt's currency reserves rose $300–400m in Oct: Newspaper', *Ahram Online*, 29 October, at: http://english.ahram.org.eg/NewsContent/3/12/56685/Business/Economy/Egypts-currency-reserves-rose-m-in-Oct-Newspaper.aspx (accessed 13 June 2015).

Reuters (2012b) 'Egypt military chief calls for "national dialogue"', *Egypt Independent*, 11 December, at: www.egyptindependent.com/news/egypt-military-chief-calls-national-dialogue (accessed 15 June 2015).

Revolutionary Socialists (2013) 'Not in our name. No to Sisi's mandate', 25 July, at: https://global.revsoc.me/2013/07/not-in-our-name-no-to-sisis-mandate/ (accessed 25 June 2015).

Rizq, Y. (2013) 'The General Sisi I know', *Al Monitor*, 28 July [Translation from *Al-Masry Al-Youm*, 25 July 2013)], at: www.al-monitor.com/pulse/politics/2013/07/sisi-egypt-morsi-ouster.html#ixzz3xtBt2uSo (accessed 27 June 2015).

Salah, F. (2012) 'Remembering Mohamed Mahmoud: The good, the bad, and the Brotherhood', *Daily News*, 19 October.

Salah, T. and Abdel Aziz, M. (2010) 'MB delegation to visit Tagammu for unified stance', *Egypt Independent*, 28 March, at: www.egyptindependent.com/news/mb-delegation-visit-tagammu-unified-stance (accessed 23 March 2013).

Salah, Y. and Ziad, D. (2011) 'Mubarak to be tried for murder of protesters', *Reuters*, 24 May, at: www.reuters.com/article/2011/05/24/us-egypt-mubarak-idUSTRE74N3LG20110524 (accessed 2 May 2015).

Saleh, S. (2015) 'Old guard eye comeback in Egypt polls', *Financial Times*, 16 October.

Saleh, Y. (2014) 'Activists who backed Mursi's fall turn against military', *Reuters*, 20 February, at: www.reuters.com/article/2014/02/20/us-egypt-politics-tamarud-idUSBREA1J1E420140220 (accessed 27 June 2015).

Sallam, H. (2011) 'Striking back at Egyptian workers', *MER* 259, at: www.merip.org/mer/mer259/striking-back-egyptian-workers (accessed 12 March 2016).

Satloff, M. (2002) 'The Arab "Street" poses no real threat to U.S.', *Newsday*, 27 September.

Sayigh, Y. (2012) *Above the State: the Officers' Republic in Egypt*, Carnegie Middle East Centre (Washington, DC: Carnegie Endowment for International Peace).

SCAF (2011a) 'SCAF Statement of 10 February 2011', *New York Times*.

SCAF (2011b) 'SCAF Statement of 14 February 2011', *New York Times*.

Schenker, J. (2016) *The Egyptians: A Radical Story* (London: Allen Lane).

Schielke, S. (2006) 'Snacks and Saints: Mawlid Festivals and the politics of festivity, piety and modernity in contemporary Egypt', International Institute for the Study of Islam, University of Leiden (Leiden University Repository), at: https://openaccess.leidenuniv.nl/handle/1887/10062 (accessed 1 March 2015).

Schielke, S. (2015) *Egypt in the Future Tense* (Bloomington, IN: Indiana University Press).

Seif El-Dawla, A. (2009) 'Torture: A state policy', in R. El-Mahdi and P. Marfleet (eds), *Egypt: The Moment of Change* (London: Zed).

Seth, R. (1966) *Russell Pasha* (London: William Kimber).

Shahid, A. (2011) 'Suez Canal workers join broad strikes in Egypt', *New York Times*, 17 February.

Shahine, G. (2008) 'Dying to live', *Al-Ahram Weekly*, 21–27 February.

Sharabi, H. (1966) *Nationalism and Revolution in the Arab World: The Middle East and North Africa* (Princeton, NJ: Van Nostrand).

Sharp, J. (2007), *Egypt: Background and US Relations*, Report for Congress (RL 33003) (Washington DC: Congressional Research Service).

Shatz, A. (2012) 'Whose Egypt?' *London Review of Books* 34 (1), 5 January: 15–17.

Shatz, A. (2013) 'Egypt's counter revolution', *London Review of Books* 16 August, at: www.lrb.co.uk/blog/2013/08/16/adam-shatz/egypts-counter-revolution/ (accessed 2 June 2015).

Shehab, S. (2008) 'Riding the storm', *Al-Ahram Weekly*, 10–16 April.

Shebab, S. (2011) 'Time for action', *Al-Ahram Weekly* 1033, 27 January–2 February.

Shehata, D. (2012) 'Youth movements and the 25 January Revolution', in R. El-Mahdi and B. Korany (eds), *Arab Spring in Egypt: Revolution and Beyond* (Cairo: The American University in Cairo Press).

Shokr, A. (2011) 'The 18 Days of Tahrir', *Middle East Report* 258.

Shukrallah, S. (2011a) 'How divided is Egypt's Muslim Brotherhood?', *Ahram Online*, 4 April, at: http://english.ahram.org.eg/NewsContent/1/64/8949/Egypt/Politics-/How-divided-is-Egypts-Muslim-Brotherhood.aspx (accessed 2 June 2015).

Shukrallah, S. (2011b) 'Egypt's Muslim Brotherhood struggles to contain cracks', *Ahram Online*, 19 July, at: http://english.ahram.org.eg/News Content/1/64/16782/Egypt/Politics-/Egypts-Muslim-Brotherhood-struggles-to-contain-cra.aspx (accessed 2 June 2015).

Sims, D. (2010) *Understanding Cairo: The Logic of a City Out of Control* (Cairo: The American University in Cairo Press).

SIS [State Information Service, Cairo] (2013) 'Hegazi: Religious fascism over, authorities combating violence', 19 August, at: www.sis.gov.eg/En/Templates/Articles/tmpArticleNews.aspx?ArtID=69445#.Vqi7p6-QGrU (accessed 1 July 2015).

Slackman, M. (2011) 'Islamist group is rising force in a new Egypt', *New York Times*, 24 March, at: www.nytimes.com/2011/03/25/world/middleeast/25egypt.html (accessed 4 May 2015).

Soueif, A. (2012) *Cairo: My City, Our Revolution* (London: Bloomsbury Publishing).

Sowers, J. and Toensing C. (eds) (2012) *The Journey to Tahrir: Revolution, Protest and Social Change in Egypt* (London: Verso).

Springborg, R. (1988) *Mubarak's Egypt: Fragmentation of the Political Order* (Boulder, CO: Westview Press).

Springborg, R. (2012) 'Egypt's cobra and mongoose', *Foreign Policy*, 27 February, at: http://mideast.foreignpolicy.com/posts/2012/02/27/egypt_s_cobra_and_mongoose (accessed 5 May 2015).

Stacher, J. (2016) 'Egypt running on empty', *MERIP*, 8 March, at: www.merip.org/mero/mero030816 (accessed 10 March 2016).

Stephens, R. (1971) *Nasser* (Harmondsworth: Penguin).

Stork, J. (2013) 'Three decades of human rights activism in the Middle East and North Africa: An ambiguous balance sheet', in J. Beinin and and F. Vairel (eds), *Social Movements, Mobilization, and Contestation in the Middle East and North Africa* (Stanford, CA: Stanford University Press).

STRATFOR (2016) 'A Dollar Crisis Threatens Egypt's Economy', STRATFOR, 10 March. Online at: www.stratfor.com/analysis/dollar-crisis-threatens-egypts-economy; accessed 10 April 2016.

Sutter, J.D. (2011) 'The faces of Egypt's "Revolution 2.0"', *CNN*, 11 February.

Tadros, M. (2012) 'Introduction: The Pulse of the Arab Revolt', in M. Tadros, *The Pulse of Egypt's Revolt, IDS Bulletin*, 43 (1): 1–15.

Tadros, S. (2012) 'Egypt's Elections: Why the Islamists Won', *World Affairs*, March–April, at: www.worldaffairsjournal.org/article/egypt%E2%80%99s-elections-why-islamists-won (accessed 6 June 2015).

Tammam, H. and Haenni, P. (2011) 'Egypt: Islam in the insurrection', *Religioscope*, 22 February, at: http://religion.info/english/articles/article_519.shtml#.ViNdvIe4m8U (accessed 6 May 2015).

Taylor, P. and Saleh, Y. (2013) 'INSIGHT-Egypt opposition can't harvest Brotherhood unpopularity', *Reuters*, 5 May, at: www.reuters.com/article/2013/05/05/egypt-opposition-idUSL6N0D90Z120130505 (accessed 23 June 2015).

Time (2011) 'A Generation Changing the World', *Time* 177, no. 8, 28 February.

Trager, E. (2011) 'The unbreakable Muslim Brotherhood: Grim prospects for a liberal Egypt', *Foreign Affairs*, September–October.

Trew, B. (2012) 'More than 70 killed in Egypt's worst football disaster', *Ahram Online*, 2 February, at: http://english.ahram.org.eg/NewsContent/1/0/33488/Egypt/0/More-than--killed-in-Egypts-worst-football-disaste.aspx (accessed 7 June 2015).

Trew, B., Shukrallah, S., Ali, R., Tarek, S., Samak, D., Haddon, H., and Rashwan, N.H. (2013) 'Live Updates 1: Protests, clashes all over the country on revolution's anniversary', *Ahram Online*, 25 January, at: http://english.ahram.org.eg/NewsContentP/1/63243/Egypt/Live-Updates-Protests,-clashes-all-over-the-countr.aspx (accessed 20 June 2015).

Trotsky, L. (1967) *The History of the Russian Revolution*, vol. 1 (three volumes) (London: Sphere).

U.S. Department of State (2006) Bureau of Democracy, Human Rights and Labor, 'Egypt', at: www.state.gov/j/drl/rls/hrrpt/2005/61687.htm (accessed 10 May 2015).

Wan, W. (2011) 'Egypt's Facebook revolution faces identity crisis', *Washington Post*, 23 March.

Wan, W. (2012) 'Muslim Brotherhood officials aim to promote moderate image in Washington visit', *Washington Post*, 3 April, at: www.washingtonpost.com/world/national-security/muslim-brotherhood-officials-aim-to-promote-moderate-image-in-washington-visit/2012/04/03/gIQApqs1tS_story.html (accessed 10 June 2015).

Wedeen, L. (1999) *Ambiguities of Domination: Politics, Rhetoric, and Symbols in Contemporary Syria* (Chicago, IL: University of Chicago Press).

Weiss, D. and Wurzel, U. (1998) *The Economics and Politics of Transition to an Open Market Economy: Egypt* (Paris: Development Centre of the Organisation for Economic Cooperation and Development).

Wendell, C. (1978) *Five tracts of Hasan Al-Banna (1906–1949): A selection from the Majmuat rasail al-Imam al-shahid Hasan al-Banna* [translation and annotation of Arabic originals] (Berkeley, CA: University of California Press).

Werr, P. and Zayed, D. (2011) 'Egyptians protest to "protect revolution"', *Reuters*, at: www.reuters.com/article/2011/04/01/us-egypt-protest-idUSTRE 73053620110401 (accessed 2 May 2015).

Wheelock, K. (1960) *Nasser's New Egypt: A Critical Analysis* (New York: Frederick A. Praeger).

Wickham, C.R. (2013) *The Muslim Brotherhood: Evolution of an Islamist Movement* (Princeton, NJ: Princeton University Press).

Winegar, J. (2012) 'The privilege of revolution: Gender, class, space, and affect in Egypt', *American Ethnologist* 39 (1): 67–70.

World Bank (2014) *Armed forces personnel, total*, at: http://data.worldbank.org/ indicator/MS.MIL.TOTL.P1 (accessed 2 May 2015).

World Bank (2015) 'World Bank Group Scales Up Support for Egypt', World Bank, December 17. Online at: www.worldbank.org/en/news/press-release/2015/12/17/world-bank-group-scales-up-support-for-egypt; accessed 10 April 2016.

Wroughton, L. (2012) 'Key IMF loan talks begin in Cairo, reducing budget deficit is focus', *Reuters*, 30 October, at: www.reuters.com/article/us-imf-egypt-idUSB RE89T09X20121030#iZebwbcz2pE5Pd15.97 (accessed 12 June 2015).

Youssef, A. (2015) 'Workers in Al-Sisi's Egypt: Muted by promises of "development"', *Daily News* [Cairo], 11 June, at: www.dailynewsegypt.com/2015/06/11/ workers-in-al-sisis-egypts-muted-by-promises-of-development/ (accessed 28 June 2015).

Zaalouk, M (1989) *Power, Class and Foreign Capital in Egypt: The Rise of the New Bourgeoisie* (London: Zed Books).

Zohny, H. (2011) 'Egyptian university professors threaten full strike', *NatureAsia*, 29 September. Online at: www.natureasia.com/en/nmiddleeast/article/10.1038/ nmiddleeast.2011.129 (accessed 3 May 2015).

Index